CU00957095

DEVON LIBRARIES

Please return/renew this item by the due date.
Renew on tel. 0345 155 1001 or at
www.devonlibraries.org.uk

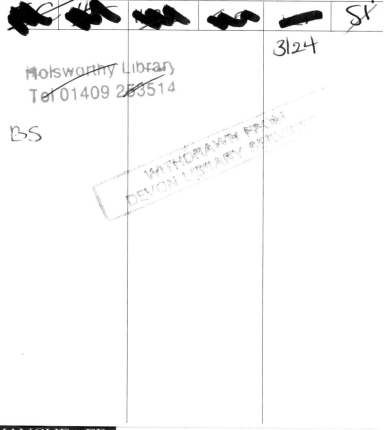

3|24

Holsworthy Library
Tel 01409 253514

BS

MANCHESTER
1824

Manchester University Press

Film modernism

Sam Rohdie

MANCHESTER UNIVERSITY PRESS

Published by Manchester University Press
Altrincham Street, Manchester M1 7JA
www.manchesteruniversitypress.co.uk

British Library Cataloguing-in-Publication Data
A catalogue record for this book is available from the British Library

Library of Congress Cataloging-in-Publication Data applied for

ISBN 978 0 7190 9928 1 paperback

First published 2015

The publisher has no responsibility for the persistence or accuracy of URLs for any
external or third-party internet websites referred to in this book, and does not guarantee
that any content on such websites is, or will remain, accurate or appropriate.

Typeset by
Servis Filmsetting Ltd, Stockport Cheshire
Printed in Great Britain
by Bell & Bain Ltd, Glasgow

For Des

Contents

Foreword

Sam Rohdie died at his home in Florida on 3 April 2015 from the effects of a severe stroke suffered a few weeks earlier. He had received the proofs of this, his last book, but was not able to correct them – a task that then fell to Des O'Rawe, his former colleague at Queen's University Belfast, and to myself.

The book is structured as a series of alphabetical entries, from Allegory to Writing. But it is not systematic, nor exhaustive, nor does it offer a single all-embracing definition of its subject. It also contains examples of what appear at first sight to be repetitions, both of argument and, in some cases, phraseology.

As far as the seeming repetitions are concerned, they turn out on closer examination almost always to have a purpose, functioning as a form of insistence reminding the reader how often in films things are not what they seem. The points on which Rohdie most wants to insist concern moments in certain films when the spectator is put in a position of uncertainty as to the solidity and coherence of the world portrayed by the film. 'Look again,' he seems to be saying. Look again at how in this film too, and in a different context, the film undermines our confidence in a stable world and the equally stable forms by which this original stability is represented. Look again, and see how the filmmaker has opened up possibilities of perception that break with habitual modes of viewing, possibly in discomfiting ways. The point being made is rhetorical, certainly, but also theoretical – though not in the context of a systematic theory.

Rohdie's distrust of system comes out also in his resistance to offering a formal definition of artistic modernism, preferring instead to approach the topic allusively and wait for a definition to emerge. While

this generally works well, in the sense that the reader soon picks up the
sense of Rohdie's argument, it also allows him to elude a paradox which
some readers at least will find surprising.

The core of Rohdie's anti-definition lies in an argument by negation.
Modernism in the arts, most dramatically in the years immediately
preceding the First World War, asserted itself above all through its rejection of the classical rules of art – notably principles of harmony, order
and proportion applied to broadly realistic forms of representation. These
principles had been undermined throughout the nineteenth century but
it was only at the beginning of the twentieth that what can be broadly
called classicism came under sustained attack across the board – in painting, music, theatre, literature. Not, however, in cinema. The cinema in
the period of early modernism around 1910 was still amorphous. It was
a field in which artists could experiment as much as they liked, but with
no guarantee of their experiments being understood for what they were.
Mostly, however, cinema was in search of rules and until it found them it
could not break them. It would be at least ten years – say around the very
end of the silent period – before the cinema established its equivalent of
classical form and a further thirty years before it discovered the value of
breaking the rules it had so painstakingly invented. Modernism in the
cinema, therefore, properly begins only around 1960, with the arrival
on the scene of a film-making generation deeply versed in a classical
tradition and equally convinced that they had to break with that tradition
and – in the famous phrase of Ezra Pound, 'Make it new'. Which they did.

Film modernism starts, then, not as one would expect with the early
avant-garde of Fernand Léger (*Ballet mécanique*, 1924), Dziga Vertov (*The
Man with the Movie Camera*, 1929) or Luis Buñuel and Salvador Dalí (*Un
chien andalou*, 1929), but a full generation later. First on stage are outliers
like Orson Welles in (or more often outside) Hollywood and the heretical
neo-realist Roberto Rossellini in Italy, both of whom broke the classical
rules and suffered for it. The book's focus then is on the cine-literate
film-makers of the 1960s and after – Antonioni and Bertolucci in Italy
and the Nouvelle Vague and its successors in France. Its protagonist is
Jean-Luc Godard, both the young iconoclastic Godard of *À bout de souffle*
in 1960 and the later Godard of the monumental *Histoires du cinéma*
(1988–98). Godard's *Histoires*, in fact, is the key to Rohdie's book, a book
that is at times pyrotechnically brilliant, at times puzzling, and always
instructively enjoyable ... like *Histoires*.

Geoffrey Nowell-Smith, July 2015

Acknowledgements

My thanks to Des O'Rawe and Geoffrey Nowell-Smith, and at Manchester University Press Matthew Frost and Polly Bentham for their help and support and advice.

Introduction

This book consists of fifty categories arranged in alphabetical order centred on film modernism. Each category, though autonomous, interacts, intersects, juxtaposes with the others, entering into a dialogue with them and in so doing creates connections, illuminations, associations and rhymes which might not have arisen in a more conventional framework. The categories refer to particular films and directors that raise questions related to modernism, and, inevitably, thereby to classicism. The book is more in the way of questions and speculations than answers and conclusions. Its intention is to stimulate not simply by the substance of what is said but by the way it is said and structured. Most attention is given to the works of Michelangelo Antonioni, Bernardo Bertolucci, John Ford, Jean-Luc Godard, Howard Hawks, Alfred Hitchcock, João César Monteiro, Pier Paolo Pasolini, Nicholas Ray, Alain Resnais, Roberto Rossellini, Luchino Visconti and Orson Welles. These directors contribute, I believe, to an understanding of modernism in the cinema, and thus to the forms of the cinema more generally. To reflect upon modernism in film is necessarily to engage with the history of the cinema, as the film directors of the French *Nouvelle Vague* did.

The apparent arbitrary order and openness of the book, based as it is on the alphabet, is indebted to Jean-Luc Godard's interrogation of History and of film history, especially in his stunning *Histoire(s) du cinema*. I make a distinction between history (as story) and History (usually understood) as history: *histoire* in French can mean either, the differentiation is usually a matter of context.

Allegory

The image of Ettore on the bed of penitence in prison in Pier Paolo Pasolini's *Mamma Roma* (1962) is seen from an extreme low angle, radically foreshortened. The perspective, the angle of view and the position of Ettore almost exactly reproduces the painting of *The Dead Christ* (c. 1500) of the fifteenth-century Italian Renaissance painter Andrea Mantegna.

A series of likenesses are posed in the film between unlike things: the delinquent, confused, miserable Ettore, child of the *borgate*, and Christ the Saviour; the whore, Mamma Roma, and the mother of Christ; the present of Italy and the past of Italy (the Renaissance) and further back a classical past at the time of Christ; a film image and a painting; low culture and high culture; the profane and the sacred. These iconological and cultural comparisons have a musical extension: the music of the baroque Italian composer Antonio Vivaldi alternates with gypsy music. There is also a literary comparison and join: passages from Dante Alighieri's *Inferno* of the thirteenth century read out in prison, a hell of its own where Ettore has been incarcerated. The noble poetry of Dante is read out loud by Ettore's vulgar prison inmates. Dante's *La Divina commedia* is the first Italian poetic epic written in the vernacular, everday Italian rather than high-culture 'literary' Latin.

The pattern of placing one type of text (painting, literary, musical) against one from another time is familiar in Pasolini's films. The films, taken as a whole are extended allegories in which a narrative and all it includes of objects, gestures and actions is equated with meanings outside the narrative. Such allegorical structures are ancient, particularly important in scholastic Christian thought that enabled writers to discover sacred significance in the most profane stories and actions. The Bible can be read as an allegory, certainly some of its parts can, like the Song of Songs. An allegory is essentially a story with a double meaning, one literal and the other symbolic. The literal story is given a moral, social, religious significance by what it points to, the story as a lesson, sometimes prophetic.

The juxtaposition of texts and the use of citations is a strategy of much of modern artistic expression, for example the paintings of Rauschenberg (his Combines), of Picasso (his collages), the density of citations in the films of Godard (his *Histoire(s)*), the music of Ravel and Stravinsky (their use of popular motifs and their incorporation of jazz), the writings of Carlo Emilio Gadda, one of Pasolini's literary models, who juxtaposed not only texts but languages and speech, as Godard does and Pasolini does (Italian, Latin, dialect, the slang of the slums), and as modern composers do. But Godard and certainly Picasso, Rauschenberg and the Pop artists, though they cite and establish associative and reciprocal relations between different and distant texts, are not allegorists and their use of citations on the whole does not function as it does in Pasolini's films as social or moral allegories or as symbolic metaphors in which the literal and the symbolic are integrated in a story of doubled inverse meanings, which make meaning opaque, difficult to grasp, problematic.

In Pasolini's *Mamma Roma*, the film opens with a parody analogy between Leonardo da Vinci's fifteenth-century painting *The Last Supper* (of Christ and his disciples), set against the marriage banquet in the Rome *borgate* for a pimp and a peasant girl attended by pimps, whores, thieves and peasants who trade insults in song and verse, drink excessively and laugh uproariously.

Allegorical relations such as these play between a surface and a depth. The surface is literal, present-day, while the depth is its symbolic charge that comes from pasts brought to the surface where a play is initiated that sets in constant motion the separate layers and dimensions of the films. *La ricotta* (1963) is a perfect example of the hide and seek of Pasolini's allegories of oscillating, echoing, fundamentally unstable, unfixed meanings. The films are more frames than stories or flat two-dimensional surfaces, where objects and texts gather, associate, permutate, touch and richochet.

Pasolini had little faith in the contemporary world. He saw modern society and especially modern capitalism as destructive, homogenising and commodifying everything and everyone, particularly languages and images, until there would be no difference, nothing other, nothing precious, no values, but that of exchange, an immobility, sameness. It is the story of all his films where the ancient world, before capitalism or what is left of it after capitalism (*Accattone*, *Mamma Roma*, *La ricotta*), is the victim of the modern and an accusation against it, with Pasolini, the prophet and critic seeing a present disaster and foreseeing something worse, the acceptance of it, compromise.

Pasolini, the poet, brings back the past and in doing so brings difference into the heart of his work, refreshing poetry, redeeming it, so that it might appear one day like a new beginning.

It is the forms of his work that eloquently speak though he loathed a formalism that might too easily serve the social ends of contemporary society that could be bought, marketed, celebrated. If for some artists, juxtaposition, fragmentation and dissonance were ends in themselves, for Pasolini they were means. For him, these strategies resulted in being difficult, scandalous, outrageous, not simply for the manner, the form of juxtaposition, disunity and contrast, but for the substance of it where form was his content. It was around these substances, like that of the condensed notions of the ancient world and the modern, that Pasolini constructed a line of resistance, a ferocity not to be accepted, the value of non-acceptance. There is no negotiation in his works. They are harsh, accusatory, the shocking made lyrical or comic, as in *Salò* (1975).

Ambulation

João César Monteiro's last film, *Vai e Vem*, was made in 2002. The central character, as with most of his films, is Monteiro himself sometimes named João de Dieu, or, as in this film, João Vuvu or simply Monteiro. Soon after the release of *Vai e Vem*, which ends with the death of João Vuvu, Monteiro died from a long illness (presumably cancer) which he was certainly aware of when he made the film. The last image is an extreme close-up on the (dead) eye of Vuvu as if the eye and the image takes in, absorbs and what is absorbed is everything that there is, as if seeing has little to do with projection, but much to do with ingestion. *Vai e Vem* translated means 'Going and Coming'. The double 'V' of the character's name 'Vuvu' refers to the ambulation of going and coming and to 'seeing' ('vu') as one comes and goes.

There are two symmetrical spaces in the film and a space between them. One is interior, the flat where Vuvu lives and where he meets, interviews and speaks and plays with pretty girls who answer his advertisement for a housekeeper; the other space is a public park where Vuvu watches the passing scene, runs after a cyclist, throws offal to the pigeons, and where he dies. The spaces are the other side of each other and the contrary of one another: the interior is closed, social (meetings, eroticism, conversations), the exterior is open and anti-social (private, hostile and misanthropic). Between the two is the bus that he travels in from one space to another. The bus space is simultaneously immobile (a fixed interior) and mobile (a moving exterior as the bus moves) as well as social (encounters) and private (isolation). Monteiro plays within this simple structure where things become very complicated. Each space has its own rhythms and music through the editing and the shooting. Monteiro plays, as one might play with a poem or a piece of music, upon the fixed and the passing, with duration and tempo, with rhymes and counterpoints.

The bus is a place where Vuvu dances, sings, joins the community and that includes, as in the other spaces, the vastness of the world, both trivial and sublime, and sometimes, in being trivial, becoming sublime. In the passage between different and connecting spaces and between the infinitesmal and the infinite, another line is drawn, fragile and delicate, between the real and the fantastic, a frontier in Monteiro's films always indistinct yet at the same time, and, because of its indistinct indefinite quality, compelling: the unimportant becomes large, the mean becomes sacred and the real transformed into the purely imaginary. The imaginary is a quality of all his images, not unlike those of Alain Resnais. In Monteiro's films, the imaginary is a passage of ingestion, observation, a sense of the preciousness of the casual and the fleeting, and hence of life. For Monteiro the imaginary is an instrument of the poetic and the sacred, where the profound is brought down to the mean and the mean raised to heaven, and where concrete realities as givens with all their disorder and messiness and energies are made into forms by as simple a gesture as intensifying them by a regard and to the smallest details (their essence) that perhaps only the camera can reveal and revere, a lesson Monteiro may have learned from Bresson, Godard, Renoir, Rossellini, and almost certainly from the Surrealists.

As opposed to social laws, Monteiro celebrates the beauty of things and of persons from which he composes his films and on behalf of whom the films are composed – it is what things give him and that he absorbs (that he views, ingests, caresses, regards) and that constitutes his films, at once anti-social and ethical-aesthetic, an ethical-aesthetic that is particular (erotic, sensual, joyous, religious) and needs to be viewed to be appreciated. That ethic-aesthetic can be called Monteirism. Monteiro was one of the great *auteurs* of the cinema, certainly a genius as some alley cats are royalty.

Archive

Jean-Luc Godard tends to break up any pattern or configuration he gives shape to in his films or whose shape he happens to encounter or discover as it is being formed or perceived through the lens of the camera or at the editing table. The images and sounds in *Histoire(s) du cinéma* (1988–98) are mostly fragments from other unities cut out from an original context and, even if recognisable, something new. Because these elements are so particular, it makes it difficult to say what precisely they represent or what they might signify beyond themselves. Their context is not actual but virtual and multiple and they are constantly being reconfigured.

The images, statements and sounds in the film belong to the past. They function in *Histoire(s)* as historical documents, material from which histories might be constructed. *Histoire(s)* itself is not a history or histories, but an archive for histories yet to take shape, in a process of being newly constituted upon each viewing.

Histoire(s) has less to do with forming a history than with *de-forming* history, disrupting classification or permanence, hence the pluralism of history with an 's' and the variety, boundaries, gaps and intersections between images and sounds of different provenances. Godard's films, because of the strategies they adopt, tend to undermine and destabilise conventions, traditions and forms that characterised and still characterise the cinema. *Histoire(s)* functions similarly with regard to history which it destabilises rather than forms. It is no more a film in the usual sense than it is a history of the cinema.

With every truly new entry in an archive, that which is not immediately classifiable, a breach is opened in the archive as conceived. In so far as every image and sound is difficult to qualify (all are plural), each has the function of declassification that corrupts secure identities such that, at every moment, the film seems to begin again, causing both the cinema, its history and *Histoire(s)* to be rethought from zero.

The film opens on to an as yet unknown world even if its elements are known and in cases familiar. It is an archive of materials so 'fatally idiomatic' (Derrida) as not to be transmittable. One thing is certain however from its view of history and of stories, that the idea of a definitive historical narrative rendering the truth of things is an illusion. Godard's film is a history of the construction of illusions, which it dismantles rather than explicates. Rather than presenting documents to exemplify a history, the film uses documents that go to work, perform, act upon history and film history, upon conventions of film, upon established aesthetics and established views which, in various ways and by various means, are debunked.

Bringing together diverse materials, rather than illustrating previously existing relations, creates new relations. It is Godard's essential undertaking and achievement.

The rapidity of cutting and, especially, flickering is noticeable as a fact and thus constitutes, objectively, the content of the film.

Since Godard's films and most radically his *Histoire(s)* lead outside itself as if the externals are its interior, it leads to a beyond of itself but, unlike, say, a Picasso collage or the Combines of Rauschenberg or the serialisations of Warhol and the works of Lichtenstein, where the outside is primarily material (paper, metal, fabric), Godard's externals are texts of one sort or another (paintings, films, poems, philosophy, literature, biography), some composed and others of a more documentary nature (war footage, records of executions, records of the death camps). In some instances the distinction of document to fiction is blurred (the false documentarism for example in Eisenstein's films), taken as fact. These textual citations however are as much matter and real as the materials in a Picasso collage and just as alive: 'la peinture est plus que jamais matière vivante' ('paint is more than ever living matter').

The power in these images to associate with an infinity of *histoire(s)* ... in a being without ends or beginnings ... like a perpetual machine.

In the classical film, determinations are internal, images follow each other, one shot as the consequence of the next, and at all levels: framing, composition, action, drama, character, tempo, colour, sound. Once something is established as a context, quite literally in an establishing shot, or as a theme, or by a dramatic event, everything follows, including and perhaps especially patterns of editing, a montage that creates and sustains continuities. Interiorisation in painting is by perspective, the frame, a fixed point of view.

Histoire(s) du cinéma has no such internal determinations, rather everything comes from the outside. It disrupts and interrupts what is established. It is a juxtaposition, a questioning, a disjunction, a breach. Images and sounds arrive from a great distance of time and space, making it impossible to speak of *Histoire(s)* in terms of an evolution between fixed points, from a beginning or from an identifiable origin to a precise end. The *film* begins but what begins is not story, plot, drama. It is not of a narrative, nor is any beginning singular. Every place is ephemeral, unstable, multiple and in flux. The film is composed of seemingly infinite, inconclusive, shifting beginning(s) as if it begins at every moment and by so doing changes everything. In that sense, the film looks back without ever becoming historical, altering what had been by what comes after, a film that is ever in the process of becoming, of being different from what it had been even an instant before. There is no *off* therefore because the place of any image and its glide of references make such categories unstable since every image is the *off* of another one.

The realist positions taken by André Bazin at the close of the Second World War, best exemplified for him by Italian neorealism, later by the films of the French *Nouvelle Vague*, was not on behalf of an internally consistent realism, likenesses to life supposed to reflect reality, but rather concerned reality as a break and disruption, the outside coming in, document in the midst of fiction, a scattering of the illusions of a realism dependent on internal consistency and coherence. As soon as the outside – the documentary real or the presence of the film as other to what it represents – enters such cohesiveness it sows a seed of dissolution by its otherness (Zavattini).

Godard's films and his *Histoire(s)* pre-eminently are marked by such interruptions from the outside that disestablish whatever is. The stutter, blink, jump and flicker of some images fragment while others fuse by superimposition, fading and condensation. Elements joined together seem extraneous to each other and unstable like some chemical compounds. Godard is physically present in *Histoire(s)* in body and/or in voice. Sometimes his voice is disembodied. He is the master of ceremonies, the conductor of an orchestra, a spectator musing, imagining, remembering, reflecting on images projected, sounds heard and the associations they call up, social, cultural, personal. Godard's roles are multiple. Their most important aspect is that they are in two places at once, within the film as characters and outside it as person. Identities are blurred, mirrored, mediated, negotiated, played upon, not only for persons-characters like Godard in the film, watching, commenting, organising, being represented, but for an audience.

Sometimes in the film, absorbed with the lyricism, tones, physical and sensual beauty of a scene or its mystery, something occurs that jars, is disharmonic, not unlike the passage of the gull that crosses the frame in Hitchcock's *The Birds* (1963) as Melanie Daniels heads back in a boat to Bodega Bay and a gull crosses the frame, of the contours of the bay and of Melanie's fixed pose. Her presence and their presence unsettle previously established patterns of the images, their carefully balanced peaceful, symmetry and harmony. The scene also creates a mirror of associations between Melanie, birds and the form of the shots. She crosses the bay, the birds cross the frame, the crossings disrupt the structure of shots, opening a tear and imbalance. The breach in pattern unnerves Melanie, the spectators, the characters, Bodega Bay, reason, order, bringing the film and us toward the chaos of the irrational, mysterious and exciting, the absolute terror of certain uncertainty, an outside element made not only part of the fiction but its dominant, that is the birds.

In *3A La Monnaie de l'absolu* of *Histoire(s)*, the birds from *The Birds* swoop down on the children as they run from the school accompanied by the piano music of the third scene (*Blind Man's Buff*) of Schumann's *Kinderszenen* (*Scenes from Childhood*) (1838) and the syncopated tolling of funeral bells from another entirely different elsewhere. The sequence is associated in *Histoire(s)* with Charles Laughton's *The Night of the Hunter* (1955), Dolores Del Rio's leap in King Vidor's *Bird of Paradise* (1932), earlier archive scenes in the film of bombings, a child wandering on a road scattered with dead bodies, Francisco Goya's *Saturn Devouring His Son* (1819–23), the destruction of Guernica (the event, Picasso's painting of Guernica, and Resnais's *Guernica*, (1950)), and with Edmund's leap to his death in Rossellini's *Germania anno zero* (1947).

The associations are multiple. They form different constellations and new patterns, some formal, some thematic. The scenes of innocence defiled, murdered, sacrificed, some from documentary footage, some from fictional films, are of violation and horror that associate them, but they also function as disruptions, fragments that transgress an order, that are always other yet never cease to be themselves, even and especially in their associations and juxtapositions: *Kinderszenen*, the tolling of the bells, Schumann and Hitchcock. Images and sounds are in more than one place, divided and joined, separate and unified, inside and out.

Two types of images. The first is produced by a fracturing into several fragments. The second is an effect of coalesence, superimposition. In both cases all the variations of linkages are in play: succession, displacement, insertion, reconnection.

There is an opposition in *Histoire(s)* between past and present. The past, narratively speaking, is the entirety of the narrative, what has been and what can be cut up and combined in an ideal synthesis. The present, to the contrary, is the coming of things, their heterogeneity, the movement of things and thus unforseeable and open to chance, to the possible. The present is by definition incomplete. It brings into play the idea of a rupture (but with what? with the past?); in the past there are details of a whole which can be brought together and synthesised. The present, however, is fragmentary. The opposition of detail/fragment. If everything is a citation, that is, a fragment, the spectator is confronted with a proliferation of signs that cannot be integrated as in everyday life. A scripted or literary film based on the text is essentially 'dead' because it wholly belongs to what is already and that it illustrates; it is already complete, finished, whereas the film of images in the present is 'alive', open, unfinished, thus the attraction of the French *Nouvelle Vague* to the incompleteness and lack of resolution in the films of Roberto Rossellini.

Historically speaking, *Histoire(s) du cinéma* appears more than a century after the first film exhibition by the Lumière brothers (1895). On the other hand, because it comes historically last and because it is a critical, indeed analytic view of the past and its history, it can be argued that the *Histoire(s)* literally reinstitutes the past and, by so doing, it comes first, as with almost all images in Godard's films which reflect on his films and their representations as the content of a Godard film, that is his *Histoire(s)* though chronologically last in fact come first as the endings of his films come first – not unlike the retrospective structure of whodunits – and, in doing so, they provide an understanding, a lesson of what has been seen, that, and it needs to be emphasised, must come *after* the *Histoire(s)* which is their comprehension and hence force a reading in reverse. And though the films precede *Histoire(s)* historically, by providing the idea of them, an analysis, an elucidation, a remembering of them, as such, the *Histoire(s)* for that reason must come first. It initiates history and is made for that purpose as reflection, commentary and question, as if only after seeing *Histoire(s)*, which changes everything, can all that had been be understood in accord with the Godardian rule that you need another image to see an image, another fragment to see the fragment before, another instance to grasp the moment that had been. Godard is, and always has been, a historian of the cinema.

Roughly speaking there are five types of images in *Histoire(s) du cinéma*: archival (documentary), fictional (from films), staged (actors speaking lines, including Godard), works of art (reproductions of paintings, sculpture), titles (a phrase, a word). There are also different kinds of sounds, some in accord with an image or sounds, others at a distance from these. The sounds are musical, natural but non-verbal (the rhythmic clicks of the typewriter or the whirr of film on the editing table, the rings of a telephone, the roar of aircraft), verbal (staged, cited or a narrative voice-over commentary). Such gatherings of differences have characterised all of Godard's films.

The Godard film is a field in which images and sounds encounter and speak to each other. Between these differences is the gap that establishes them. The material of the classical film was disengaged from varieties of possible styles, images and sounds and from the differences and otherness of the world in order to form a homogeneity, a fictionalised and fictional unity in which gaps, as interruption, discontinuity, elisions, rather than stressed were effaced. The ellipse, for example, functioned not as a breach through which difference could enter but as a transition between likenesses and thus the gap was unnoticeable and difference blocked. This was the case of the shot/reverse-shot system in exchanges of dialogue where the presence of the camera and an outside to the fiction was suppressed by binding the spectator within the scene, hence within the fiction. In reality (in the process of the film), there was a gap, but fictionally (in the projection of the film), there was none.

Godard's films frequently cite the films of Italian neorealism, especially, directly and indirectly, of Roberto Rossellini, in particular Rossellini's earliest films of the 1940s and 1950s, *Roma città aperta* (1945), *Paisà* (1946), *Germania anno zero, Stromboli* (1949), *Francesco, giullare di Dio* (1950), *Europa '51* (1952), *Viaggio in Italia* (1954). In *Histoire(s) du cinéma* there are more than twenty-five references to Rossellini and citations from his films. Characteristic of early Rossellini is a difference posed between the fictional and the reality exterior to it, between cultures, languages, and persons who cannot be easily assimilated into a fictional world. The 'other' is not simply difference but scandal, confrontation and mystery. More importantly, perhaps, it is a lesson learned from Jean Rouch. Every instance of Rossellini's films that seem to be document is impermanent and immediately appears as fiction, and this also dissolves into document. There is not one *or* the other or even one *and* the other, but a movement *between* that fluctuates constantly (as with Godard's films and above all *Histoire(s) du cinéma*) and that movement is what you see, each instant the clarification of every other. As the film moves, it is in constant redefinition. Nothing remains what it was as if the film becomes other than it had been and does so forever.

Histoire(s) with an 's' is the variety and quantity of stories told by the cinema and cited by the film, the relation of these to each other and the relation of the stories to the wider story of history. Most Godard films centre on two dimensions, the couple and the outside world that impinges upon them. It is an echo of the films of Rossellini, especially those with Ingrid Bergman, a Hollywood actress out of place in a real setting. It is present in *Histoire(s)* not as a fictional love affair subject to the vagaries of reality but in terms of the inadequate response of the cinema in general (its fictions, its stories) to the horrors (massacres, wars, the Holocaust, terror) of the century in which both, cinema and historical horror, grew apace, though not together, as if their separate existences were a guarantee for the horrors to continue and the cinema to be sustained as it was (to be profitable), hence a link between a certain form and historical occurrences. In order to account for historical realities, as Rossellini did, an alteration in film form (a way of thinking therefore) was necessary.

With the exception of a few films, *Histoire(s)* suggests that the cinema ensured that history (external realities) was excluded. The question raised by Godard in *Histoire(s)* is why the exclusion, especially because of the capacity of the cinema, not only to bring the outside in but to reproduce reality, not as fiction and illusion but as the real in all its heterogeneity, mystery and untidiness, a real as other and disruptive for the good reason that the fictional in the past history of the cinema was made coherent while reality is never so.

Film, it seemed, was doubly condemned to isolation from the real: it was condemned to narrative and by that fact to the script, to writing in which to film was not an opportunity to respond to accident, immediacy, contingency, sentiment, commentary, the personal, in short to difference, but rather the illustration of a premeditated plan in which uncertainties, intimacies, chance, providence, the miraculous were prevented from entering. The cinema was closed to such possibilities rather than an instrument for their introduction.

It is not difficult to understand the enthusiasm of the French *Nouvelle Vague*, and of Godard especially, for the films of Jean Rouch of the 1950s and early 1960s such as *Jaguar* (1954–67), *La Chasse au lion à l'arc* (1957–64), *Moi, un Noir* (1958) and *Chronique d'un été* (1960), where real people acted out their own stories in real settings as they responded to those settings, to the selves they projected and to each other. Fiction and reality were posed as complements whose borders however were obscured, the fictional seeping into the real and the real into the fictional.

The disjunctions between cinema and reality are not in *Histoire(s)* differences to be overcome but rather differences to be found and sustained. The problem is formal and meeting it required not a discourse on historical horrors or an interpretation of history still less a direct, unmediated representation and recording of such events, than it does the invention of forms to highlight and question the relation of fiction to reality, in order to keep things alive, refuse cohesion, embrace chance, flexibility, otherness, even obscurity, so that the world may be allowed to create disturbances and these in turn knowledge, in short, what according to Godard, the cinema historically failed to produce.

Histoire(s) du cinéma is not thereby a rejection of what the cinema has been but the transformation of a past that still survives, though in ruins, fragments of memory and sentiments where it can be repositioned, saved, reconceived, made part of the future, part of histories where stories and the world can come together differently, as it does, returning to Rouch, in Marceline's walk along the Champs-Elysées in *Chronique d'un été* tracked by Rouch's camera and a Nagra recorder, as she remembers her father helplessly having to watch an SS officer slap her face, or the shock of Landry, the black African, learning the significance of the numbers tattooed on Marceline's arm, the real suddenly making its appearance, as it does in Rossellini, disturbing lunch and laughter, a shifting of tones.

As Jacques Aumont says, there are two essential 'histories' involved in the title 'histoire(s) du cinéma': History proper (political, social, cultural), and stories (narratives). History itself is a narrative and one of the tasks of the historian is to sort out events from narrative. For Godard, the cinema is involved with the events of history (history proper) and with narratives (*histoires*) and at the same time in so far as the domain of the one necessarily involves the other. The fact that film can tell stories is itself the result of a certain historical situation. And if it has a relation to the wider history, it is in having related stories. *Histoire(s)* is an encounter between History and stories. For example, 1A *Toutes les histoires*, the reflection of the studio system on the one hand, and the presence of the real in the Second World War and in the Holocaust.

It is impossible to argue that the fragments of works by filmmakers, painters, poets, composers, novelists, philosophers, historians, inventors, intellectuals cited in *Histoire(s) du cinéma* are direct influences on Godard or on his film. They are instead filiations, none causal, unmediated, ordered or precise. They arise and meet at moments in *Histoire(s)* in a flash, a sudden arrest, an interruption of what was, or was coming to be, dictated by the immediate present, calling to the past and retrieving it. These fragments, which intersect and thicken, often impossibly and in unlikely ways, are always in attendance. Their appearance can never be planned, and, when their time comes, an evanescent time that will never come again, like a thought that arrives or a gesture caught, is temporary, genuine, to be cherished, to make you pause, that halts continuity and disrupts stability.

All images in *Histoire(s)* are historical, pieces of time, not because every image everywhere has a history (though it does), but for the fact that in *Histoire(s)* the past contained within its images is more than a field of reference or a mark of influence, and more than history as commonly presented. They are disconnected images from narratives no longer with a subject to narrate or a story to tell. The Godard image, in addition to having a past or pasts, has the past as its subject, the past made evident, conscious, framed, whose presence, not sense, is attested to, insisted upon, yet impossible to absorb, resistant to historicise, because the past it comes from is already in tatters, disorganised, made of stories that no longer hold, philosophies reduced to a line, musical compositions of which only a few bars remain, events that cannot be summarised or fully represented, a phrase here, a phrase there, a fragment of a painting, flotsam, jetsam, bric-a-brac, a field strewn with litter seemingly thrown together, accumulated, piled up.

The connections to the past in *Histoire(s)* are unplanned, often inconsequential, indefinite, without causality, boundaries, perspectives or a frame. As such, every image that appears is called into question as is History, the cinema, the history of the cinema, its traditions, precisely because direction is eschewed and tradition ignored. The past in *Histoire(s)* is a heap of debris, chaotic and disestablished, not a field for historians, but, following Walter Benjamin, for collectors, *flâneurs* there to find foregathered Jerry Lewis, Nick Ray, Robert Bresson, John Ford, Fritz Lang, Roberto Rossellini, François Truffaut, Ludwig Wittgenstein, André Malraux, William Faulkner, Virginia Woolf, Franz Liszt, Riccardo Cocciante, Leonard Cohen, Jean-Paul Sartre, Wolfgang Amadeus Mozart, Giuseppe Verdi, Sam Fuller, Cocteau, Cervantes, Rilke, Homer, Chaplin, pornography, Hitchcock, the Holocaust, hangings, shootings, executions, monsters, Henri Langlois, Picasso, Charles-Ferdinand Ramuz, Beethoven, massacres, Goya, Chopin.

The list is infinite, unclassifiable, unsystematic and random, its value is in the singularity of each name, figure, person, portrait, object, event. Rather than representing an established tradition, musical, filmic, literary or philosophical, the list is, by its heterogeneity and disorderliness, directed against tradition, history, the authority the past might once have had.

Perhaps all histories of art should be unstructured in this way, unlike political and social histories. Since the mid-nineteenth century, art has been less about continuing traditions than about overturning and displacing these, not with another tradition but with none at all. Such a history, without a tradition to establish, but rather traditions to dismantle, has become a norm of twentieth-century modernism and with Dada and Pop above all.

Histoire(s) is an anti-traditional, anti-historical, destructive, anarchic work, not history, but a witness to contemporary historical impossiblities. In it, the past rises up in the present to shatter all that is ordered, institutionalised, connected, systematic, reasonable, customary, more exactly to expose the true existence of these conditions as current since the destruction (historically speaking) has already occurred.

For Godard, true history is not the traditions inherited from the past but the break with these, that which checks the progressive movement of history. What his names, images, sounds, sayings from the past have in common, their true filiation and sign of genuineness, their power and fraternity, is their *function*, to break, decompose, destroy and for Godard (and us) to stroll through the ruins that remain, gather up what is left and what we might fancy, that catches our attention and might be useful. All this depends on the depth and extreme of disconnectedness, of the separateness that *Histoire(s)* creates in some cases, but recognises in all, where montage is the privileged means of perception. History is not in *Histoire(s)* a representation, structure, text, discourse, reasoned argument, but an activity.

Every citation is a document and every citation belongs to a fiction (at least a construction): there is a double history in every citation (the history of it as a document – HISTOIRE – and the history of it as fiction and story: histoire).

The histories that *Histoire(s) du cinéma* evokes and belongs to go beyond the boundaries of the traditional history of the cinema. Godard's history of the cinema places the cinema with the other arts, philosophy, anthropology and the discipline of history. What makes the excess of histories possible in *Histoire(s)* is a reconception of the way in which film is structured (a new cinema) and the way in which history is structured (a new history).

Histoire(s) is a new cinema by its forms, and a new way of thinking history as a consequence. The practices of tradition, influence, development, evolution that mark both history and cinema – the history of the cinema having been subject to existing models of history writing – are displaced by contrary practices of discontinuity and rupture. Just as *Histoire(s)* takes apart and dismantles a certain history of the cinema (as orderly progress, as genres, as styles), it also dismantles traditional practices of the cinema (its classicism, narrative, the dominant role of the script, linearity), and it dismantles traditional historical narratives. The film accomplishes four levels of dislodgement: of the practices of cinema, of the practices of the history of it, of the practices of history, of the perception of events. Taken together, these constitute reconceptions of reality and its representation.

The excess in *Histoire(s)* by the presence within it of heterogeneous histories, events, objects, figures, disciplines, that intersect with the cinema, is the consequence of the intersections (the history of the cinema is greater than itself) and what makes them possible in the first place (discontinuity and rupture are openings). Different times, practices and substances necessarily come into contact with each other, causing homogeneous, continuous conjunctions and the linearity associated with them to fall away. The most evident difference is that the past in *Histoire(s)* is seized upon in the present, made present, not by logic or progression but by memory, by association and by the fact that in the film the past never passes or disappears. To regard a work in terms of progress and development is effectively to leave it behind as progress overtakes, as one style or set of forms displaces another. *Histoire(s)* obliterates nothing, on the contrary, it accumulates, recycles, reassigns.

To recover Griffith, Eisenstein, Lang, Rossellini, Ford and hundreds of others as *Histoire(s)* does is to pay homage to the excellence of their films. If the disjunctive manner of Godard is different from the narrative continuities of Griffith, these are viewed not to be displaced but as a stimulus, an accord of attitude and commitment, of metaphors, Godard would say.

The passing of the past is not only a consequence of progressive history, but relates to a vision of what the cinema *should* become: in effect, it is a manifesto. Godard, by accepting the past, highlighting, remembering and making it present, is not defining a direction but reordering the cinema beyond any historical framework, in excess of it, on the other side of any definitions or of a clearly marked future vocation.

The richness of *Histoire(s)* is a function of its correspondences, not of accords exactly, but of sodality (Rembrandt and Jean Vigo) that give the film depth and volume, literally constitute it and declare, by a *rapprochement*, that no film is alone, and the best of films least of all.

Arrangements

Bernardo Bertolucci's films can be divided roughly into two categories. One is operatic: spectacular, melodramatic, colourful, passionate, films that take place in multiple settings, often in exteriors and with large casts. Time in these films is historical time, inexorable, moving forward. The films that most clearly belong to this category are *The Last Emperor* (1987), *Novecento* (1976), *Strategia del ragno* (1970) and *La luna* (1979), orchestrated and lavishly staged. The other category is chamber music and chamber theatre. The films that belong to this category are *Ultimo tango a Parigi* (1972), *Besieged* (1999), *Stealing Beauty* (1996), *Agonia* (1969), *The Dreamers* (2003), *Partner* (1968) and Bertolucci's latest film, *Io e te* (2012), his first in a decade. The films are intimate, confined to limited spaces, often a single interior setting like a flat, hallway, basement, corridors, with muted colours and tones and limited light. The cast of players is small, sometimes as few as two or three. Characters seem imprisoned in narrow, cramped spaces. The effect is claustrophobic, an enclosed world, tense, shadowy, haunted by memories. Neither category, however, is absolute. There is a sense of confinement and imprisonment in every Bertolucci film from the most grand, like *The Last Emperor*, to the most minimal, like *Io e te*. And though the melodramatic characterises the larger films, it is not exclusive to them. *Ultimo tango a Parigi* with its grieving, passion and violence is both a melodrama, and a chamber piece.

Bertolucci's characters seek an escape, a liberation from where they are, to an elsewhere, hence their journeys to that elsewhere or their hiding out (*The Dreamers*, *Ultimo tango a Parigi*, *Partner*, *Io e te*). The journeys are sometimes physical (*The Sheltering Sky* (1990), *The Last Emperor*,

Little Buddha (1993)) or internal and psychological (*Il conformista* (1970), *Prima della rivoluzione* (1964), *Partner*, *Agonia*, but, usually, they are both.

The interplay and juxtapositions between characters, especially in the chamber pieces, are like differences between musical instruments in a duet or a trio, while the variations between characters and their divergence from each other are tonal, harmonic and rhythmic whose contraries almost always fade away. The visual is musical and the musical visual and gestural. At these moments, Bertolucci turns away from explication and narrative and turns toward the purely emotional and expressive by means of gestures, music, dance as in *Io e te*.

The enigma, the labyrinth are typical figurations in Bertolucci's films. They create a situation of a quest for resolution, clarity, settlement, discovery, a perpetual longing and desire for climax, for settlement. The two directions are contraries, and also complements, one pulling forward, advancing, seeking out, on the verge of elucidation, the other pulling back, both inextricably tied and mutually necessary to each other, like Giacobbe 1 and Giacobbe 2 in *Partner*, the two sides to Marcello in *Il conformista*, Athos the father and Athos the son in *Strategia del ragno*.

Bertolucci's films are films of cleavages, divided identities, doubles in search of singularity and unity. On the one hand, there is expectation and fulfilment, on the other, there is delay and hesitation, each at the threshold of the other. These are matters of time and its passage, at once emotional and sexual, seeking culmination, but detaining it, a perpetual postponement and irresolution, about to come, but not yet. This back and forth of essentially temporal contraries is the source of the vividness and pleasure of the films, at an edge between desire and its satisfaction, the definite and disintegration as if to seek out something too difficult to achieve and to seek it out too intensely, for too long and thereby to risk its existence. Writing sometimes is like that, a seeking to grasp something and by that effort to lose it.

In *Io e te*, there is a sense of an unavoidable passage of time, because so much in the film is repetitive, a scene or a note played over and over again, or held for too long, or so slight and undramatic as to appear insignificant, as if nothing much occurs, no events to speak of, no climax, no resolution, nothing to narrate, only tonal shifts, like hints, or a caress, grazing, nothing unequivocal, changes that are difficult to perceive because subtle, as if time stands still both eternal and relentless, urgent and resistant. Sex has only the merest suggestion in *Io e te*, a flirtation with incest, but not an issue, unlike the place of sex in Bertolucci's other films, some more, some less. Yet, because of its play on time, desire and uncertainty and the way it is played, *Io e te* is one of the most erotic of Bertolucci's films, the one most dependent on expectation, and by that fact most suggestive of *Viaggio in Italia* (1954), if not of all of Rossellini's films of the 1950s in which waiting and anticipation are central as are actual or spiritual imprisonment. The principal question in Rossellini's films is 'when' joined with a hope 'if only': will the couple in *Viaggio in Italia* come back together? and if so 'when?'; and there is the wait and expectation in the tuna fish sequence in Rossellini's *Stromboli* (1949), and the scene of revelation and surrender at the top of the volcano when Karin quite literally gives herself, surrenders. The most exquisite moment in all his films is at the moment of death when the young boy Edmund leaps from the ruins of a house in *Germania anno zero* (1947).

The scenes are reversals. It appears that the films are moving in one direction or not moving in any direction in particular and then suddenly, without a clear motive or warning, they move in an opposite direction or, as with Edmund, a leap into nothing expected. The surprise and the shock require a complete reconsideration of the films and of oneself. The reasons for what occurs are not evident before the act, but only after. *Io e te* is that kind of film.

The events in *Io e te* occur in a single week in Rome in the basement of an apartment block. There are two principal characters, Lorenzo, a boy of fourteen, and Olivia, his half-sister, in her mid-twenties. The basement, dark, dingy, dirty, messy, essentially a single room, is where Lorenzo hides out. He had been scheduled to go on a skiing trip organised for his class at school. But at the last minute, instead of giving the money for the trip to his teacher, as the other students had done, he pockets the money, has a spare key made to the basement and stocks up on supplies for a week.

Alone in his basement, he listens to rock music on headphones, moves in rhythm to the beat of the music lying on his back on a makeshift bed, a kind of squirming, and observes a colony of ants, an observation which gives him immense pleasure. Lorenzo's journey is a solitary exile rather than a journey 'away' in the usual sense, like what happens to Paul in

Ultimo tango a Parigi and like Kit's incarceration in the protected cell-like room of the Tuareg after the death of Port in *The Sheltering Sky* (1990). In these instances confinement is liberation and what happens to Kit is like what happens to the couple in *Viaggio in Italia*.

What Lorenzo travels to is nowhere, a hideout beneath the block of flats where he lives, and he does everything he can not to be discovered. It is a retreat from his mother, from the school, from the outside world, from everything that might be called 'normal'. His retreat is his private world, a willed solitary detention, almost a shipwreck, where Lorenzo appears most happy, most himself. His mother, over-protective and intrusive, believes he has gone skiing and that such socialising and activity are positive psychological signs in contrast to Lorenzo's isolation and unsociability. Now and then, Lorenzo's mother rings him up and he concocts a narrative of skiing and snow and companionship with his classmates and teacher to defend the integrity of his hideaway.

Into this paradise, Olivia suddenly (and noisily) appears, shouting, banging. Hers, and in every sense, is literally a new note, a different and contrary music. Olivia is a heroin addict, beautiful and alone. Nowhere else to go, she lands on – invades – the happily isolated hideaway of Lorenzo. The invasion is pure chance. Olivia has come to the basement to find a box of things that had been left there for her. Within a day of her arrival, Olivia, who is trying to break her heroin addiction by going cold turkey, becomes ill and in agony, vomits over herself. Lorenzo cares for her, himself another casualty.

Initially, Lorenzo wants Olivia to go away and leave him alone. But there is nowhere else for her to go and she becomes more ill and scared. He becomes sympathetic, as if, despite her otherness to him, Lorenzo finds in her a likeness of himself.

The Edenic hideaway has a limit of one week before the two must leave when Lorenzo's fictional skiing holiday will end. So, over seven days in the messiness and squalor of Eden, the two unlikely and in every way utterly different figures, must find a means to be together, to form, and almost against their will, a duet, a manner to be together, play together, understand each other, make music, trust, dance. Both are in need of salvation and each rescues the other. Each of them enters the world of the other one and there they improvise. *Io* (I) becomes *te* (You) and *te* becomes *io*, like the two Giacobbes become each other and the two Athoses do as do Kit and Port.

The music between them follows the same beat, rhythms and song. Olivia promises to give up drugs and Lorenzo to stop hiding. These are the preconditions for playing together, for a duet, despite everything, *malgré tout*. At that point, the week is over. Lorenzo and Olivia separate, go their own ways.

Olivia is the other side, the other half of Lorenzo, his contrary and his double. What happens between them is like a miracle of a conversion, or a spiritual revelation. The ending is Rossellinian, a sign of a past more than a half century ago in Rossellini's films with Ingrid Bergman that gave birth to the modern cinema after which, according to Jacques Rivette, everything in the cinema aged and nothing was the same again. It is that beginning and that end that Bertolucci's film pays homage to. If *Io e te* proves to be Bertolucci's last film, it is a most perfect beginning and perfect end, indeed, a perfect circle.

Authorship

Je fais ... de Hawks, le plus grand cinéaste, Griffith excepté, naquit en Amérique, bien supérieur à mon goût à Ford, généralement plus estimé. Ce dernier m'ennuie (qu'y puis-je?) tandis que l'autre me ravit ...

... j'aime le cinéma, parce que je crois qu'il est le fruit non du hasard mais de l'art et du génie de hommes, parce que je pense qu'on ne peut aimer profondément aucun film si l'on n'aime profondément ceux de Howard Hawks.

(I regard Hawks as the greatest filmmaker born in America with the exception of Griffith, far superior in my judgement to Ford who is generally more esteemed. The latter bores me (what can I say?) while the other enthralls me.

... I love the cinema because I believe it is not the result of chance but of art and the genius of men, because I believe that one cannot deeply love any film if one does not deeply love those of Howard Hawks.)

Eric Rohmer[1]

Jacques Rivette's essay in *Cahiers du cinéma* from the 1950s 'Génie de Howard Hawks' ('Genius of Howard Hawks') and the 1996 anthology

1 Maurice Schérer (Eric Rohmer), 'Les maîtres de l'aventure', *Cahiers du Cinéma*, vol. 5 (29 December 1953), p. 44. (This and subsequent translations of quotations are by the author, unless stated otherwise.)

of writings on Hawks edited by Peter Wollen and Jim Hillier, *Howard Hawks: American Artist*, are polemical in their titles.

The American cinema is first and foremost an industry producing goods for mass consumption and profit. Filmmakers, like Orson Welles and John Cassavetes, who experimented with new forms of film outside the conventions of Hollywood, were not welcome in Hollywood. Though Hollywood has always supported innovations that its commercial system could make profitable, it has not welcomed innovations with limited appeal to audiences, innovations that went too far. Welles and Cassavetes supported their own films by working as actors in other people's films or in commercial advertisements. Their films were too far removed from popular taste and established forms to be profitable. Essentially they spent their own money on their films rather than earning money with them. When they made films for the industry, they lost money for the studios. Other filmmakers, like Nicholas Ray, Sam Fuller and Anthony Mann, were either destroyed by the Hollywood system (Ray) or forced to compromise with it (Fuller and Mann) or had to bear the intrusions of the studio who remade (butchered) their films (Ray, Fuller, Mann and above all Welles, for example, with *The Magnificent Ambersons* (1942), *Touch of Evil* (1958), *The Lady from Shanghai* (1947)).

Hawks was the quintessential Hollywood filmmaker who conformed to its conventions while helping to establish them. To speak of Hawks's artistry in this situation is of a different order from speaking of the artistry of Welles or Cassavetes, whose artistry was defined by opposition to the Hollywood system and its forms. Hawks's 'genius' and artistry resides in his skill at using a traditional system and making it his own.

'Genius' and 'artist' are essentially terms about the assertion of a subjectivity making its presence felt in the work and often brilliantly, remarkably and evidently. If classical forms are remarkable for their objectivity, rules and clarity, modern forms are celebrated essentially for their subjectivity, an artistry that goes beyond the norms and establishes a new set of forms and language. Modernism is messier than classicism and norms are more difficult to establish – there is no agreement about what is beautiful or meaningful nor even an agreement that beauty and meaningfulness are values at all, nor is there an agreement about forms and traditions. An *auteur* is someone who creates his or her own system rather than putting into play an existing one (not their own). An *auteur* in this sense is a modern artist whereas those who put into play what already is established might be thought of as traditional skilled craftspeople and it is also perhaps what, initially at least, the critics of the French *Nouvelle Vague* liked and deemed important. Auteurship was a reward for excellence. A classical system is primarily imitative (of nature, of existing forms) and the great classical artist is someone great for his or her ability to imitate not innovate, who obeys the rules with grace and style.

The critical writing of *Cahiers du cinéma* in the period of the 1950s through to the early 1970s was dominated by the *politique des auteurs*. For the most part, the *auteurs* of Hollywood for the *Cahiers* critics (later film-makers) were primarily found within the Hollywood system not outside or opposed to it: Hitchcock, Hawks, early Nicholas Ray, Sirk, early Fuller, Ford, Preminger, Mankiewicz.

A notion of *écriture* (literally, 'writing') became central to both the films and the criticism of the French *Nouvelle Vague* in their formulations of *la politique des auteurs*. In the American film tradition and especially that thought of as classical, the entire means of the cinema (the use of the camera, dialogue, characterisation, movement, editing, settings) were subordinate to narrative and story. In that sense the forms of the American classical film were essentially forms for the realisation of a narrative, to make it clear, comprehensible, exciting, dramatic and enter-taining. A precondition for the success of such narrative dominance was the effacement of the forms which realised the narrative (invisible editing, narratively motivated, shifts in angles, in scale, in scene transi-tions, in the movement of the camera), as if, for the sake of the narrative, the film and its forms had to be invisible in order not to be disruptive. *Écriture*, in the sense of a visible writing, was an idea tied simultane-ously to that of authorship (subjectivity) and to the visibility of forms (expression as no longer subordinate to the demands of a narrative, but to a degree independent of it). Thus, for *Citizen Kane* (1941), the narra-tive, rather than being the purpose of the film, what the film put in the foreground, became instead a background for a noticeable display of cin-ematic means and hence evidence (indeed privileging) of the presence of Welles. After all, Welles was being 'sold' by the studios as a star-genius and *Kane* was the vehicle for that, a moment when Welles's ambitions and the commercial interests of the RKO studio roughly seemed to coincide.

The notion of Hawks as 'genius', '*auteur*' and 'artist' represents an important moment in the transformation of the understanding of Hollywood
and beyond Hollywood, the understanding of the cinema more generally.
Effectively, the *Cahiers* critics, and Rivette in particular, disengaged the
formality of Hawks's films from the story and narratives in which they
were embedded and which they served, and made them visible. Hawks
was praised for the formal grace and elegance of his work, at once giving
his work classical status while naming classicism as only a form, as a certain tradition that was 'written', a 'writing', an enunciativeness and in its
polemical edge and that neon, an *écriture*, thus opening up the classical
cinema to the cinema more generally, taking from it its supposed objectivity and informing it (subverting it) with a subjectivity that was foreign
to it. The individuality of Hawks, unlike that of Welles, was perfectly in
accord with the Hollywood system, yet, in a surprising way, the identification and equalisation of Hawks and Hitchcock (in the Hollywood system)
with Welles, Renoir, Dreyer (outside of it) as all *auteurs* made of the
Hollywood system something it possibly was not while suggesting that it
belonged to a more heterogeneous field of individual expression, artistry
and genius and the manipulation of forms (*écriture*).

In a curious way the Hollywood system for the French was only something to be cited and if it was imitated (as it was by Demy, Truffaut,
Rohmer and Godard), it was more like a reference than a duplication or
at least every duplication was surrounded by quotation marks and set
alongside other styles, other conventions. The classical system became
central to the modern cinema by being reduced to a citation, part of the
heterogeneous texts of modernism, a tradition not so much to oppose
(as Welles sometimes did, or was thought to have done) but to set off
and play with (the gangster film in Godard's *À bout de souffle* (1960) and
Truffaut's *Tirez sur le pianiste* (1960), the American musical in Demy's
Les Demoiselles de Rochefort (1967) and Godard's *Une femme est une femme*
(1961), Hitchcock in virtually all the films of Rohmer and Chabrol, and
of course the presence of *film noir* in Welles's *The Lady from Shanghai*
and Cassavetes's *The Killing of a Chinese Bookie* (1976), and not as a con-
tinuation of these genres but as the resurrection of them as pure forms to
be interrogated, rewritten, subjectivised and transformed, from films of
genre to films of *auteurs* – in short, American film genres, but made into
the 'idea' of them. In the case of Hawks, there is no such distinction –

genre and *auteur* happily coexist). This change in consciousness and in films occurs at the moment when the Hollywood classical system was beginning to decline and the studios to break up. If subjectivity and all the terms that are associated with it in French criticism – *auteur, écriture* – are a central constituent of the modern cinema, its other aspect is *réalité*.

Bodies

Two 1964 paintings by Francis Bacon are reproduced in the credit sequence of Bertolucci's *Ultimo tango a Parigi* (1972) : *Portrait of Lucian Freud* (1969) and *Study for a Portrait of Isabel Rawsthorne* (1966). The portraits in the film first appear separately, then, towards the close of the sequence, are framed together.

Both Freud and Rawsthorne were painters, and, like Bacon, concentrated on portraiture and figures. Their paintings are expressionist, distorted by colour, light, line and position, at once realistic because figurative, and unrealistic by their deformations, defigurations, exaggerations, unnatural colouring and deframings bordering on the grotesque. Bacon acknowledged a debt, evident in his paintings, to Van Gogh and also to Cézanne, and Velazquez.

While making *Ultimo tango*, Bertolucci took Vittorio Storaro to an exhibition of Bacon's paintings in Paris; Storaro was the cinematographer of his early films, and of *Ultimo tango*. Bertolucci called Storaro's attention to the orange hues in Bacon's work, hues that dominate Storaro's images of the interior of the flat on rue Jules Verne where Paul (Marlon Brando) and Jeanne (Maria Schneider) encounter each other. Bertolucci also took Marlon Brando to the same exhibition. He remarked to Brando the intensity of suffering evident in Bacon's paintings, as if the figures were crying out in an agony that twisted their bodies out of shape. Brando duplicates that agony in the film during his walk along the metro bridge in Paris, and in his pose at the Jules Verne flat just before Jeanne enters.

Many of the scenes and depictions in *Ultimo tango* concern the isolation of figures by the use of shadow, the alternations of dark and light, the use of silhouette, the contorted pose of bodies, huddled in corners, often naked, caught in love-making, sitting, lying down, astride each other, curled up, stretched out, on their backs, face down, face up, Jeanne's arse waiting, inviting, Jeanne masturbating, her orgasm. The figures seem to have issued from Bacon's canvases as if the figures in his portraits had wandered into the film, like lost travellers cut adrift from the world.

Bertolucci's films are not equivalents of Bacon's post-expressionism, not a simple matter of borrowing, of influence or of inspiration. Bacon's portraits and bodies seem to have taken up residence in the Bertolucci film, doubling them. Bertolucci was fond of duplicating themes and images from paintings, literature, theatre, sculpture and opera, in short, from the arts. For example: Dostoevsky's *The Double* in *Partner* (1968), Antonio Ligabue's *naif* paintings in the credit sequence of *Strategia del ragno* (1970), Giuseppe Pelizza da Volpedo's late nineteenth-painting *Il quarto stato* in the credit sequence in *Novecento* (1976). And the references to Stendhal and Flaubert in *Prima della rivoluzione* (1964). And Giuseppe Verdi is everywhere in Bertolucci's films.

What is important in the doubling of Bacon's paintings by Bertolucci in *Ultimo tango* is less the specific duplications in his work and their re-creation in film than a more general practice in Bertolucci's work at once classical and resistant to classicism. Bertolucci's narratives turn back on themselves, are enigmatic and elliptical, sometimes obscure, often unresolved, as in Ingmar Bergman's films, especially *Persona* (1966) where identity and doubling are central as they are in the films of Orson Welles.

In Bergman's *Persona*, for example, the subject within the film for the characters and for the spectator is to resolve the enigma of Elisabet's silence. The film is that dilemma. Its narrative is obscure, puzzling and intense. Bertolucci narrates, describes, represents (as Bergman and Welles do). At the same time, he struggles against the narratives he portrays. Bacon, more insistently, engages in that struggle of representation and against representation, the subject of his paintings and the subject of Bertolucci's films.

Bacon was not a formalist. His paintings are not abstract. They are dominated by figures, some, like his portraits of Freud and Rawsthorne, are recognisable, however defaced. Though his work relates to a classical, representational, realistic tradition, it is also in conflict with it. Bacon disintegrates, distorts, against illustration and representation. What classicism affirms, he subverts, making it difficult to constitute a narrative or an anecdote. His figures are cut off from likenesses, from contexts. No story is recounted, no connectives hold, instead there is isolation, decomposition, indecisiveness and imperceptibility, the indescribable marked by disfigurement.

Bodies, objects that enter Bacon's paintings, their origin dimly present, emerge scarred, battered, mutilated, stripped bare by their journey to another world. They belong to the classical world that has been left behind, and to the new world where they find themselves, discomfited, fragmented, in pain, not a substitute, or an erasure, but warped. The real in Bacon's paintings is not resemblance or appearance or story or significance. Instead, devastation, already lurking inside the image, to appear when summoned forth by Bacon and set free, often by an inversion, interiors on the surface, purified, not alternative reality, but real reality, found in painting as its unavoidable subject.

It is less important that Bertolucci imitates Bacon's images in *Ultimo tango* than that Bertolucci deals with similar problems, produced by an unease in the gap within which he works, between representation and a modernity that challenges it. Bertolucci incorporates both without surrendering to either, not to easy representation and illustration, nor, and certainly not, to what might be easier still, abstraction and the formal. The works of Bacon and Bertolucci, as Gilles Deleuze has insisted, are concerned with sensation where boundaries are bridged by colour and rhythm, and whose terms of warmth and energy are of greater moment than line or exactitude, logic or sense. Neither artist is an illusionist, both are dis-illusionists, like Welles, Bergman, Resnais, Van Gogh, Cézanne, artists who construct by deconstructions.

Bricolage

One of the consequences for Orson Welles of working in Europe was that it took a long time, often years, for him to complete a film once begun, and, because he was subject to constraints imposed by a lack of funding, these productions had a 'make-do' quality to them, not exactly improvisation so much as resourcefulness. When costumes did not materialise for a scene in *Othello* (1952) because they had not been paid for, Welles shot the scene in a Turkish bath where costumes were not necessary. Similarly, studio set-ups were often not available to him, making it necessary to use perceptible cardboard sets (*Macbeth* (1948)) or, because of gaps imposed on shooting, collages of different real locations (*Mr Arkadin* (1955)). *Mr Arkadin* documents not only the itinerary of Van Straaten but the itinerary of Welles in putting the film together over a number of years. Actors who had begun with him in shooting a film, because of the interruptions in shooting, often were elsewhere when shooting resumed. In those instances, Welles would either rewrite scenes to accommodate their absence or make them present by shooting them in shadow or from the back and thereby rearranging relations and occurrences.

The make-do, hodge-podge, bricolage quality of his films was not simply a consequence of conditions of production in his non-Hollywood work but also a quality in his Hollywood productions, one reason his films were unfamiliar to audiences and not successful. Rather than sketchiness, fragmentation, lack of finish and heterogeneity being merely a result of economic difficulties, they were characteristic of Welles's style.

If *Citizen Kane* (1941) (where Welles had complete freedom given to him by the studios) is compared to *Mr Arkadin* (where freedom was tempered by lack of money), similar stylistic effects and procedures are noticeable: multiple narratives, the joining together of disparate elements and different conventions, cutting that emphasised the discontinuity between shots and the events they depicted. In *Mr Arkadin*, Van Straaten sets out on a journey to find Arkadin's 'true' identity, his secret, similar to the investigation pursued in *Kane* by the reporter Thompson and resembling too the enigmatic qualities of Bannister and Elsa in *The Lady from Shanghai* (1947) and the identity of Quinlan in *Touch of Evil* (1958).

Within the narratives of these films there is an internal narrative (Thompson's, Van Straaten's) and within these the separate 'stories' (narratives) told by the characters encountered by Van Straaten in *Arkadin* and by Thompson in *Kane*. The different narratives, overlapping and intruding upon each other and located at different levels in the films, rather than clarifying the object of the quests (the secret of 'Rosebud' the identity of Arkadin), tend instead, by their differences and interruptions, to make the enigma of identity and hence of person, more obscure and the search labyrinthine. The multiplicity of the narrations is not only contradictory but fragmentary, incomplete. Neither Kane nor Arkadin is reflected as unity or coherence, and they are instead, like the films overall, constructed as discontinuities of multiple reflections. Alongside every story, every view, every perspective, there is another, just beyond it, that is its distortion, parody or contradiction. The sense of this otherness to whatever is remains a disquieting presence and not only in stories but in sequences and shots, as if whatever you see or hear contains another view of itself as in multiple mirrored views of the same as occurs at the close of *Kane* and in the closing sequence of *The Lady from Shanghai*. In Welles's films, the fragments prevail over continuity, the image over what it represents, as if the film and its images, not its representations, are the only realities, the exact reverse of the Hollywood film. The enigma presented in these films is a threat to clarity, continuity, singularity, identity, the stability of any representation as the reality of the image overcomes the realities it seeks, but fails to represent, hence the uneasiness of Welles's films, their failure to satisfy, to secure. In a Welles film there is no final, resolute reality that unmasks appearances, but rather only the uneasy reality of appearances and these are marked as such.

Characters

Ho eliminato ... tutti quelli che potevano essere nessi logici del racconto, gli scatti di sequenza per cui l'una sequenza faceva da trampolino alla successiva proprio perché m'é sembrato e ne sono fermamente convinto, che oggi il cinematografo debba essere legato più alla verità che alla logica.

(I have eliminated ... all that could be considered the logical connections of narrative, the sudden high points of a sequence in which a sequence functions like a trampoline for the successive one precisely because it seemed to me, and I am firmly convinced of it, that today's cinema must be linked to the truth of things rather than to logic.)

Michelangelo Antonioni[2]

In the silent period, more than in the 1930s with the coming of sound, the directors of films were recognised as authors, directors like Griffith, Chaplin, Murnau, Flaherty, Eisenstein, Pudovkin, Stroheim, Lang. The reason for that recognition was directly related to the relative openness of film, the uncertainty and lack of institutionalisation of its rules and forms of construction. The silent period, almost more than any other, was a time of experimentation. For that reason the personal was more a factor than the industrial, and films were more fresh, more apparently

2 Michelangelo Antonioni (colloquio con), 'La malattia dei sentimenti', *Bianco e nero*, vol. XXII, nos 2–3 (February–March 1961), pp. 75–6.

individual as if directors were in search of their particular expression and the means and possibilities of film to realise it.

The coming of sound altered the relation of director to film. It was a period, particularly in the United States (though not exclusively), of large studios, huge capital investment (and profits) and industrialised production. What is noticeable about the films of the 1930s and in instances up to and including the early 1950s is their conformity to a certain set of rules and conventions. It is these rules and obedience to them that has been referred to as 'classical'. What was valuable in that classicism was not the personal expression of the director but rather the ability of a director to follow the rules. The great directors were those who followed the rules best – not invention, but imitation, skill, not innovation or at least not innovation outside the rules. It was never the rules that were to be changed. It was not that directors were not appreciated nor recognised, but rather that appreciation and recognition were of a different order and on behalf of different qualities. To ignore what was industrially institutionalised was perilous, for example the experience of Orson Welles, originally given complete and almost unheard-of freedom under the assumption that he would simply bring some novelty and celebrity to what was already established rather than seek radically to disestablish what was the norm. Welles went too far.

The classical cinema was marked by technical procedures related to the industrial nature of its production. There was a clear division of labour and a division of stages in the making of a film: from idea to treatment, to script, to filming, to editing, to distribution, to marketing. In that system, the studio had the final say about a film project – what was or was not to be filmed, what types of film were to be made and how the film once shot was to be edited and all of it done to a schedule of so many weeks for one process and so many weeks for another. The script was not just an outline of events and the marking out of dialogue and of character but a *découpage*, a pre-editing of the film into sequences and sub-sequences and at times even into shots and suggestions of placement and movement (of actors and of camera) that determined the building of sets and the provision of decor and of costume. Films (and production schedules) were organised according to relatively fixed genres or types of film not unlike fashions or models of motor cars.

One of the qualities that these films had was predictability and a determinate structure (economically manageable and easily planned for).

What they lacked was the reverse of these, openness and indeterminacy (economic chaos). Films had to proceed clearly in a definite direction and means were invented to secure such direction, what has been referred to as continuity: a lucid and at best elegant succession of events leading to a conclusion. It was a cinema of theorem and logic. What these films also lacked (though their absence was considered a virtue) was anything that might disrupt or disturb the logic of continuity, in short qualities of spontaneity, or obscurity or hesitancy. Everything had to be known beforehand and therefore nothing was, strictly speaking, fragile, uncertain or fresh.

There were other rules associated with these, for example the invisibility of the film in relation to its story and drama. If the drama was to be transparent and coherent and the characters believable and identified with, then the film had to make sure that its presence was not felt because such presence would be an interruption and disruption of the fiction and because such a presence could have no fictional motivation, no justification. If you look at the films of the 1930s, they are marked (from film to film, director to director) not only by their conventionality but by the modesty of their conventions – few if any close-ups, no action or gesture or word that was not clearly motivated and understood, no truly objective shooting so that, in the movement from one shot to another, a dramatic reason or an exchange of looks or a continuity of points of view would be established (the shot/reverse-shot was a crucial instrument for maintaining the coherence of the fictional world and involving the spectator in it, not as an outside observer with the camera, but rather as a direct participant in that world).

Antonioni was among the new *auteurs* of what would become the future of the cinema where the rules of the past and its procedures no longer held. It is not that Antonioni's cinema is polemical in the way in which I think the films of Godard, early Truffaut, Rohmer and Rivette were, in which built into their films were comparisons, references and citations to a cinema that had been and also, in contrast, a programme for a cinema that they hoped would appear in which the past would be present but transformed, that is, their cinema as a consequence of a tradition but not traditional. Antonioni, like the *Nouvelle Vague*, did things differently, however not as an argument. His films are not posed as a contestation.

Antonioni's *Le amiche*, made in 1955, is his fourth feature, based on a novel by Cesare Pavese. It begins with an attempted suicide by Rosetta

(Madeleine Fischer) and ends with a successful suicide by Rosetta. Between these two events are a series of other events essentially of relations of the characters to each other and to the places in which the events occur: the streets and squares of Turin, railway stations, restaurants, bars, fashion houses, hotel rooms, the beach. The use of locations by Antonioni was, relative to the period and certainly relative to Italian neo-realism, unique. The locations were not decor background, fixed and intert, or atmosphere, or metaphor, or realistic background to a drama, but a relationship of the characters to where they were. The relations of characters to each other complicate Rosetta's situation without explaining it. In fact, they seem to be casual, unlinked to each other, and that determines nothing in particular. The film is essentially a document of these characters and what they do, but not as exceptional or dramatic occurrences, instead as normal, daily, even monotonous, almost unarticulated, at least not joined in any clear succession or development; nor are motives made evident. The film is posed, like *Cronaca di un amore* (1950), as an inquest, to decipher a situation rather than to interpret it, still less to dramatise it. The inquest, the seeming purpose of the film, dissolves and with it the sense of events that accumulate around it. This is a film without a centre and hence no event is strictly determined and every action is open. Rosetta's suicide has no greater import than Clelia's (Eleanora Rossi Drago) fashion show or her decision to leave Turin for Rome and thus to leave Carlo (Ettore Manni), or the fliration between Momina (Yvonne Furneaux) and Cesare (Franco Fabrizi).

The story, despite its complexity, seems less a plot or an intrigue than an observation of comportment and relations, almost formless without determinate ends. All of the relations are relations of dissolution, incomprehension, as if without substance, certainly without clear meaning or anything very positive. The triangle of Nene (Valentina Cortese), Rosetta and Lorenzo (Gabriele Ferzetti) is emptied of any dynamism, hence the relative blankness and lack of dramatic force of Rosetta's attempted or completed suicide.

It is extraordinary, certainly extraordinary in relation to the classical past of the cinema, that amidst all these characters and all their relations there seems to be no instance of a shot/reverse-shot to bring an audience into the interior of the fiction. On the contrary, Antonioni's camera and his editing (the sequences are lengthy, mostly in real time and only minimally fragmented – characters are followed, observed rather than constructed in the usual way) are rigorously objective, outside the film, looking in, interested without being directly engaged, at least not in the taking of a position or identifying with one, or even being sympathetic.

Antonioni was concerned to film his characters as they responded to the situation and locations they were in, hence a camera that followed and observed and hence too actors who were not unduly prepared or rehearsed in order to 'catch' their reactions, to document them and above all the rejection of the script and the primacy of a story in order to sustain the immediacy and freshness of the film and to allow a gesture or a sound or a movement to open up possibilities and to lead the film in a multiplicity of directions. In this circumstance, not to know beforehand was a virtue, and instead to be ready, attentive, aware, in short open and responsive.

The film emerges as an object and the characters and events as its forms, a different kind of notion of reality than had prevailed in the cinema, the classical one and the neorealist one (with the exception of Rossellini).

Classicism

Je ne m'intéresse pas tant aux acteurs qu'aux 'personnalités.' Un acteur lit le script et joue la scène comme elle est écrite, ou suivant les indications que lui donne le metteur en scène. Tandis qu'une 'personnalité' a une façon à elle de le faire et c'est ça qui fait les scènes intéressantes. Je ne me soucie pas d'une intrigue, je suis intéressée par des personnages et par les rapports qui peuvent exister entre eux. Mais pour avoir des personnages sur l'écran, il faut que vous ayez des 'personnalités' sur le plateau, alors les choses marchent bien, vous pouvez improviser, élaborer des scènes nouvelles ...

J'ai fait deux films avec lui [Bogart]; c'était facile et amusant de travailler avec Bogart, car lui, c'était une 'personnalité', et pour moi c'est ça qui fait l'intrigue.

(I am less interested in actors than I am in 'characters'. An actor reads the script and plays the scene as it is written, or follows directions given to him by the filmmaker. But a 'character' has his own way of doing it and that makes the scenes interesting. I am not so concerned with the story as I am with the characters and the relations they have with each other. But in order to have characters on the screen, you need to have 'characters' on the set, thus when things go well, you can improvise, develop new scenes.

... I have made two films with him [Bogart]; it was easy and fun to work with Bogart, because he was a 'character' and for me that is what makes the story.)

Howard Hawks[3]

The central theme of Howard Hawks's films is the itinerary. A journey needs to be taken by the main character or is entered into or endured by the main character. Along the way obstacles threaten the success of the journey and may force a change in it, not of its ends (to bring the cattle to market) but of its means (one trail rather than another, to Kansas rather than Missouri). More specifically, as in *Red River* (1948), *To Have and Have Not* (1944), *Only Angels Have Wings* (1939), *Rio Bravo* (1959), *The Big Sleep* (1946), the journey is about the overcoming of obstacles (means to an end). It is a journey at once of action and of character (inventiveness, resourcefulness, intelligence, tenacity, courage and dignity in the face of hopelessness). The actions that occur are tests of character and the films alternate (and bring together seamlessly) relations between characters and the actions they engage in. In Hawks's films, how characters act reveals their 'character'. The completion of the itinerary resolves differences within characters and between them. For this reason, in part, Hawks chooses actors with 'character' (Humphrey Bogart, Lauren Bacall, John Wayne, Montgomery Clift, Walter Brennan, Jean Arthur, Noah Beery Jr, John Ireland).

The beauty of a Hawks film is its simplicity and straightforwardness. Hence, the importance of the itinerary as a ready-made continuity whose obstacles, at once objective (a distance to be covered, a mystery to be solved) and matters of character (refusing to give up, facing danger), are exciting and dramatic.

Hawks is the perfect classicist. It is as if the films objectively imitate nature and invent nothing, going along with what occurs and what is necessarily met on the way exactly as his characters do. The events seem to be the consequence of action interior to the narrative and not the consequence of a construction externally made by Hawks. Nothing disrupts the apparent exact overlay between images and what they represent nor

---

3 Howard Hawks in an interview in Jean A. Gili, *Howard Hawks*, Cinéma d'Aujourd'hui (Paris: Editions Seghers, 1971).

is any join between images felt as anything but a continuity of actions, largely because the film moves along at the pace of the itinerary and the events set within it, at the pace of its action and the pace of the characters in dealing with obstacles they find in their path. There are no ruptures, nothing to suggest an externality because every action and every image of action is directly functional and their succession smooth and orderly.

Lev Kuleshov admired the virtues of the American cinema of the 1910s and early 1920s: their narrative and illusionist mechanisms and, in following them he brought these mechanisms to a level of awareness that helped create the conditions of their undoing by the Soviet cinema. Rather than it performing the same magic, it revealed how the tricks were done, the illusions constructed and by that revelation developed new principles of editing and film construction that were not illusionist or subordinate to a narrative. The *Nouvelle Vague* did something similar by its enthusiastic appreciation of Hawks's qualities and his classicism: a classicism that it viewed as outstanding in its skill and whose central aspect was its own self-effacement before the objectivity and power and grace of what it represented). By naming it and revealing it, Hawks's style was made evident. As a consequence, his images (his means) were recognised as both integrated with but separate from their narrative ends. What Hawks had joined together (continuity) the *Nouvelle Vague* critics tore asunder (gaps, ruptures), at once rescuing the American cinema by highlighting its classicism, giving it new life and making it part of modernism (the forms of film) while also undermining its classicism (forms were made visible and had a life of their own, no longer merely to serve a narrative). The lesson it drew from Hawks was primarily formal and cinematic, about his skill and the potentials of the cinema.

In a Godard film, segments of the films of Hawks are cited, but out of their narrative context, out of the itinerary and its continuities. They literally become fragments excised from the classical system as examples of it to be given a home in the new forms and awareness of modernism.

Colour

There is a passage of 43 seconds toward the end of *Histoire(s) du cinéma: 1A Toutes les histoires* which alternates black-and-white archival images of a condemned man being secured to a post by a soldier for execution with images in technicolor of Gene Kelly and Leslie Caron dancing their dance of love in the evening on the banks of the Seine in sight of the Pont Neuf in Vincente Minnelli's *An American in Paris* (1951). The images of the condemned man are stuttered by jump cuts creating a musical rhythm choreographed to a poem in recitative by Robert Brasillach, *Le Testament d'un condamné* from his collection *Poèmes de Fresnes* (1945). Brasillach was a writer and film critic who collaborated with Vichy and the Nazis. He was executed in 1945. The Brasillach recitative is over-laid by a lyrical Italian nineteenth-century love song from the Abruzzi, *Addije, addije amore*, of parting and death. Kelly and Caron dance to the same polyphonous 'music' of the combined Brasillach and the Italian song that accompanies the securing of the condemned man. Over the Kelly–Caron images is a written title by the Russian filmmaker Friedrich Ermler: 'Jamais je n'oublierai le sang que préfigure en carmin le baiser' ('I shall never forget the blood whose colour of carmine foreshadows a kiss'). And over these images and sounds, Godard speaks: 'C'est le pauvre cinéma des actualités qui doit laver de tout soupçon le sang et les larmes comme on nettoie le trottoir lorsqu'il est trop tard et que l'armée à déjà tiré sur la foule'. ('The poor newsreel cinema must clean away the blood and tears of all suspicion just as the streets are cleaned after the army has fired on the crowd').

This passage, and I believe it is true for the entire film, is based primarily on fraternities, similarities, the formation of constellations whereby
something in one element forms a continuity with something else in
another element, each sharing aspects of love and death, embracing
and parting, a recitative and a love song, kisses and blood, hence their
partial not completely aligned overlaps as layers or sheets of similarities
that emphasise accords and also differences in gaps of time, space,
place, action, substance. They are like circles to be viewed vertically
from above, superimposed and slightly out of true so that each layer is
visible. You can sense the connection, in fact see it, but it is difficult to
articulate or interpret because there is also a breach. If each layer has
points of coincidence with others, they associate as well with things
beyond. The structure is like that in *Le Mépris* (1963) which accompanies
Alberto Moravia's *Il disprezzo*, the films of Fritz Lang, the *Odyssey* of
Homer, an accompaniment and a set of transformations and transitions
that intermingle topographically rather than function as adaptations or
imitations.

Godard took existing images and sounds, cut them up, disrupted, dis-
sected them, then reassembled them. Some reassemblies are alternations
(execution/dance of love), some superimpositions (titles/dance of love)
(poetic recitative/dance of love/execution/love song), like overpainting,
a pictorial world, a world of sounds, another of words, still another of
writing that coalesce only momentarily, as if impulsively, touch, graze
by, then separate as if every join is also the beginning of a break. It is
this irresolution of structure based on similarities and on differences of
substance and temporality and on odd, disturbing juxtapositions (a dance
of love and an execution whose detailed gestures are interchangeable and
compelling) that conspire not only against stable meanings but against
the stability of the film.

It is difficult to find a clear frame or boundaries for this passage,
indeed 'passage' is too definite a term for *Histoire(s)* (1988–98) because
the layers that compose the film's images flow beyond its borders, are
at different tempos moving toward diverse connections and affiliations,
and yet are similar and continuous. Perhaps, the film is best described as
'symphonic', as a piece of music, or, like the overpainting of the works
of Max Ernst where nothing in time is lost and things are close and
distant simultaneously, thereby hallucinatory as with *Histoire(s)* and its

dreamlike effect of layered, almost transparent universes, close to one another and spinning well away.

Moments in *Histoire(s)* are contradictory because they are plural and unresolved. Some push, others pull (Resnais would say, 'absorb', like a sponge). They can scatter things and incorporate them, fleeting two-sided impressions like love, death, the olives and leaves that fall from the trees in the Abruzzi, like the passing frames of a projected film, like slight gestures caught by the camera or spied upon at the editing table, Leslie Caron, close and far away, yielding and resistant, offering and refusing, holding out a hand and withdrawing it, a turn of her head caught in a Rembrandt-like illumination and then, just by her side, the execution played out to the same sounds.

A montage that too closely connects, that leaves no room, that binds and constrains, renders clarity of meaning by reduction. Godard's montage is a rupture, an undoing. It creates resonances, echoes, also irresolution, nothing definitive. It accumulates, agglutinises, overlays, intersects, also disperses. Most importantly, it renders back to the things of the world their opacity and thereby their fascination and mystery, their resistance to explanation. It enables them, for the first time perhaps, to be seen.

It is not only that there are no barriers or boundaries between images, sounds, writing, and that everything is porous, permitting the everday to enter and combine, for likenesses to be discovered, connections formed, but the polyphony of *Histoire(s)* extends to its own overlap of forms: film, video, poetry, music, painting, drawing, the essay, philosophy, history, narrative – it is all these things – and of the different types and times and histories of these as diverse and expansive as contained in the museum or archive, but less ordered, more open to chance, not the organisation of things into categories though not exactly new categories or no categories either, or confusion, or bric-a-brac, but rather the temporary, the approx-imate, the ambiguous and the uncertain.

Each shot is plural, contradictory, multi-dimensional, multi-directional. Everything includes other things, which is the state not only of each shot, each frame but of the film taken as a whole, the shot as a kind of magnet or point of attraction. Since the different lines and elements in a single shot spill over the boundaries of the shot and with different tempos and constituents, the result within the shot is an interaction that is more sensual than it is intellectual, the closest analogy to which is the symphony.

Contradiction

I do the shot and then cut it because I feel in general that we ought to work against what we have done. You do something and contradict it, then contradict the contradiction and so on. Vitality is precisely due to the ability to contradict oneself constantly, to deny oneself and eventually you discover that you haven't contradicted yourself but rather followed your very own truth.

Bernardo Bertolucci[4]

Contradiction is fundamental in structuring Bertolucci's *Partner* (1968). For example, though events are represented as actual, in fact they are unreal, illogical and inexplicable, like the arbitrary shooting of the pianist, the 'romantic' drive in a stolen car by Clara and Giacobbe, sex with the soap-suds girl with her false eyes and her fake and grotesque murder. The central figure in the film is Giacobbe 1 (Pierre Clementi), while the central unreality is Giacobbe's double, Giacobbe 2 (Pierre Clementi), each the shadow and substance of the other, imaginary projections and, like a dream. The doubling is inconclusive and indefinite: Giacobbe's shadow pursues Giacobbe and kicks his arse. Doubling, characteristic of *Novecento* (1976) (De Niro, Depardieu), *Strategia del ragno* (1970) (Athos Magnani, father and son) and *Il conformista* (1970) (Pierre Clementi

---

4 In Fabien S. Gerard, T. Jefferson Kline and Bruce Sklarew, 'Bernardo Bertolucci: Partner', in *Bernardo Bertolucci: Interviews* (Jackson: University of Mississippi Press, 2000), p. 41; originallly in *Cinema e film*, nos 7–8 (Spring 1968) (translated by Fabien Gerard and T. Jefferson Kline).

twice over as if returning from the dead, also Trintignant, Dominique Sanda). Doubling is a play with identity. It occurs so frequently and insistently that it ends by turning back on itself, becomes what it had opposed, changing places with its opposite, only to return to itself, in a state between reiteration and denial. As a result, who is who, what is what, what real, and what natural, what unreal and what artificial are never clear. The film is in a state of forever becoming, of commentary and reversals, hence the difficulty in seizing hold of it, slowing it down or halting its repetition machine.

In interviews, Bertolucci stressed the fact of improvisation in *Partner*. From one shot to the next, one sequence to the next, one identity to another, the mechanics of the film seem to take control as if the film was writing itself and impulsively, improvisation as self-made film. The film is a shadow of itself: not only are characters doubled but the film is doubled, like an apparition pursued by its shadow. The result is one of incompletion, indistinction, a paradoxical in-between where what is denied is also affirmed and what is affirmed also denied.

The film cites a phrase from the May Events that Clementi brought back with him to Rome each week from a weekend spent in Paris: 'Prohibitions are prohibited'. Just as there is Giacobbe 1 and his double Giacobbe 2, the film has its double, its artifice displaced by reality and reality is displaced by artifice, a generalised impermanence where no position is secure and everything is temporary. The real is present and absent simultaneously including a final unresolved 'resolution' where opposites come together and difference is dissolved, Giacobbe 1 and Giacobbe 2 reconciled and unified. Even so, and even then, questions of identity, of false and true, theatre and cinema, real and artifice, natural and unnatural persist within their contraries and duplicates.

Such movement between and amidst opposites with a consequent blurring and instability is a constant in Bertolucci's work. The most realistic of his films (*Via del petrolio* (1965), *Sheltering Sky* (1990), *Ultimo tango a Parigi* (1972), *Stealing Beauty* (1996), *Besieged* (1999), *La tragedia di uomo ridicolo* (1981)) are also the least realistic, like dreams, fairy tales, legends, masquerade, fantasies. *Partner* is perhaps the most anti-realistic of Bertolucci's films by its excess and the least illusionist, because the most open. Nothing is hidden. The film never pretends to be what it is not. *Partner* is a comedy as *The Nutty Professor* of Jerry Lewis is a comedy, but it is also an ordeal by its relentless irresolution and enigmas. At the party and the dance from which Giacobbe is forcefully ejected, the events, including the music, the pursuit of Clara, are so declaratively theatrical and absurd as to be true, as a Chaplin or Keaton gag is true, and, emphatically, film theatricalised, conscious of its fiction and their semblance and which the film declares.

Partner was shot during the May Events in 1968. It is a film of shot sequences rather than frames as if each sequence is an autonomous film. The shot sequence historically has been thought to provide greater realism than the classical film of a tight editing of frames. André Bazin asserted the greater realism of the shot sequence, typified in the films of Italian neorealism (De Sica, Rossellini) and in the films of Orson Welles, where reality, for Bazin, remains intact spatially and consistent temporally unlike their violation when broken down into shots to be recombined into a 'false' illusory reality.

Bertolucci, in 1968, was hostile to editing. *Partner* is its illustration. His hostility was not because he believed it more real to shoot in sequences (Godard had demonstrated this was not true) but rather because the shot sequence and the continuous presence of the shot seemed best to lend themselves to a position from which Bertolucci never wavered either in this 1968 period in which editing was his *bête noire* or later when his editor was Franco Arcalli, and Bertolucci became less averse to editing. Bertolucci's concern was with blurring differences between fiction and reality.

Bazin's 'realism' linked to an uninterrupted space and time which he attributed to the cinema of Orson Welles and its supposed realism. In fact, few film directors have been as committed to artifice, theatre, make-believe and fakery as Welles. Welles was an anti-realist like Bertolucci. What Bertolucci and Welles brought into play was an apparent contradiction between film as a duplication of the real and film as artifice and theatre.

The shot sequence and the moving camera, opposed to editing and to laboratory manipulations and 'effects', suited Bertolucci because by such means he could more easily approach the theatrical without compromising the cinematic and could do so smoothly, thereby proceeding from the natural to the unnatural and back again in a single sequence. Bertolucci's anti-realism and his theatricality are founded on an anti-illusionism, and, like Welles's films, have less to do with the reality of the shot sequence as with the mobility of the camera to negotiate between opposites.

What is noticeable in Bertolucci's films, and *Partner* is exemplary in this regard, is that every film has a political dimension that depicts a political-historical situation. In *Partner*, it is the 1968 May Events. Such politics, however, are not easy representation or a simple message or crude commitment. Bertolucci's films veer without exception towards theatre, spectacle, melodrama and the operatic, that is, his 'political' is not primarily representational, nor a message of political radicalism, but a choice of means (the subject of *Prima della rivoluzione*) at the interstice of the representable and the unreal. The means chosen is anti-realistic, an interrogation of cinema, in an in-between, not a political position (definite, ideological), but a cinematic one, necessarily contradictory.

On the other hand, there has been nothing more radical perhaps than André Bazin's question, *Qu'est-ce que le cinéma?*, nothing that has opened up the cinema more even if Bazin formulated an answer linked to a prescriptive ontological reality. What is radical in the question is that there is no definitive answer to it, no line, no proposition, rather that the cinema is what you make it to be. It is the end of rules, formulas, the end of conventions, the opening of film instead to anything it might be or anything it might be thought to be. Bertolucci's cinema belongs to that Bazinian question, but without a precise answer, certainly not the restatement of modernism which is already a manifesto, but with what goes beyond it. The Bertoluccian project refuses the answer including that of the modern, instead seeking to keep the question open and by doing so keeping the cinema open, rejecting any closing of any kind whatsoever, and to posit, on the contrary, doubles, enigmas, impossibilities, paradox, that is, obstacles, further questions, nothing in any case resolved.

Desire

Io stesso sono dell'epoca di Mann, Proust, Mahler. Sono nato nel 1906 e il mondo che mi ha circondato, il mondo artistico, letterario, musicale, è quel mondo lì. Non è un caso che mi ci senta attaccato. Probabilmente ho anche dei ricordi visivi, figurativi, una specie di memoria involontaria che mi aiuta a ricostruire l'atmosfera di quell'epoca. Oggi è tutto diverso. Se dovessi fare oggi un film moderno non so dove andrei a cercare i miei ambienti; mi sembra tutto molto meno interessante, mi sembra, come dire, molto meno stuzzicante. La società europea fino alla prima guerra mondiale è stata quella dei più grandi contrasti e dei maggiori risultati estetici. Il mondo contemporaneo invece è così livellato, così grigio, così poco estetico, non le pare?

(I belong to the period of Mann, Proust, Mahler. I was born in 1906 and the world that surrounded me, the artistic, literary and musical world was of that time. It is not by chance that I feel attached to it. Probably, I also have visual, figurative recollections of it, an involuntary memory that helps me reconstruct the atmosphere of that period. Today, everything is different. If I had to make a modern film, I would not know where to seek my settings; it seems to me that everything is less interesting, that is, less stimulating. European society up to the First World War was one of extreme contrasts and significant aesthetic achievements. The contemporary world is so much the same, so grey, much less refined, wouldn't you agree?)

Luchino Visconti[5]

As most narrative films develop their story and move forward to the conclusion of that development, they create their own past. Each event consigns preceding ones by a system of consequence to the past as what has occurred is displaced by what follows and what it leads to thereby effacing it, and it in turn is effaced by its consequence. In such narratives, the sense of the film is that the events that take place, however compelling and present on screen, have already happened and the narrative is their recollection. The entire film belongs to the past and all events it depicts have already occurred. Because they have occurred, they can be narrated. The film simply unfolds what has been, and what has been is the precondition of its representation.

This is in contrast to say a film by Claire Denis (*Chocolat* (1988), *Beau Travail* (1999), *J'ai pas sommeil* (1994)) where it seems that every event is the beginning of something new and the film rather than reaching an end is rather a series of (endless) beginnings to which there are no pasts either fictively or of the film. You can say only that scenes precede each other but none seems exactly consequent to another nor determined by a logic of linearity however much the movement of the film is horizontal. It is also in contrast to a film by Jean-Luc Godard which seems to be composed at the moment of filming and for which there is no 'before' that the film represents or illustrates or a past that it constructs. His films, like those of Denis and of Rivette and Rohmer are rigorously in the present.

There is a considerable gap in the classical film and in Visconti's films between what fictively is represented to have happened and the instance of the representation-narration of it. The film transforms (represents) past events, words, gestures, characters into a fictional immediacy (as if they are in the present). In fact, such narratives are primarily an evocation and memory of the past expressed in the present.

Though Visconti's films are constructed in this way, they are also very different since, rather than seeking to make the past present, it is the

5 In Pio Baldelli, *Luchino Visconti* (Milan: Gabriella Mazzotta Editore, 1973), p. 278.

pastness of the past, the fact of its passing, that Visconti emphasises and not simply because his subjects and settings are sometimes historical, as with *Il gattopardo* (1963), *Senso* (1954) and *Morte a Venezia* (1971), but because there is a contradictory struggle that takes place at the heart of his films. Not only is the world Visconti recreates, remembers and narrates set in the past but the story he tells of it is a story of the disintegration of the past, the past at the moment of it becoming so. Not only are the events completed and hence can be narrated as in the classical film but what is narrated is the passing and destruction of the present into the past. Pastness is what is represented rather than being brought to life. The past is retained for what it is, only a memory, immobilised and eternalised as such. There is then a double passing: the passing of events common to all narratives and the passing of events that concern the passing of time, hence the melancholy of his films.

Aschenbach in *Morte a Venezia* turns into a marionette of himself, an object that is essentially lifeless. The Prince in *Il gattopardo* becomes a shadow of himself lost in a darkness where Death had been. Visconti's characters want to hold on to beauty, exquisiteness, sensuality as part of a world threatened with extinction. Their story is the story of that loss and their failed attempt to hold on to their world and thereby of themselves. Almost always they lose both – characters, families, relations disintegrate – and it is important that individuals and worlds simultaneously are stricken since what keeps the world of the characters alive is their vision and imagining of it, their rendering it into an ideal and an image.

The Visconti narrative is a recognition that it is a memory of what once was (and is valued) and the initiation of a process of temporal destruction that erodes the realities it seeks to retain. These realities are as fragile as the images of the past that they depict. The films are two-sided: they evoke and treasure a past moment of beauty (visual, aural) and they gnaw at it by time.

The structures of Visconti's films are mirrors of what occurs to the characters in the films, a record of those events and a reflection of them. They are stories of impossible, hopeless attempts to preserve sensibilities that cannot be preserved in reality and instead decline into the grotesque and pathetic (*Morte a Venezia*, *Ludwig* (1972), *Ossessione* (1943), *Senso*), or the murderous (*La caduta degli dei* (1969), *L'innocente*

(1976), *Rocco e i suoi fratelli* (1960), *Lo straniero* (1967)), or the nostalgic (*Il gattopardo, Senso*), or the perverse (*Bellissima* (1951), *Vaghe stelle dell'Orsa* (1965), *Gruppo di famiglia in un interno* (1974)) or the lonely and isolated (*La terra trema* (1948), *Il gattopardo, Gruppo di famiglia in un interno*). All that is left is the unreality of images and in these images often no more than a glare of light or a powdery substance. The sense of reality, the obsessive attention to it and its details in Visconti's films are always marked by temporal decay. They can be preserved only in images, stories, remnants, reflections, in matter and forms that are intensely friable: melodrama which is the story of that fragility and film that is the physical matter of it.

Visconti chose classical narrative and lyrical-romantic melodramatic forms because they perfectly suited the stories he told. The forms he used to tell his stories *are* the stories. Equally the settings of his stories, their objects, *palazzi*, hotels, hovels, gowns and rags, *are* the stories. The forms reflect what they tell and the settings reflect what occurs within them. The fact of making a choice as Visconti did for these forms within a social and artistic context of European modernism was a step backward into the past, but taken by Visconti with the full awareness of the choice like Aschenbach's choice to return to Venice for a last glance at the beauty of Tadzio. But what Aschenbach desired was only to gaze at that beauty, not to touch it as flesh, but preserve it as a pure aesthetic ideal. What he sought was contemplative and it is in the contemplation that the intensity and passion of Aschenbach is concentrated.

What is regarded is simultaneously voluptuously close (because it is real, fleshy, opulent) and out of reach (only an image, only a look) like the Prince's regard of Angelica in *Il gattopardo* in the ball scene and his first sight of her at Donnafugata and for 'Ntoni and Nedda in *La terra trema* where 'Ntoni's image and dreams of wealth and his image and dreams of sexual desire overlap. What Aschenbach sought was not the substance of things but the shadows they cast, so too with N'toni.

Morte a Venezia regards itself in a manner not unlike the regard of the Prince in *Il gattopardo* (of Angelica, of his class, of his own death) and of Aschenbach in *Morte in Venezia* (of Tadzio, of the whore, of his face in the mirror, of his reflection in the grotesque encounters with the gondolier, the musician, the barber). It is a regard of one's own passing and disintegration, of death, of solitude, of irrelevance even, of belonging to a world that was ceasing to exist. All that is left of it is the memory of its scent, taste, feel, like Proust's Madeleine, and a nostalgia and melancholy, for moments rescued from time as in a photograph. The final images of the film are of a still camera.

Tadzio at the end of the film is bleached out of existence by the glare of light on the water and sand as Aschenbach dies just as the Prince in the final scene of *Il gattopardo* is absorbed by blackness. Tadzio was never much more to Aschenbach than an image of himself. Tadzio exists only so long as Aschenbach is looking at him.

Most regards in Visconti's films turn back upon themselves, as in the hotel lounge at the Lido where Aschenbach's look is taken up by the camera that overlaps with it only for the camera to later separate itself from him when Aschenbach's glance rests on Tadzio and the camera comes full circle to look at Aschenbach looking, becoming objective and detached from him. The play between the objective and the subjective is a constant feature in Visconti, a shifting of perspectives and points of view and, at extraordinary moments, superimposing them as in the lounge scene in the Hôtel des Bains. It is the perfect expression of the choreography and exchange between the close (subjective, desirous, longing, imaginary) and the distant (objective, out of reach, impossible, real).

Visconti's central characters are the victims not of fate or circumstance but of their own conscious choice and sad awareness. They never try to escape the destruction that awaits them, but instead embrace it and not only fully sensible to their choice, but at times joyously and triumphantly welcoming its consequences. It is the past they seek, as does Visconti, and that, by definition, is unreachable, however desirable, palpable and sensate (Angelica, Tadzio). These figures belong to a future from which the Prince and Aschenbach are necessarily excluded. The only place these differences of the real and the desired can be reconciled and the struggle that Visconti engages in be resolved is in film, theatre, lyric opera, in short in art, in the pursuit of beauty not in life where it is perilous and fatal, but by restating the dilemma and contradictions of the pursuit in the forms of his art (that eternalises). It is the dilemma that stimulates him to make things, to put ideals into scenes in his fabulous, and magnificent *mise en scène*. For a moment, in the reality of performance, sound, voice, music, movement, gesture, he can find and create the imaginary spectacle of a life that can no longer be lived except in an intense play between the fabricated and the real.

Visconti is not a modernist, but he is not thereby a classicist. What makes him neither the one nor the other is his ability and the opportunity to choose. Paradoxically, it is not that Visconti was behind the times. On the contrary, he comes 'after' the modern and can choose thereby to look back with passionate regret.

Destructuring

In a Ford or Hawks film images follow one another in accord with the action that is taking place. Whatever may be discontinuous between the images is 'covered' by a logic of events, drama or action. Thus, discontinuity is unnoticeable and the film, however fragmented it may be, appears seamless. The seamlessness has an effect of appearing natural (realistic) and therefore transparent (clear). If what is represented in an image seems to be the consequence of a prior action and set of events, the system is a closed one, closed off from anything exterior to it (the world outside, the instance of forming the image).

This 'classical' system has prevailed in the cinema for a long time (until today). Critics and filmmakers in the late 1930s and particularly after 1945 were able to see within that classicism another, apparently contrary system that they called 'modern'. What was seen was a sense of unrealised possibilities, of a cinema (and world) other than the one that prevailed. That sense of possibility had to do with the fact that the classical system was neither stable nor coherent and thus possibility was in effect a realisation of instability and incoherence.

The structure of the classical system depended on the continuity out of discontinuous fragments (shots), the more discontinuous the better to link one thing to another in a chain of logic and events. If the discontinuities that the system 'covered' by finding accords between the fragments held within it, it also held within it its own contrary. If the discontinuities were made invisible, nevertheless they existed and indeed were crucial to the architecture and artifice of the classical system. A shift away from the continuities that rendered the architecture of it invisible would reveal it, would reveal the reality of the image against the seeming reality of events and thus make the invisible visible, would give a presence to the film, a threat that the techniques of classicism sought to avoid.

If, at the same time, the practice of editing fragments, all of which were assumed to be part of the homogeneous reality represented by the film, was replaced by more fluid and genuinely continuous strategies (moving camera, moving lenses, shooting in depth, extended surfaces), the image became more difficult to define and control and the reality thereby represented more ambiguous, more plural, less centred and most important, the interaction and overlap between such manners of filming with the editing patterns of classical cinema in a single film (*Citizen Kane* (1941), *Touch of Evil* (1958)) made it clear and visible that films could be composed not only of different and plural realities but by different and plural practices of films and images (Welles, Godard).

The effectiveness of the classical system depended upon an overlap between the image (the representing) and reality (what was represented). If the discontinuities between images in the classical system were no longer held together by either logic or action, then the more fundamental accord in that system between image and reality could not be sustained. On the one hand, the image was liberated by being no longer subject to the demands of representation, sense, clarity or accord and on the other reality was no longer confined to fit into these needs.

Accords of a linear and continuous kind between images and the actions they represent were revealed as simply a convention. Other kinds of structuring became possible once structuring itself was made self-evident.

The notion of deconstruction is not exactly a taking apart of structures as it is the awareness that all structures contain within them their contrary, and hence an instability. It was not that the French *Nouvelle Vague* critics dismantled classicism but that they perceived another system within it, another possibility, hence another cinema. Thus, classicism was not to be denounced, contested or displaced, but appreciated not simply for what was there but for what could be in what was there.

For example, the liberation of the image depended on loosening representational patterns, and the constraints of narrative and story and the constraints of coherence demanded by the insistent presence and awareness of thematic accords in a film and as well a loosening of representational clarity for the sake of formal experimentation. The French *Nouvelle*

Vague is more concerned with the forms of cinema as its content than its representations thereby dissolving a conventional distinction between form and content. To see a cinema that was different as the French did in the cinema of classical sameness was breathtaking.

By most standards, Hitchcock is as classical a filmmaker as Hawks and Ford. His films are built upon an architecture composed of short, discontinuous shots (the attack of the birds in the attic; the shower scene in *Psycho*, the crop duster sequence in *North by Northwest*). His pattern of editing is rigorously continuous and the audience is taken into the fiction and bound within it by a clearly articulated shot/reverse-shot system (between Melanie and the birds as they gather outside the schoolhouse, between Scottie and Madeleine, pursuer and pursued between the photographer and the salesman across the way in *Rear Window* (1954) that binds the spectator by fear and suspense along the editing line that creates an accord between on-screen and off, object and regard). There is no external to a Hitchcock film. It is a closed structure. No matter the play of doubling, of deception, of suspense, these remain rigorously objective in their presentation, that is, they appear to belong to the world of the fiction rather than imposed upon it as forms from outside or as a subjective projection from within. What makes the birds terrifying in *The Birds* (1963) is their objective presence, like the presence of the crop duster in *North by Northwest* (1959). What Scottie sees in *Vertigo* (1958) (or does not see) may be a result of his projections, like the murder unseen but imagined by the photographer across the courtyard in *Rear Window*, but they nevertheless actually exist: Scottie is being fooled and deceived by others and by his own (mis)perceptions while the photogapher's imaginings, however projected by his desires, have a basis in fact. Madeleine is not Madeleine and we know it, nor is Judy Madeleine (she has to be made over); the birds are really birds and they are malevolent; the salesman did indeed kill his wife. Doubling, voyeurism, suspense, perception and instability are the themes of the films and these as they bunch up and combine with the essential linearity of the narrative give the films their consistency, sense and (classical) coherence. They do not intrude on the action as forms but rather are the transfer of forms into action and themes, forms objectified, materialised. The Hitchcock image is no more than the Hawksian or Fordian image abstracted from the material it presents.

Hitchcock does not propose a criticism of what is being represented in his films, does not undermine what he represents. At most, he wants to create disquiet, hence the play on perception and misperception. Fundamentally, Hitchcock wants to involve his audience, and involvement (necessarily in the cinema) involves deception. There is no question for Hitchcock of setting at odds the forms of the films and the objects and materials from which he constructs his forms. Perception is at once a formal play with the audience and the film and a theme interior to the fiction and the objects and persons and actions that constitute it.

Nevertheless, and it is one of the central reasons he was so much favoured by the French *Nouvelle Vague* critics, Hitchcock's films depend on finding a flaw in all images of reality and in all perceptions of reality and thus another possibility in them beyond their appearances (the upsetting of the natural order of things that Melanie brings to Bodega Bay with the lovebirds; the menace in the banal in *North by Northwest*; the obsessions that corrode and distort normality in *Vertigo*). In *Rear Window*, it is perfectly possible that the imaginings of the photographer have no substance and that the salesman did not kill and cut up his wife except in the photographer's head and that reality therefore is not objective, but subject to projections and therefore neither stable nor orderly. But Hitchcock never takes this path in which reality and the image of it are separated out and misperception becomes a norm. To the contrary, if order is once disturbed by Hitchcock (and the terror is that it is being disturbed or might be or could be or will be), it is always fundamentally restored: the image and action realigned. Nevertheless, no event in a Hitchcock film is innocent, secure or stable and no image that is not liable to misperception. In order to threaten stability in the fiction, the stability of the film is placed under threat (image and action not in accord or their relation placed in doubt).

In that flaw and within that gap of uncertainty, misrecognition, suspension and obscurity in Hitchcock's classical cinema, the modern cinema could enter.

Drama

Bertolucci had worked with the cinematographer Vittorio Storaro for nearly twenty years but for *La tragedia di un uomo ridicolo* in 1981 he chose a different cinematographer, Carlo di Palma. He explained the break from Storaro thus:

> I wanted a very sharp image. Vittorio is never truly sharp. His way of lighting comes from a school which uses very little light ... This film concerned the absolute blurring of the question of terrorism in Italy. One didn't understand anything. The story was very hazy. I thought it was necessary to counterbalance that with a very well defined image.[6]

The main character in *La tragedia* is Primo Spaggiari (Ugo Tognazzi), whose business is agriculture: the manufacture of Parmigiano cheese, of salami and of prosciutto. The plant is large and the business considerable: six thousand pigs, many employees, servants, up-to-date equipment. Spaggiari is a self-made man. The factory is in the Parma countryside where Primo lives with his wife, Barbara (Anouk Aimée), a daughter of the bourgeoisie. She had admired Primo for his energy and commitment, for his not being satisfied, his hard work, his not being bourgeois. She was attracted to him and they married.

The Spaggiari house, next to the factory, is a medieval stone castle on a hillside. It has two paintings of note: a *naif* Ligabue (probably a

---

6 Jean A. Gili and Christian Viviani, 'Interview with Bernardo Bertolucci', *Positif*, no. 424 (June 1996).

reproduction) and a Camille Pissarro (certainly fake though Barbara would try to sell it as an original). The Spaggiaris have one son, Giovanni, in his twenties.

The film opens on Primo's birthday. He is alone in the house, unwraps a gift from his son while talking to himself. The gift is a yachting cap and a pair of binoculars. Primo likes the idea of himself as the captain, the agricultural factory as a yacht under his command. He tries on the cap. With the binoculars he can spy on his employees, especially women. He shouts out marine orders to himself: 'weigh anchor'. Primo is a voyeur, a spectator of his possessions and proud of himself. The masquerade of being other than he is (the captain of a yacht) and his factory other than it is (a medieval castle) delights him.

He focuses the binoculars on a car chase between a grey sedan seemingly in pursuit of a small red car, a mini Cooper or a Fiat, as if the binoculars have been given to him for that purpose. From a distance the chase seems to be a game, a scene from a film. The car flips over and rolls down a hill. Those in the sedan drag the driver from the car, appear to force him into their car. They drive off at speed. Primo realises that it is his son, Giovanni, who was in the car and was abducted.

The action in the film occurs during a period of the late 1970s in Italy of Left-wing terrorism, political assassinations (Aldo Moro), kidnappings, bombings (the Red Brigades). Primo and Barbara assume that the abduction of his son is an event of political terror and is motivated to secure a ransom. They begin to count their assets: the plant, the stored cheese, the pigs, their personal possessions. Primo has a meeting with the bank to mortgage everything.

The film is roughly based on a Dostoevsky short story, *The Diary of a Ridiculous Man*, whose main character, like Primo, has a dialogue with himself. The same occurs in Bertolucci's *Partner* (1968), also based on a Dostoevsky story: *The Double*. The dialogue is like a confession of Primo to Primo. There are two Primos: the one who interacts with others (industrialist, employer, father, husband) and the one who reflects on his own actions (confesses, imagines the opinions others may have of him, realises his fragility, part autobiography, part confession, part make-believe).

Identity as problematic and as divided is a Bertoluccian theme where characters are often in opposed positions to themselves like the bereft

Paul and the erotic Paul in *Ultimo tango* (1972); the all-powerful and powerless emperor in *The Last Emperor* (1987); Athos Magnani, the hero and Athos Magnani the traitor, and also Athos Magnani the son not wanting to betray the legend of his father, who therefore sustains the deceit of a false heroism, like father like son. Identity, unity and narrative are, by these doublings, placed in doubt.

The multiple roles assumed by Primo, like his changing of costume, waver, become indistinct and blurred. Primo reacts to what he projects and what others might believe of him, exactly like Dostoevsky's *Ridiculous Man*. Because of Primo's lack of certainty and his imaginings, he is a perfect target for deceit, confidence tricks, fictions, imaginary kidnappings, as if he himself is fictional. His actions, though governed by an apparent reality, seem like play-acting (his sudden and inexplicable rock dance with a servant, his sexual embrace of Laura). Who are these kidnappers? What might they want? Is Giovanni alive or dead? What is the story? And, most serious of all, the kidnapping, the ransom demand as they turn out to be, the assumed threats are as fake as the Camille Pissarro painting that Barbara wants to sell as an original. 'Captain' Spaggiari's life, however serious the drama that is taking place, is also farce and ridiculous and, because ridiculous, pathetic.

Giovanni's gift to his father is more than a binocular and a yachting cap. It is the gift of fiction. Primo is the parody of Primo. What occurs is a scam. Primo is Primo mocked, Primo the gullible. He becomes his own object and that object is something less than true and especially when Primo appears to be most troubled and the events that occur most real.

What occurs (or does not occur), the effort to discover what really is taking place, the attempt to free Giovanni, the organisation of the ransom, its actual payment has all the elements of make-believe and play-acting. The kidnapping raises questions while the response to them creates a labyrinth of uncertainties, suppositions, fragments, doubts and thus possibilities (and impossibilities), like a self-generating story machine before which Primo and Barbara are helpless and, by their helplessness and what they imagine and improvise, add to the machine, become part of it. Other stories are initiated and begin to form a web, 'the plot thickens'. Barbara receives notes (signed by Giovanni) instructing her, in detail, how, when and where to deliver the ransom to free him. Notes arrive, inexplicably, at the Spaggiari castle as if having been planted there. The notes and instructions seem constructed like a film scenario or a Shakespeare play, theatre as mystery, maze, artifice, serious and farcical at once. It is the realm of Wellesian fake making believe to the unwary that it is real, but is more like the landing of aliens from Mars.

The Carabinieri arrive after dusk: helicopters, vehicles, flashing lights, uniforms, salutes, speculations. The two principal Carabinieri are played by Vittorio Caprioli (*Zazie dans le métro* (1960), *Tout va bien* (1972)) and Renato Salvatori (*Rocco e suoi fratelli* (1960), *La luna* (1979)), well-known actors, acting out a self-parody. Caprioli is a comic actor, ridiculous, excessive, exaggerated, almost by nature. The Spaggiari castle reverts to what it perhaps principally is, a stage or a film set pretending to be a castle. The Carabinieri pursue a line of inquiry that implicates Giovanni, who, it seems to them, rather than being the victim of a terrorist plot, is its culprit, the perpetrator of a hoax that he arranged and staged, relying on the myth of terrorism for the credibility of his game of make-believe. Giovanni, who is abducted, is also an other Giovanni who is the abductor, doubled, trebled even in contradictory roles. None of this is clarified in the film, not even at its end. Actions and events are difficult to decipher. It can be thought of as a repeat performance of *Strategia del ragno* (1970). The duplicity in the one film is re-enacted in the other as if one film is a citation of another film. Such inter-citations are not confined to these two films, but are ubiquitous in Bertolucci's work as if every one of his films is only a variant and duplicate of another.

Added to the theatre of real-seeming is the revelation of an earlier plot by Giovanni to abduct his father Primo, later rejected by him for being too unbelievable to be accepted. What occurs and what Primo witnesses is a revision of Giovanni's original scenario, another variant like a first draft of a text or a film script. The theatrical in the film is layered by deceits, falsity, impersonations, performances within performances. What is revealed, and seemingly concluded, obscures rather than clarifying. *La tragedia di un uomo ridicolo* is farce in the mask of tragedy played to its finale. Primo, and the other characters, especially Barbara, Adelio, Laura, are unaware (or it seems that they are unaware) that they are enacting a script prepared by Giovanni with the help of the actuality of terrorism in Italy. It is not unlike the realisation by Athos Magnani, the son, that he is enacting an already written script by Athos Magnani, the father, and that out of loyalty to a myth of his father and to the reality of his father (who is a myth-maker), he is constrained to accept. And there is a further echo of that situation in the duplicity and false identity at play in Welles's *Arkadin* (1955), where Arkadin (a fiction) must be sustained in order that his other and secret identity, Athabadze, is not revealed. And when it is revealed that Arkadin and Athabadze are the same person, Arkadin/Athabadze has no other choice but that of suicide to protect the name of who he is not while who he is not is who he is. His reality is that he is a fake and that the film is a fake, merely a performance.

Any clash of father and son is historical and often mythical, as is the father/son relation in every Bertolucci film, despite an apparent reality. What takes place in *La tragedia* also occurs in *Strategia del ragno*, *The Last Emperor*, *Il conformista* (1970), *La luna* (1979) and *Stealing Beauty* (1996), characters playing preordained theatrical roles in real cities and actual squares and piazzas to help create make-believe to seem true or the reverse to make the real seem imaginary, for example Tara for Sabbioneta, or the oil tankers, rigs, crews in *La via del Petrolio* (1965) as ghosts imagined by Arthur Rimbaud. Dostoevsky and Borges have their place in these tragedies and operas of artifice, deception, trickery, divided identity and role-playing. The farce of *La tragedia* also belongs to the theatre of the absurd of Luigi Pirandello's play *Sei personaggi in cerca d'autore*. Antonin Artaud and his theatre of cruelty are Pirandello's heir apparent while Artaud's theatre resonates in the theatre of Julian Beck displayed in Bertolucci's *Partner* and *Agonia* (1969).

There are multiple stories and narratives in *La tragedia* that encounter each other, move in parallel, add to each other, contradict each other, coagulate. The images of *La tragedia* are crisp and crystalline in contrast to the obscurity of its narrative of hiding, denying, dissembling, in effect, which is Shakespearian, a comedy of errors. The clearer the image, the more puzzling, opaque and confusing are the events depicted. Is it fact or fiction, document or fantasy, an actual abduction or not?

Clarification, the resolution of the enigma of the kidnapping, the conclusion of the fate of Giovanni, the result of the inquiry by the Carabinieri, the settlement of the fortunes of the Spaggiari business, the blur between real and artifice, move in tandem, some as contraries, as an affirmation and a positive on one level are denied and negated on another, either because they are opposed or because there is an overload, or because occurrences are fragmentary, and, sometimes, because all of these are concurrent, belong to a woven tapestry of different many-coloured threads.

The film ends with the return, mysterious, unsuspected, of a smiling delighted Giovanni in the midst of a communal dance. Everyone dances, the entire cast dances, all the employees of the Spaggiari dance, Giovanni dances.

The play is over.

Duplication

Bertolucci's *Strategia del ragno* (1970) is based on a short story by Jorge Luis Borges, 'The Theme of the Traitor and the Hero'/'Tema del traidor y del héroe' (1944). The Borges story concerns a narrative of the assassination of an Irish rebel and hero, Fergus Kilpatrick. Borges's story – and it is central to his fiction – is not exactly a narrative of what occurred as it is a narrative of the narrative of what happened, strictly speaking the narration of a narrative, or, and more precisely, of narratives. The multiple narratives are duplicates of each other that proceed in parallel and are simultaneous in time. There is no linear thread, but rather circularities and reversals that mirror each other. The narrative related by Borges is a narrative of duplicity while the narrative as a narrative of a narrative is doubled, the substance of what is related (doubling) and the form of what is related (doubles) are reflecting mirrors, the content of the story is its form, and the form, of the story its content, the told and the telling are likenesses. When taken together they form a labyrinth from which there is no exit.

Kilpatrick's death, which occurs in a theatre, is the death of a hero. The hero, however, is a traitor whose heroism is a myth, more exactly an invented fiction, concocted to make the death of a traitor appear as the death of a hero. The story is hatched by James Nolan, one of Kilpatrick's rebel comrades, who discovered, at Kilpatrick's urging, that Kilpatrick, an Irish hero, is instead a traitor to the Irish cause. The story of the treachery is devised by Kilpatrick as if it is he who is organising and staging everything that will occur, a future that at once confirms the past (Kilpatrick is a hero) and its opposite (Kilpatrick is a traitor).

Kilpatrick is the stage director of his own death (suicide as murder) to take place in a theatre, with the audience as participants (spectators as actors). Nolan, assuming no one would believe Kilpatrick to be a traitor, arranges for Kilpatrick's death as the hero he is believed to be by the audience, a mythical fictional hero, all the more emphatic and believable since Kilpatrick dies a legendary death. The outcome that creates heroism out of treachery is suggested by Kilpatrick, his fictional murder guaranteeing the Revolt and saving the cause of Ireland. Kilpatrick, a traitor while he lived, is a hero in death and doubly so.

Neither Nolan nor Kilpatrick depended on reality to make their fictional false story convincing, but had recourse instead to theatre, to Shakespeare – the quintessential *English* dramatist – as their model, the death not only a fictional effect but a literary citation. The assassination of the traitor Kilpatrick as hero is built upon masks and deceits (theatre), an enigma and a story of such multiplicity and differential origins that it is a puzzle, not so much false, as incomprehensible, closest perhaps, to another parallel time zone narration, Orson Welles's *Mr Arkadin* (1955). Welles, like Nolan, found his inspiration in Shakespeare, and, specifically, as Nolan did, in *Macbeth* and *Julius Caesar*, though there are also other Shakespeare citations in the Welles: *Othello* and *Chimes at Midnight* and the ubiquity of Wellesian (and Shakespearian) masquerade, trickery and false identities. Kilpatrick is in fact murdered, but at the hands of his friends not his enemies. The significance of his death, however, is hidden, *in order to mislead*.

It is not difficult to see Bertolucci's attraction to Borges's story with its presence of stratified time zones and multiple, conflicting identities and dead ends, derived from theatre and structured as theatre. Bertolucci's *Strategia*, like many of his other films, is a theatrical operatic spectacle modelled on Giuseppe Verdi's melodramas and on Shakespeare's tragedies (models also for Nolan and Kilpatrick) from which there is no way out to reality.

The events surrounding the death of Kilpatrick are stated in the Borges story as having taken place in 1824 in Ireland, though, as Borges commented, they could just as well have occurred in Poland, Venice, the Balkans or South America. By noting fictional alternatives, Borges creates parallels and echoes that take his narrative beyond itself, toward their reflections, rather than going beyond these to anywhere in particular. It is a mirror mirrored in perpetual returns.

The story narrated by Borges is the story told by Ryan, the great-grandson of Kilpatrick. Ryan's story in turn is based on a document written by James Nolan, discovered by Ryan in his quest to find the 'truth' of the death of his legendary great-grandfather. Since Kilpatrick is an invention of Nolan (or of Borges), it could just as well be that Nolan is an invention of Ryan (or of Borges). Bertolucci's adaptation-contribution is the addition of a further layer of fictional duplications already layered. Almost all of Bertolucci's films are inquests to uncover a mystery or solve an enigma, as the films of Welles are, especially his *The Lady from Shanghai* (1947) and *Mr Arkadin*. It might be said that Bertolucci's films mirror the films of Orson Welles and that Welles's *F for Fake* (1973) is a film in a hall of mirrors like his *Touch of Evil* (1958) and *Citizen Kane* (1941), investigations of elusive reflections and testimonies, of obscurities that, rather than being clarified, become more opaque, more playful, like Borges's story and Bertolucci's films, in a game with their audiences. What is at stake is a crisis in identity, at once serious and trivial. Such crises are indicative of works that consist of parallel occurrences and duplications that are self-contradictory and thereby oblique, calling into question not only what is represented but representation *tout court*.

Nolan and Kilpatrick were revolutionary conspirators whose conspiracy was betrayed (but by whom?). Kilpatrick gave Nolan the task of discovering the identity of the traitor, which, as it turned out, was Kilpatrick himself. If the truth of his treachery were told, if it were believed, then the Irish Revolt, whose hero was Kilpatrick, would have been compromised. The truth then would be unbearable. Only fiction would serve. To preserve Kilpatrick's good name and in so doing preserve the Revolt, Kilpatrick's fellow conspirators, with Kilpatrick's assent, and by his suggestion, stab him to death, staging the assassination as the work of unknown enemies, thus upholding, by a false story and staged action, a veritable *mise en scène*, namely that Kilpatrick was a hero. The staging is crucial. The manner by which Kilpatrick dies is adapted by the conspirators, including Kilpatrick, from Shakespeare's *Julius Caesar*.

Nolan had translated Shakespeare into Irish in 1814, or so the story goes. Borges's tale is one of doubled contraries, the hero and the traitor, and Borges's narrative of the traitor as hero is the double of the story told by Nolan, who knew the 'real' truth, namely that Kilpatrick was a traitor. Borges's story, a fiction of multiple internal citations from Shakespeare including Nolan's role in Kilpatrick's contribution of concocting heroism out of betrayal, involves external references and citations to G.K. Chesterton's *The Man Who Was Thursday*. Chesterton was one of Borges's favourite writers.

In discovering Nolan's manuscript, Kilpatrick's grandson, Ryan, discovers the truth, that his revered grandfather was a traitor, a truth Kilpatrick and later Nolan tried to cover up. Ryan chooses to maintain the myth of Kilpatrick's heroism and thus the myth of the Irish Revolt and, perhaps most telling, the mythological dimension of History.

Nolan's staging of *Julius Caesar* is more complicated than having its origin in Nolan's acquaintance with the works of Shakespeare that he had translated. It seems that Nolan believed that Kilpatrick was in fact Julius Caesar, not simply his duplicate or a reference to him, but literally Julius Caesar in person who 'returns', with Kilpatrick thereby a ghost of Caesar (ghosts and prophecies being crucial to Shakespeare's *Macbeth* and his *Julius Caesar*). In the name itself, 'Kilpatrick', can be found a prophecy of Kilpatrick's fate. History, in this context, is no more than a fiction of intersecting parallel lines, duplicates of literary works, of myths, stories, inventions, not reality, like a novel.

Criss-crossing and parallelism between fiction and history and between multiple, but similar, narratives, historical or fictional, are familiar in Bertolucci's films where history, fiction, biography, autobiography, politics and eroticism duplicate each other like rhymes. The duplications give Bertolucci's films their density and create similitudes that swell events while compressing time. Bertolucci's citations are not exterior to his narratives nor mere illustrations at the periphery of a central story, but at the centre of his films, part of a fabric that resists unravelling, as with Borges's narratives, woven of contrary citations, references and doublings as their essential material, which, if unknotted, the entire edifice of his works would crumble were they to be resolved and made, like the story of Oedipus.

Elsewhere

Godard's *For Ever Mozart* was made in 1996. It refers directly to the civil war and massacres in ex-Yugoslavia (Bosnia, Serbia and Kosovo) that were taking place. It was a situation *away* from Europe, *elsewhere*, yet *here*, on its borders, in a European country that most of Europe seemed unable or unwilling to do much about.

Here and *Elsewhere* have been a central preoccupation in Godard's films. One of them, which concerns the situation in Palestine/Israel, has the title *Ici et Ailleurs* (*Here and Elsewhere*) (1974) and there is as well *Made in USA* (1966), *La Chinoise* (1967) and *Loin du Vietnam* (1967). *Passion* (1982) has a number of 'heres', that is to say, a number of 'elsewheres', each here being an elsewhere to another here: Paris, Poland, Germany, the Studio, the Hotel, the Workplace, seventeenth-century Europe and also eighteenth- and nineteenth-century Europe, real light, studio light, paintings of the past, a film in the present, the minuteness of earth and the infiniteness of the heavens, the 'Passion' of the worker, the Passion of Christ. Much of the film is a coming and going between these distant, other places that characters run, dance, dash, drive towards. The central *here* for Godard is the film that is being made (*Passion, For Ever Mozart, Une femme est une femme* (1961), *Vivre sa vie* (1962)) and the crucial *elsewhere* is the films, books, paintings, music to which they relate (Velazquez, Goya, Rembrandt, Delacroix, Fauré, Mozart, Beethoven, Ravel, Marivaux, Musset, *Singin' in the Rain*, John Ford's *The Searchers*, Edgar Allan Poe, etc.). These relations are essentially historical, that is, they raise the question of what is the elsewhere (the history) that the here (the present) belongs to or contrarily what is the here of the elsewhere.

Belonging, for Godard, is not a line of connections but an overlapping and telescoping of associations such that relations over vast distances of space, time and context are brought together, for example, Mozart, Marivaux, Musset, Godard, Sarajevo, palaces, hovels, Switzerland, and in this bringing together something is released and both are saved. Godard, brings the far near and pushes the near to the far, Sarajevo *in* the Mozart of the eighteenth century and the Mozart music, a moment of peace and sublimity, in contemporary barbarity and slaughter. There is nothing 'easy' about Mozart, nothing 'light', or rather the melody and lightness of the music does not come easily, but only after a struggle, like the passions of *Passion*, and the experiences that are fundamentally journeys of Nana, in *Vivre sa vie* through Zola, Renoir, philosophy, *film noir*, the Three Musketeers.

Until the late 1930s and for the most part well into the 1940s, the stories that films told, were organised such that every part of those stories cohered. Time was made to be continuous and space homogeneous. One event followed the next in a line of consequence and in a space within which all things belonged to all other things. In such films, there was only a *here*, no *elsewhere* outside it, that opposed it, that was different from it, and no gaps in that here, especially not the gap between it and an elsewhere. Everything fitted, meshed, and what was shown to an audience had no mystery to it since the fit of everything included its comprehensibility. There were not simply events but events plus their significance as if there was nothing not only out of place or elsewhere but nothing that was not explicable, nothing that could not be resolved and made to cohere. In that situation, there was never any grace, miracle, coming, nor exactly struggle, in effect no Mozart in Sarajevo, more precisely no Mozart anywhere, or at least not a Mozart that could be *heard*. Because to hear Mozart or to see a Rembrandt, or to feel a Delacroix, or to experience passion, it has to be achieved for Godard. What makes some of the moments of Godard's films as intensely beautiful and rich and condensed and filled with energy (passion) as they are has to do with the journey that is taken to arrive at that point.

The editing patterns of an earlier cinema, before the 1950s, were structured on accords, so that one shot not only followed each other but followed as a logical consequence, as if a response and answer to what had preceded it. The single most important aspect of that editing was the shot and counter-shot so that a succeeding shot was melded to a previous one, not naturally, so much as logically, and so logically that the binding of the shots was unnoticeable and therefore their relation appeared as continuous and seamless though built upon endless seams (shots, cuts). This system of accords and returns and invisibility brought an audience into a film (*here*), taking them from *elsewhere* where they really were, on the outside, to inside where they only were fictively and imaginatively, in make-believe.

There is a wonderful moment in *For Ever Mozart* when the situation in Bosnia and Kosovo (in the 1990s) is conceived as a rehearsal for the 1930s (Fascism, Spain). In a grotesque and thereby amusing way, Bosnia and Kosovo are like stars in the sky through which you see what has disappeared, what no longer exists.

In *For Ever Mozart*, three young people, Camille, Jérôme and Djamila, leave Paris to go to Sarajevo to put on a play by Musset. They are accompanied at first by a filmmaker, their grandfather (a dinosaur), Vitalis, who is trying to make a film, *Boléro Fatal*. When he sets about it, he can never find the right shot. *For Ever Mozart* is a record of their journey and, in the end, of their death, caught up in the Yugoslavian conflict. Beneath, within, along the side of, yet necessarily elsewhere is a trace, echo, resonance of John Ford's film *The Searchers* (1956). And, in some scenes, especially when Camille falters in the journey and later during the shooting of *Boléro Fatal*, when the lead actress similarly falters, whose resuscitation and salvation resonate with a similar scene from the end of Robert Bresson's *Les Dames du Bois de Boulogne* (1945). In both cases these are films of suffering, courage, resistance and will. The Mozart instance in *The Searchers*, that *For Ever Mozart* makes one see, is the moment when John Wayne picks Natalie Wood up in his arms to take her home near the close of the film. There is a similar instance that recalls *The Searchers* and the films of John Ford in *For Ever Mozart* when Camille is picked up all stiff and hard and when the actress, immobilised, frozen, is later picked up and both of them revived, brought to life, brought 'home'. Two opposites, unresolved, of different universes, are reconciled. Similarly, *For Ever Mozart* breathes life into *The Searchers* and *Les Dames du Bois de Boulogne*. The Godard film allows you to see the other films.

In *For Ever Mozart*, everything returns under a different form. New characters in *Boléro Fatal* retake the phrases already said by those who have disappeared in the film. Characters who die in the course of the film acquire a different sense if other characters resuscitate them in a different form and renew a narrative and sense that has never truly been effaced. And this too is the sense of Godard's appropriately named film with Alain Delon, *Nouvelle Vague*. It is like the return of Cyd Charisse as Nana in *Une femme est une femme* and in *Le Mépris* (1963), the return of Rossellini and *Viaggio in Italia* (1954), and the return of Fritz Lang as Fritz Lang. These are not revivals or anything so pale as a citation, but transformations where figures that have passed are revivified by others who take their place, and this happens in Godard with images as well. Such transformations depend on being here and elsewhere, *ici et ailleurs*, and that in order to see either place requires their juxtaposition and that juxtaposition depends on strategies of telescoping, overlapping, inter-ruption, disjunction as the only way to maintain the life of things, not a history that makes things of the past into a narrative but a history that reverses the order so that here and now are rehearsals for then and else-where, marks of disappearances, reappearances, of shadows, in short, of images, of the cinema. Bertolucci's *Partner* (1968) is their rhyme.

The restlessness and constant movement in a Godard film, seemingly useless and pointless, without goal, resolve or settlement, is a movement between the poles of here and elsewhere, now and then, and in attaining one, compelled toward the other, as between fiction and documentary, the real and the image of it. The final moment (conclusion) in *For Ever Mozart* of grace and peace and sublimity of the Mozart concert is (neces-sarily) attenuated, not unrealised, but not completed either.

In *Passion* (1982), there are a number of centres between which the characters move frenetically (set, hotel, factory) and between these differ-ent states of desire and passion; in *For Ever Mozart*, there are the many (seven) houses in the journey of first Camille, Jérôme and Djamila and then of Vitalis and the movement between war (reality), theatre, film and music, movements in representation and its forms (parody, burlesque, circus, tragedy). Each place gives birth to another, war as theatre, theatre as film and film as the purity of music, in a perpetual passing and rebirth where nothing is lost.

Film noir

Film noir derives essentially from popular *noir* literature: the writings of Raymond Chandler, James M. Cain, Dashiell Hammett and others. It is the reverse of the American dream whose promises of happiness, prosperity and security are confronted by a sordid reality conditioned by money and the amorality of it, weighed down at every level by cynicism, despair, violence, murder and hopelessness.

Film noir is essentially a style, a night-time film where shadows and murky greys predominate. Dim reflections and shimmering electric lights create an unstable, uneasy, disquieting space, a nightmare world of insecurity and danger. It was the qualities of unreality and threat in *film noir* and the themes of power and money that attracted Welles.

Ultimately, the Hollywood *film noir*, despite its anomalies, darkness, instabilities, ugliness, sordidness and violence, was a genre of action, explicit plot, organic development and symbolic sense. Though it could be argued that in *film noir* and the German cinema of the 1920s, to which it is a direct heir with its plays of light, shadow, menace and distortion (the early films of Fritz Lang, for example, especially his *M*), the world is created as disquieting by the images of it rather than the images being a creation of a disquieting world that they mimic and hence there would be an explicit discontinuity or gap between image and reality. It could further be argued that this gap is the very source of the insecurity, of the disturbing sense of unreality evoked by these films.

This may be true of Lang and Murnau in the German cinema, but it is less true of American films of the late 1930s and early 1940s whose narrative systems are perfectly coherent, linear and explicit and easily absorb the disquiet of lighting and atmosphere whose object in the case of *noir* films is to make the films appear as realistic as possible, more real in fact than the films that depict a happier and brighter reality (the musical comedy, for example, or the family romance). The image in the American films does not disturb what is presented, does not appear as exterior to the action and the drama, but as interior to it, part of it.

Though Welles may in *The Lady from Shanghai* (1947), in *Touch of Evil* (1958), and to a degree in *The Stranger* (1946) and *Citizen Kane* (1941), use conventions of the *noir* film, they are used as conventions whose conventionality is stressed rather than the instrumentality of them in creating a real-seeming world. Welles 'mixes' and contrasts genres, thus highlighting their artificiality (documentary, court-room drama, rise and fall of the great man, *noir*, comedy) and their aspect as film language rather than as a representation of what might be real. Welles's films may use a genre like *noir*, but it is broken and incoherent and thereby made conscious and thereby opened up to criticism by the flamboyance of his camera (distorted, grotesque angles, unnatural highlights), the mannerism of his compositions (where the 'manner' rather than the substance prevails), the discords created by his editing (discontinuities, false matches), the mismatch between sound and image, the grotesque nature of performances (overblown, excessive, caricatured), roles are 'out of character' with the conventions (the 'hero' of *The Lady from Shanghai*, O'Hara, is a romantic innocent). These breaks and resulting incoherences make the films difficult and uneasy.

For example, Rita Hayworth, rather than integrated into *The Lady from Shanghai*, is by her beauty and star status an anomaly within it. What she is in the film is less a character in a real-seeming fiction than the image of a star, max-factored and made artificial from outside the film, and, while her beauty within the drama of it is the lure that attracts and traps O'Hara, it proves as empty and fragile as the money and power of Bannister, both of which are shattered in multiple, mirrored, unidentifiable fragments, the twin supports of the Hollywood system: money and desire.

Much of the *film noir* tradition has within it a social commentary and criticism. Welles goes a step further. What is discomfiting about Welles's work is not that he criticises values like power and money, but that he criticises the money and power that makes images of them, the mechanism of reality that created Welles and almost destroyed him, the system of filmmaking that he loved to make use of and hated to have to leave.

Frames

Godard's exhibition in 2006 at the Centre Pompidou in Paris, *Voyage(s) en Utopie, Jean-Luc Godard, 1946–2006: À la recherche d'un théorème perdu*, was in three rooms each consisting of a number of installations and a collection of objects at first sight seemingly set out higgledy-piggledy. It was as if each room constituted in itself an installation. As with his *Histoire(s) du cinéma* (1988–98), the materials were cited (images, sounds, phrases), found (a bed, a broom, steps, a model electric train) or reconstructed and miniaturised (the *maquette* of the unrealised original exhibition for the Pompidou, *Collages de France*). These various materials from different provenances were brought together as in a super collage (the entire exhibition), not exactly a parody, but certainly a commentary on traditional museum classifications by genre, artist, period, nationality. The disjunctions between what was displayed, because of their apparent arbitrariness and the unfamiliarity of the joins (not unlike Surrealist experiments from the 1930s), provoked memories, associations and surprising unlikely connections. For example, the toy electric train that ran in a loop through a tunnel variously seemed to cite Hitchcock's *North by Northwest* (1959), the Lumière brothers' *L'Arrivée d'un train en gare de La Ciotat* (1895), Orson Welles's ecstatic comment on the studio machinery offered him at RKO for *Citizen Kane* (1941) ('This is the biggest electric train set any boy ever had!'), and, as well, the trains that transported the victims of the Holocaust to Auschwitz and Bergen-Belsen, images which Godard earlier had reproduced in his *Histoire(s) du cinéma*, some taken from Alain Resnais's *Nuit et brouillard* (1955), others from George Stevens's home movie that ends with his entry into the death camps in 1945, others from Claude Lanzmann's *Shoah* (1985), and still others that were archival. Some of the material, such as the *Collages de France* miniature (like a model for a film set), was reduced in size and projected (looped on flat small screens of fragments from films by Godard and others – Nicholas Ray, Sergei Eisenstein, Otto Preminger – placed alongside anonymous pornographic images and those from sport), an odd collection, as you might find in a junk shop and be provoked by to dream and imagine, to be transported.

Though objects and associations tended to coalesce on contact, they also tended to disperse, going off in different directions to their origins and beyond, making of the exhibition a map of pathways and possible journeys that exceeded it, defying any presumed unity. No one thing sufficed, each was particular (none 'served' an apparent function) and all were plural because they suggested multiple places and entries.

The exhibition, because of its apparent disorder, citational density, heterogeneity, evocations and the banality of the collection of its found objects, echoed works of Dada, particularly Kurt Schwitters's *Merzbau* and of the common objects, or odd conjunctions, some scandalous, displayed by Marcel Duchamp (his urinal, for example and the moustache on the *Mona Lisa*). It also resonated with the Combines and installation pieces of Robert Rauschenberg which in turn echoed strategies in Cubist collages, those of Picasso, for example, and before Picasso the purified, almost abstract, sculpted and geometric paintings of Paul Cézanne. There was as well an echo of the Surrealists, their art works, literary works and films, not only the Buñuel–Dali films and their improbable juxtapositions but also Joseph Cornell's film *Rose Hobart* (1936), a remake/citation of *East of Borneo* (1931), like the Pompidou exhibition and Godard's *Histoire(s) du cinéma*.

It was the 'reality' and everydayness of things in the exhibition, as if 'documents' of the real, also true of the cited images and sounds of *Histoire(s) du cinéma* whose organisation and connections are often as obscure as these are in the exhibition, that are disorienting by the fact of their 'reality', the lack of any single precise narrative or 'line' to contain them and their resistance to 'sense'. The 'real' and its contrary multiple openings to possible other arrangements and references, including an opening to fictions not-yet-formed or articulated (in *Histoire(s)* to films that 'might be'), is disruptive of any unified coherence while the dailiness and casualness, the sense of chance encounters between different materials (as in Surrealist *rencontres*) gave the exhibition and *Histoire(s)* a sense of travelling (*voyage*), a wandering within an indeterminate geography without guidance or precise purpose or destination. It is not exactly Godard who is the *flâneur* but rather the film that almost seems as alive and palpable as a person.

The earliest drafts of *Histoire(s) du cinéma*, based on lectures given by Godard at the Montréal Cinémathèque in 1978, were divided into twelve voyages. The title of the Pompidou exhibition was *Voyage(s) en Utopie*, multiple wanderings to nowhere very exact, a vagabondage of memories, chance and an expectation-readiness for occurrences that might happen. These works are exciting, wonderful and open precisely because nothing definitive can be deduced. They are also uncomfortable for their apparent chaos and fortuity, their refusal to arrive or to come, like being lost.

Cubist collages not only recruited fragments excised from reality, as the Godard exhibition did, and mixed them together with paint and graphic lines (as in a 'painting'), but they did so as to compromise the traditional two dimensions of painting which historically had created a third dimension by the use of perspective, that is, an illusory one at the interior of a painted scene whose model was theatrical and dependent upon a strict respect for framing. The fact that these works recruited real objects constituted an intrusion into an imaginary, essentially fictionalised, representational space which the real compromised simply by its alien presence, as the will towards abstraction in Cézanne, pared down as it was, disturbed a prevailing naturalism, still evident in Impressionism. It too presented a new, 'other' note in a heretofore homogeneous space. What had been traditional was now confronted with radical differences (abstraction, the actual, the found, commentary, a remaking which was disruptive and parodic, signs of reordering that were neither beautiful nor even 'skilful' but instead questioning as different forms of questions and as questions of forms, articulated by Nicole Brenez in her *The Forms of the Question*).[7]

The Cubist collage created discontinuities (gaps) between the various items 'in' the collage and by the addition of real material (cloth, wood, feathers, toys, matchboxes, newspaper clippings rather like the

7 Nicole Brenez, 'The Forms of the Question', in Michael Temple, James S. Williams and Michael Witt (eds), *For Ever Godard* (London: Black Dog Publishing, 2004), pp. 160–77.

miniature boxes of scenes and objects in the work of Joseph Cornell), but there was no glue (continuities) to hold these differences together. The Cubist work moved beyond its pictorial boundaries to an exterior third dimension (as opposed to a traditional illusory one interiorised within a frame by perspective, by *trompe d'oeil*, and by a carefully wrought scenic composition). The actual 'third' dimension in the Cubist collage brings the exhibited work (like a painting) toward sculpture (cut-outs) and later what would be installations. The Cubist collage, because of its mix of materials (paper, wood, metal), its straining beyond the boundaries of the work and its resonance with the origins from which real objects that constituted it had come or which they could be associated with, seems unfinished and infinite, in part for the fact that the frame had been traversed, focus endangered and thus painting, as it traditionally was, put at risk. For Picasso, it seemed that anything could become a subject for a work, could be a starting point. It was making do, an improvisation, the creation and transformation with whatever happened to be around, no object having a necessary permanence or definiteness, no reality thereby stable.

The collage was perpetually going away, going 'off', away from itself, beyond the framed limits that had been crucial for creating the illusionary scenes and figures of traditional painting that had framed beauty and indicated skill. Even Picasso's purely painted canvases seemed to be like cut-outs not because of their diverse materials (everything in those paintings is paint) so much as by its diverse and overlapping-intersecting volumes. The Cubist 'scene' not only lacked a fixed perspective and point of view but was not, strictly speaking, representational and, where it was, it approached parody. It neither described, narrated nor illustrated. Instead, it simply demonstrated (and sometimes cited).

Francis Bacon's work is also interesting in this regard. Bacon's frames, rather than being traversed toward an outside beyond them, have the effect of constraining their subjects, tearing them apart by placing them under extreme pressure as if the painting, and everything represented within it, were about to explode and disintegrate and along with it the fact and idea of representation itself, its fragility and temporariness. Certainly, the frame, rather than being a frame of perspective, depth and clarification, tended towards so extreme a distortion that whatever was represented became purely form, shape, paint, rhythm, imbalance, as if the painting was dissolved into the pureness (chastity) of its constituents

at the price of the coherence, stability or focus of any subject, as occurs
with Picasso's art.

The installation work, Rauschenberg's Combines, Schwitters's *Merzbau*,
are the heirs to Cubist experiments and innovations and the revolution
in painting it had initiated. A number of things were accomplished: the
frame was discarded, the anecdotal narrative-theatrical scene dissolved,
points of view multiplied, the centre destroyed, a heterogeneity of material put into play and completeness and originality compromised. The
consistencies and homogeneities characteristic of painting were made
inconsistent and its unities (scenes) shattered into fragments by disjunctions in matter, temporality and dimension. These works spilled over
boundaries and definitions that might contain or fix them, exceeding not
only the practices but the categories, understandings, ideas, discourses
and criticism that had served to define the art work: frame, centre, point
of view, perspective, description, meaning, significance, originality,
beauty and sometimes narrative. As a result, what had previously simply
been accepted and enjoyed for its skill and beauty and had given comfort
by its sense (the represented, the anecdote, the piece of theatre) was now
open to question ('what is art?'), to doubt and to uncertainty that went
to the heart of the traditional art work (pierced it) and its institutions as
Duchamp's urinal and Warhol's Brillo Boxes and serialised images later
provocatively made clear as if such questioning was one of the purposes,
if not the principal purpose, of the artistic strategies of Surrealism, Dada
and later their heir, Pop.

Godard's films in general, and *Histoire(s) du cinéma* in particular
echoed these accomplishments (which were also evident in the Pompidou
exhibition), especially the use of the art work to bring itself into question
and by extension all art where the work and the commentary upon it ('a
musical and the idea of a musical' as in *Une femme est une femme* (1964))
were brought together, thus making every element, image, sound concrete and discursive, representational and critical, focused and digressive.
One of the achievements of *Histoire(s) du cinéma* is to so isolate images
or sounds that these are refreshed, like seeing or hearing them anew
and for the first time, no longer part of their origins nor immediately
'connected' to what surrounds them or is contiguous to them, and by
so doing, by giving back to images, sounds, objects their autonomy,
it freed them for any number of associations and encounters, none of

which would cause them to lose their identity, as a continuous narrative might by restricting movement into fixed directions, by holding elements in place. In this multiplication of identities and possibilities nothing is lost and what has been can be seen once more (returns, memories), but differently, newly, for example, Ethan Edwards taking Debbie in his arms in Ford's *The Searchers* (1956), fragmented, pulverised, retimed, broken down in *Histoire(s)*, but with nothing destroyed, to the contrary enabling one (almost for the first time) to see the scene (because remade differently) and to bring it into a relation with other scenes elsewhere as if the function of *Histoire(s)* is not only for the film to be open and ready (attentive as in Rossellini's cinema) but for it to open up the cinema in general and in its details.

Historically, the questioning of the cinema – what it was, what it could become – an act of criticism and therefore necessarily a historical undertaking, had been the achievement of the films of the *Nouvelle Vague*, of the reflections on film in *Cahiers du cinéma* in the 1950s and 1960s, and coincident with both, perhaps even their source, certainly their inspiration, the writings of André Bazin and his philosophical pursuit of the cinema, *Qu'est ce que le cinéma?*, which made of films and their forms instruments of thought, giving them thereby an unaccustomed and extraordinary range and density.

In film, the frame has been defined by three interrelated aspects: the frame of the shot, the frame of the narrative which it served (a beginning and an end) and the continuities between shots that established scenes and sequences within a narrative to provide not only coherence and unity, a focus, but fictionality as a constructed simulacrum of the real. In other words, the frame or frames in film, as they had functioned in painting (and in theatre), were to contribute to the construction of an ideal illusory space within which a scene could be described, enacted and performed.

The frame was functional for narrative and therefore crucial to it. The destruction of the frame or at the very least compromising it, a deframing (the *Nouvelle Vague* was central in this process), affected an entire range of practices, ideas and histories where film and the commentary on film, contemporary film and the historical past of film were no more distinct or distant than was fiction from documentary precisely because borders were crossed and separations interconnected. One of the virtues of Godard was to bring into doubt categories and their (false?) oppositions, in order to begin to bring together what had been apart and in doing so propose differences as disjunctions that worked upon and with each other, active rather than fixed, in movement rather than fixed and classified. This freedom (almost casual and instinctive, like the freedom and curiosity evoked in Surrealist encounters) and the intensity of play involved are the reason that Godard's films are so exhilarating.

Histoire(s) du cinéma accomplishes a massive deframing of the cinema and in doing so initiates a new history while not exactly closing a previous one, as *cleansing* it, as Cézanne cleansed painting. The traditional history of the cinema has been presented as a chronology (a progressive narrative) where each film or group of films cited is made to belong to some kind of order, that is, the cited work as exemplary and illustrative (the 'silent' period, neorealism, the *Nouvelle Vague*, national cinemas, realism, formalism and so on), part of a classification system where every film represents and illustrates the history of the cinema and can be accounted for (counted). Such a history *typifies*. What *Histoire(s)* cleanses from the history of the cinema (and therefore from its practices) is the *typical*. The citation in Godard is a form that acts, one of whose functions is to disturb and dismantle every order. His *Histoire(s)* is, unlike most histories and stories, no longer dependent on structures of reference and direction or a narrative, that is, on a frame.

History

The necessity of history. You need to have the sense of the history of the cinema even if you know it only imperfectly so that every shot you take, every cut you make has the sense of the presence of the past and that sense of the past is what constitutes it. This work, a work Godard calls 'documentary' has been lost or abandoned and the American cinema is particularly guilty of that.

Alain Resnais's *Nuit et brouillard* (1955) opens, in colour, on the ruins of Auschwitz and Majdanek. Colour is the sign of the present. The ruins are traces of a past, a means of entry to it, of remembering and imagining. The past in the film is represented in black-and-white, by archival footage, that is, the past is cited.

Between the beginning and the end, the film moves back and forth between two times, the black-and-white of the past of what is remembered belonging to a store of images, the colour of the present, the remembering, and the narrative that negotiates between the past and an imagined future. Three different times then and an extraordinary accumulation of details from diverse origins.

In the ruins of Auschwitz and Majdanek, the camera tracks through the landscape, the gates, the fencing, the labyrinth of dormitories, latrines, torture chambers (hospitals), crematoria. As in other Resnais films, there is an assemblage, an amassing of things, objects. The way of presenting them is almost musical, as if it is set to a beat and tempo. Either the newsreel images interrupt the track of the camera (in the present), halting it for an instant (in the past), or the track is continued between past and present, elaborating a rhythm, as if scanning the past, and then returning to the present again, seamless in movement, but distinct in time. In both instances of the continuous track over heterogeneous times and places and the interruption of movement, it seems as if the different times both coalesce and separate. These movements and counter-movements are like itineraries of memory and imaginings. The instants are their pauses, a stillness almost, an intake of breath.

The ruins are an archive of breaks, shards, dispersions, silences, mutterings, things hidden, invisibilities, immobilities. It is among these and by means of them that the past is sought and, literally, re-membered. The temptation with such material is to fill in what is left out, to construct with hints and traces a true, definitive narrative of the camps, to make the unspeakable speak, the incomprehensible clear, memories, true, and to reinstate continuities for gaps, plausibility for questions.

Resnais resists the temptation. The ruins, both physical and in reproductions in photographs and films from archives, are witnesses, memories, not a story but the intersection of documents, an *errance*, a wandering through debris of various kinds from different origins, not unlike what occurs in Resnais's film *Toute la mémoire du monde* (1956) on the Bibliothèque Nationale in Paris, memories stored in books, coins, etchings which his camera traverses, tracking as if inside the pathways of the brain. These are the most compelling sequences of the film and the most rhythmic.

The simplest object is a source of a new path, a new encounter, new evidence. There is no pretence to reproduce the experience of the camps, not because it is unthinkable but because it is beyond a final, comprehensive grasp. There is always more and especially when there seems to be nothing but debris and a temporal and ethical void.

What is singular about the camps is the comparison between the physical destruction of them (by war and time), the dispersion, disappearance of their material existence, their status as ruins and, in contrast, the durability of the memory of them, for example Jean Cayrol's voice-over, the photographs, the films cited. *Nuit et brouillard*, though only ten years distant in time from the liberation of the camps by the Allies at the end of the war, the freeing of those who remained, the capturing of those who had guarded and murdered the interned, and the sight of the horrors of it, is less about the camps directly than about a memory of them, both its resistance to time (remembered) and its transformation by time (forgotten, imagined). What Resnais presents is not a reflection of the experience or even exactly a proof of and testament to it, still less an interpretation, but rather a montage of memories, not a fiction, but comparisons and associations at the interior of real events, not one thing or another but their joins and gaps including the gap in memory that imagination fills. This montage, anything but continuous or logical, in turn creates a space for another montage, one accomplished by the viewer.

The depth and expanse of the film is less in what it shows than what it cannot and does not show.

It is as if reality provokes an imaginary, even dream, and the imaginary illuminates reality, not only helping to uncover it but giving it force and presence, making the real appear out of its traces, between the stones, along the empty paths and beside Resnais's glorious labyrinthine tracking shots. The imaginary is in the present blended with a future. It is what provokes the return to the past, what summons it from the depth of the forgotten and the dead. There is no true nor exactly false in the film or at least that is not the issue. It is rather what is and what is not that is at stake.

What is given in recollections, narratives, photos, buildings, towers, fences, barbed wire, ovens, gas chambers, trains, piles of bodies, dormitories, objects, tattooed flesh, identification cards, is not a reflection of reality, still less a transparent story of it, but left-over fragments, a juxtaposition of real matter, the stuff of memory, disordered, atemporal, alogical, out of which the film provokes not truth but reappearances, interweaving the imaginary and realities, the poetic and the document, yet avoiding any false aestheticism or exploitation of the historical occurrence of the camps.

The film is a history of a strongly present absence, as the best histories are.

In *Histoire(s) du cinéma* (1988–98), its montage of extreme disconnections, differences, juxtapositions, overloading and opacity simultaneously calls out for understanding yet frustrates the very need for understanding that it provokes. Effectively, the film is a journey through a landscape of thoughts, words, images, sounds made by others, whose geography is always on the point of being reconfigured, remapped, because the cited material is impermanent, and even more so its significances, because each new image and sound change everything. It is as if the film, Godard and the viewers are condemned to wander perpetually in a strange, mysterious world among the no-longer living as Orpheus or Ulysses do. The film articulates a forgotten dead past by means of a language made to bring the past back to life, to rescue it, a language essentially and necessarily unfinished because the resurrection is ongoing, disorderly and haphazard.

Godard's contribution to history is that language.

Images

Most of the images and scenes in *Histoire(s) du cinéma* (1988–98) are citations. If their origins cannot be found, it is probable, nevertheless, that in time they will be. Some scenes in the film are staged, for example monologues by professional actors: Alain Cuny, Sabine Azema, Julie Delpy, Juliette Binoche and Godard. The monologues are quotations from philosophy and poetry either directly or in a collage of phrases from different sources.

There is an argument in *Histoire(s)*, or allusions to one, that historically the cinema did not realise its true potential of registering the real (this is the History of *Histoire(s)*). For example, it failed (except in rare instances) to foresee or engage with the horrors of war, the death camps or Sarajevo. For Godard, it seems, this failure has to do with a history of film as a history of narratives, that is, as illusion, a verisimilitude enacted by means of continuities and motivated connections. Thus, to reinstate the real to the cinema requires the dissolution and break up of narrative that *Histoire(s) du cinéma* accomplishes, not simply of small narratives but of the grand narrative of History and the narrative in between, the history of the cinema. The dismemberment is the work of citation (extraction from a context, from some kind of narrative) and montage (a recombination of forms).

French Impressionism, even if it had precedents in an earlier history of painting, created images out of doors, *en plein air*, in touch with the direct experience of nature, not an idealised view but an actual one, the immediacy of the sketch, in order to capture the effects of light and mood, not eternal or immobile or idealised but found, encountered, if not exactly in a moment of time, within time in an actual present and in the reality of its passing. The paintings of Impressionism mark out temporality and the subjectivity necessarily attached to it in the capturing of an instant (like a photograph). What comes after Impressionism – Manet, Cézanne, Matisse, Picasso – is less an attempt to capture the real (though it is that too) than, as Foucault has pointed out, to create paintings for the museum, paintings related to other paintings, to forms and hence freed from reproductive demands, demands that photography and later film, would better satisfy. What occurred was not an either/or, either reality or artifice, reality or abstraction, but rather a play between the two, and hence an awareness of both at the heart of painting so that being in the one place (of experience, of reality) necessarily led to the other (the image, consciousness), as with Godard's comment (and practice) whereby the document becomes fiction and fiction the document, neither of them stable and brought together less as an opposition than a difficult-to-define difference because of their closeness.

Disaffection toward narrative fiction or more precisely the felt need to question it belonged to a historical necessity. The film documentaries of the late 1920s and 1930s were in part provoked by political and social events which it was felt the fiction film did not adequately address (if at all). For the sake of the coherence and effectiveness of its fictions, reality, however defined, was a disturbance to highly organised, coded and institutionalised fictional practices. The forms of narrative fiction were, if not threatened early on in the history of the cinema, certainly called into question: the result of this (Renoir's films in this regard are exemplary) was a cinema that juxtaposed reality, the everyday, the casual and the incidental with the fictional and theatrical, either within a film, as with the films of Renoir, or as an entirely different kind of film such as the documentary or the works of the avant-garde (Dada and Surrealism specifically), something in any case radically 'other' to the conventional. Some documentaries veered off into the fabulous and dream, at once under the spell of reality and aware of its subjectivity and hence of the magic, wonder and possibility (flexibility) in the document and the everyday within it. The films of Vigo, Buñuel, Franju and Painlevé were exemplary in this regard, and perhaps Chaplin as well. Given the fact that all of Godard's images and sounds in *Histoire(s) du cinéma* are cited (he is dealing with 'history', with the past), his material is necessarily second-hand, is already images. There are no images in the film of direct experience, no 'real' in the usual documentary sense of the real, no Eskimos hunting seal, except perhaps as memories, that is as already having been fashioned and which Godard can only 'cite' and 'remake' or rearrange.

If the real is impossible to attain, why accuse the cinema of having betrayed its nature and vocation to register it? And why accuse it of failing to confront the actuality and horror of historical events? The problem for Godard is not that narrative fiction is fictional, but rather that it created an illusion as if it were not fictional, but like life, as History-writing created false continuities and homogeneities as if true. The force of Godard's cinema and the work of his montage are to break up anything that immobilises and certifies, including, or above all, an answer or strictly determined oppositions. The real is not an object but a relationship or, better, relationships, *Histoire(s)*, History with an 's', that fluctuates and is constantly subject to being reconfigured at every (historical) moment. Nothing for Godard stands still, least of all his films. At best, the real can only be glimpsed, momentarily, in the in-between of perpetual rearrangements. It has no fixity any more than the past has, always subject to the vagaries of a present, to reconsiderations, to time, memory and the moment, no better demonstrated than by Godard's reinstatement of the past in the future by the activity of his citations and their montage that causes what comes 'after', the next shot, to be what the present resurrects from the past, a transformed future as if the film is moving backwards snatching the past, exhuming and projecting it forward. It involves an extended temporality like that which belongs to memory, reflection and thought.

In no sense, however, does *Histoire(s)* unfold time by means of events but rather it points to time as an element of the shot and thereby makes everything ephemeral, always on the verge of disappearance, all the more so by the fact that the shot is an already pre-existing image, a citation, and thereby it is a return summoned by the present whose future is behind it and every shot belonging to multiple temporalities and directions.

Immediacy

Alain Bergala distinguishes between the *disposition* (the arrangement of a scene) and the *attaque* (the shooting of it in the choice of angle, distance, perspective, focal length). For the most part, in most fiction films, these two elements come together. In Godard's case (and also in painting), the two procedures are usually disjoined so that the *disposition* and the *attaque* are at odds with one another. – allowing for improvisation, a sudden sight, the invisible becoming visible, an inspiration, a matter of an instant, a moment. In most films the scene is derived from its function in the script and the shot from its function in the scene, and the *disposition* from its function in the shot and the shooting from the readability of the *disposition*. Godard is resistant to this logic. His openness is to the visual, to the moment, to the unexpected. As Dominique Chateau said:

> Je m'intéresse surtout à la relation qui s'établit entre la posture discursive de Godard et son idée du cinéma. Le principe du fragment renvoie au principe de la fragmentation cinématographique: l'instant, dit Godard, 'c'est ce qu'il y a de beau au cinéma. C'est pour ça que le cinéma a été inventé. C'est qu'il les enregistre certaines qualités de l'instant et qui les conserve.

> (I am particularly interested in the relation established between the discursive posture of Godard and his idea of the cinema. The principle of the fragment brings us to the principle of fragmentation in the cinema: 'The moment', Godard said, 'is what is beautiful in the

cinema. It was for that reason the cinema was invented. It is that it records certain qualities of the moment and retains them.)[8]

The shot sequence in early Godard films was a means to render the immediate and casual, not exactly to create an image as to find one and in finding one to duplicate it. This concern with improvisation and the casual real would become, in editing, a concern with composition.

A shot sequence conceived as an opportunity to register 'flashes' and 'moments' by Godard is montage by another means and it too is primarily 'linguistic' and ideational ... the immediacy of something and the idea of it, the presentation and the interrogation ... a reality and a discourse, but not as interpretation, rather as enlightenment, which is something entirely different.

In the classical film, linearity creates a past in so far as every image depends on the image that has gone before. The new image is always the consequence of the previous one. The past is what has been passed by and the present is what is passing. Godard's film is a history which is neither chronological nor singular. Though Lumière came before Griffith and Griffith before Murnau, and Murnau before Rossellini, and so on, in *Histoire(s) du cinéma* (1988–98) such succession while assumed is not important. Instead, at every present moment in the film, what belongs to the past reappears in the present and, as it does, it becomes a point, an instant that summons other pasts in the present such that, strictly speaking, nothing ever passes.

The achronological structure of the film multiplies histories. There is no single history in *Histoire(s)* since every moment is a starting point for some series or another, a chain of associations that spread, divide, call up, disperse, circulate, trace, explode. Each instant creates new instances and within these, everything, the whole of the past, appears as entirely new, different from itself, having been reconfigured, refreshed in its journey towards a present moment. *Histoire(s)* does not unfold or advance in the usual sense. This accounts for the fragility and precariousness of each instant, each present: these are images of time and memory neither of

8 Dominique Chateau, A. Gardies and F. Jost (eds), *Cinéma de la modernité: films, théories* (Colloque à Cerisy) (Paris: Klincksieck, 1981).

which can be constrained or fixed in place. Each moment is a shift in a point of view and a change in patterns of association, hence a new image makes its appearance from out of a store of pre-existing ones, every repetition never being the same. No image is definitively in the past but rather in attendance, watchful, like Nanook waiting for the seal to appear from under the ice. Hence too, the alternation in *Histoire(s)* between images within which new images come into sight by layerings, fades, superimpositions, parallelism, and other images broken into and shattered by stutterings, flickerings, interruptions, writings, black leader. The two strategies though different are variants of each other, as is the movement of the film where images cohere to form a constellation and then dissolve to form another as if without apparent cause.

Behind the practice of the script is a notion of being able to plan, lay out, order, calculate. Godard calls it accounting. As the cinema accepted or courted the entry of reality within it and thereby opened itself to chance, accident, memory, sketchiness, to the unheralded irruption of time, the central function of the script in the creation of a film diminished, replaced by various degrees of improvisation, the immediacy of reactions to the unexpected and the momentary, to a glance, gesture, shift in light, accident, a sound, a word, or an image, that touch directly on memory and on the vagaries and accidents of life. Film became more like life, that is sensitive to the unexpected and aware of the need to respond, to be open and flexible to what might arrive. To Godard, Antonioni, Cassavetes, Kiarostami, Rouch, Rossellini, Rivette, the experience of making films ought to be similar to life: unpredictable, surprising and dynamic.

For these filmmakers the distinction between life and film is difficult to sustain. The border between them is porous and, more often than not, breached. For Godard, living, working, loving involve the same gestures, or gestures and words, that intermingle and interact (love to work, work to love, the subjects and play in all his films). In his method no plan is assumed to be definite but rather as tentative and provisional, making a film as an activity of reacting to the film as it is taking shape and at every moment of it. It was the method of Jean Rouch. It is not that in *Histoire(s)* the past never passes and the present is always fragile, but that the process of the film which is its subject is both a way of working and a way of living.

Effectively, there is neither present nor past in *Histoire(s)*. The instant is a terminal point for both and in an unexpected way. What comes after is not determined by what precedes it. In fact, causation and its linear consequences do not come into play. Instead, because the instant calls up and reconfigures what comes before, what comes after can be said to have come first. It is the 'after' that brings forward the 'before', not as consequence but as association and questioning. Each is both separate and within the other. Simultaneity, where present and past continue to exist and are demolished, while difficult to speak, is perfectly perceptible. Time can be seen to stand still and be in motion.

Inertia

The title of the Bertolucci film *Prima della rivoluzione* (*Before the Revolution*, 1964) is a reference to the French aristocrat Charles Maurice de Talleyrand (1754–1838): 'Ceux qui n'ont pas vécu avant 1789 ne connaissent pas la douceur de vivre' ('Those who have not lived before 1789 cannot understand the sweetness of life'). Talleyrand lived before and after the French Revolution, which he supported as he later would support the Empire under Napoléon whose government he served.

Two nineteenth-century French novels, Stendhal's *The Charterhouse of Parma*/*La Chartreuse de Parme* (1839) and Gustave Flaubert's *L'Education sentimentale* (1869), are cited within the Bertolucci film, though the story in the film is different from the events in the novels.

What was 'sweet' before the revolution? The 'before' the revolution in the Bertolucci film refers to two revolutions, one not yet in an indefinite future, a socialist revolution; the other recent and constituting the cinematic revolution of the French *Nouvelle Vague*, especially the films of Jean-Luc Godard.

Before the cinematic revolution, films tended to be governed by conventions, by rules. The rules that dominated were those of Hollywood. Before 1789, everyone had their assigned social place in a class system and, though for some that place seemed untenable or uncomfortable, demanding change, even abolition and revolution, it could be said, nevertheless, that things were clear. Sweetness was a taste of nostalgia for a past that was or was only simply imagined. The Revolution, when it came, had unintended consequences. The Stendhal and Flaubert novels concern two young men in a post-revolutionary France seeking their place in a new world in the process of being formed. It is the subject of Bertolucci's film, whose central character, Fabrizio, is faced with a choice between lovers and political loyalties, a past that needs to be changed or a past to be acccepted. He is unsure about what to do. The film is the story of that uncertainty.

Godard's cinema was a model for Bertolucci, and *Prima della rivoluzione* is his most Godardian film. It has Godard's looseness, openness and sense of the casual, his episodic structures, jump cuts that compromise continuity creating associations and rhymes and doublings rather than a narrative of consequence, linearity and causation. Classical cinematic rules are overturned and violated. The Bertolucci film, like Godard's films, digresses from a centre, deviates, wanders, migrates. His films lack the unities of conventional ones. Many of the shots and sequences are built on the basis of citations which are multi-directional and associational. The Bertolucci film depends, like Godard's films, on disruption, interruption of a line, changes of direction, focus, tone and action. The usual boundaries and categories that defined films, defined what they are or should be, become blurred, upset or parodied. Instead of resolution there is inconclusiveness and lack of finish, instead of clarity there is ambiguity. Oppositions and contrasts are constant. Bertolucci tended to edit between sequences, sequences tended to be filmed by an incessantly moving tracking shot as in Godard's films, for example in *Vivre sa vie* where Godard's camera follows Anna Karina dancing as it follows her in *Le Petit Soldat* (1960).

A cinema built on citations necessarily returns to the past, to before the revolution instituted by Godard and still being instituted by him and continued by Bertolucci, that is, revolutions that in essence are nostalgic and thereby sweet. If the new cinema departs from an older classical one, the departure is made evident only by the arrival of the new. What comes after, the most new, the latest, forces a retrospective view to what had been before. The last shot then comes first and the first shot last, because the action of film is to be understood not successively nor chronologically, but retrospectively.

Though classicism predates the modern, it is only with modernism that classicism is truly born, is made conscious, pointed to. Though modernism undoubtedly comes after classicism, modernism comes first since it is only with the modern that the classicism that preceded it fully comes into being. Classicism then comes *after* and, like the sweetness of life, is an aftertaste.

In disrupting classicism and by doing so necessarily marking its presence, modernism looks back – there is no comprehensive reordering of the debris left over by revolution. The disruption, often in the form of citations, confounds continuity, makes style noticeable. Modern art and film, by disordering the classical, inevitably disordered itself so that, try as it might to re-establish a new order from the one displaced, there could no longer be a definitive order. Instead, there is an array of styles and displacements. The accomplishment of contemporary art has been its destructiveness, not of art but of the rules which define it.

Almost all the films of the French *Nouvelle Vague* are nostalgic and bitter-sweet, bitter because the classical cinema it cites is only of the past, but because the *Nouvelle Vague*, by its stylistic innovations, was responsible for that passage, in effect, for the loss of a classicism that it admired for its elegance and whose loss it regretted by its passing, hence the bitter taste for a cinema no more and one whose demise the *Nouvelle Vague* had hastened. On the other hand, it also resumed that classicism, reinstated it, not by imitation or duplication, but by something exceedingly more profound, by citation, a refashioning and a commentary, a remodelling, as a way not to lose it, rather to commemorate it and go beyond it, hence the sweetness. The films of the French *Nouvelle Vague* are Hollywood genre films revisted, reconfigured and, by virtue of this, brought up to date.

Prima della rivoluzione is constructed by mirror relations and transformations: of time (past to present), of novel to film, of film to theatre, of theatre to opera. These relations never conclude, never 'settle'. Since everything is subject to mirrored reflections and nothing stable or certain, the film seems constantly *between* categories in a nowhere of uncertainty, indecision and restlessness. And, when a decision is arrived at, for example by Fabrizio to end his affair with Gina and to marry Clelia or to turn his back on the Communist Party, what also arrives is a mark of the temporary, of impermanence and tentativeness. Held at bay, suspended, autonomous and disconnected, the film opens to new combinations, to a further restlessness. All you can say about the revolution is that it is revolutionary, that it liberates, a reason in Bertolucci's films perhaps of the ubiquity of prisons, barriers, confinement and the difficulty of escape.

If everything in *Prima della rivoluzione*, indeed in all Bertolucci's films, is subject to doubling (and it is), and to false identities and theatrical masquerades (and it is), there is no one thing that is final, but there are instead multiple comparatives between multiple likenesses, relations that are essentially formal rather than substantive, forms of contradiction and repetition.

Fabrizio can never decide, or, when he seems to decide and marries Clelia, it is as if he is not there, his presence an absence that never was present, an inability to act, action that is divorced from will and desire.

Towards the end of the Bertolucci film, the Parma bourgeoisie take their place at the opening of the opera season of the Parma opera house. The bourgeoisie of Parma, bejewelled, elegantly dressed, enter the opera house, as if on parade, certainly on display, for the opening night, Giuseppe Verdi's *Macbeth*. Their entry is like a scene from another Verdi opera, *Un ballo in maschera*. The audience of the opera resemble figures from an operatic fancy-dress ball.

There are two stages and two performances, the stage for *Macbeth* and the stage for the drama of Fabrizio unable to choose between Clelia and Gina and the jealousies that the drama creates, like scenes from the films of Jean Renoir, especially his *La Régle du jeu* (1939) and *French Cancan* (1954).

The question for Fabrizio: should he or should he not marry the bourgeois, blonde-haired, statuesque, churchgoing Clelia or carry on his affair with the seductive, dark, energetic, sexually compulsive, neurotic, not at all respectable Gina that might place at risk his possible marriage and his far from unambiguous future of integration with the Parma bourgeoisie. Besides, Gina is his aunt. At the Parma opera house, the two melodramas, in reality and in opera, are placed side by side, mirroring each other, regarding each other.

Clelia is in the family box in the balcony watching the Verdi opera. Gina and Fabrizio are in the corridors and at the entry to the opera house playing hide and seek with each other and their emotions. Bertolucci's camera moves from one to the other in counterpoint. In addition to the Bertolucci/Renoir mirror, there is another mirror: Bertolucci/Visconti, and its comparisons.

In Visconti's *Senso* (1954), a drama in life (and politics) is played out against a performance of Verdi's *Il trovatore* and, at the end of the film, against a musical passage from Anton Bruckner's 7th Symphony. In both cases life imitates art and art imitates life as if two operas, two melodramas, two musical accompaniments in the Visconti are being performed exactly as occurs in *Prima della rivoluzione*, mirrors mirrored within which it is difficult to find your way. *Macbeth* is pure opera, melodrama, artifice. The scene off stage of Fabrizio and the two women is by contrast realistic with political overtones. What happens, however, is that the two melodramas, on stage and off, begin to resemble each other as if Fabrizio, Clelia and Gina are performing, and that theatre and opera are part of life, the border between them is almost interchangeable.

The finale of *Macbeth* is also the finale of the love affair between Fabrizio and his aunt Gina. The scene which follows, almost as if incidental, is one of surrender: Fabrizio, at last, marries Clelia. The rejection of Gina and the marriage to Clelia are social acts and political ones. Choosing one rather than the other is a choice between revolution and conformity, the Communist Party and the bourgeoisie. The finale to the affair of Fabrizio takes place in the corridors and at the entrance lobby of the opera house. Upstairs, on stage, the opera continues. Downstairs another is being acted out and to the same Verdi music.

Gina, Fabrizio, Clelia are caught by their class, society, history, a condition they are unable to alter or reconcile. Their dreams and fantasies cannot be detached from the oppressive weight of reality nor are they able to distinguish between the two. Instead, fantasies become more fantastic, realities more burdensome, reinforce each other, the real made more real, the fantastic more fantastic and unattainable.

The present, because already a past, becomes nostalgia for what has been lost even as what has been lost comes into being, a future already of the past, that reaches out towards the moments of its disappearance. Sweetness, perhaps something closer to ecstasy, is to seize these moments.

Insufficiency

How is it possible to encompass all films with a single film, to tell the history of the cinema totally in one film without being a complete encyclopaedia of it? If every image contains within it all images (virtually) then the task of such a film would be to touch that virtuality and release it and to do so by montage.

There are *no* essential images in *Histoire(s) du cinéma* (1988–98). Every image in it has a certain irresoluteness. Every image can be undone and often is undone by the next. Generally, Godard does not distinguish in this way between 'essential' and 'inessential' images. Unlike most film directors, he doesn't use some images as weak links in a narrative chain leading to strong ones, but only images which, in addition to serving a narrative function, also have independent value.

There is a play in the title of *Histoire(s) du cinéma* between the one and the many, the singular and the plural, the cinema and the other arts, film and cinema, the history of the cinema and the stories (*histoires*) narrated in films. These ideas are restated in the titles of four of the eight sections of the film: *1A Toutes les histoires, 1B Une histoire seule, 2A Seul le cinéma, 4B Les signes parmi nous.*

Every history of the cinema is faced with an abundance of films and the inadequacy of a history to account for these, to put them into some acceptable order which can do justice to their range and complexity without the loss of their singularity as often occurs when films are regarded as illustrations of a movement, epoch, genre, nation or author.

If the cinema is thought of as a means to encompass the real, the real will always be greater than any film or images and sounds used to describe it, perhaps the lesson of the citation, forever pointing to more than itself, at once less because it is a fragment and more because it is no longer constrained within a context and thereby free to associate. Once Godard decided to create histories of the cinema in film, he necessarily confronted the insufficiency of his means to relate a history and to relate the real. How do you account, for example, for all the things the cinema has accomplished and been over time? And how do you say with film what actually happened?

In some of Godard's earlier films, there are a number of takes of the same situation, a kind of hesitation, repetition, stutter, not in order to find the right perspective but to assert the multiplicity of perspectives on any one thing and the uncertainty with regard to any particular approach. For example, in *2 ou 3 choses que je sais d'elle* (1966), the red Mini Cooper being driven into the car wash repeatedly; in *Vivre sa vie* (1962), Anna Karina trying out the same line in different ways; in *Le Petit Soldat* (1960), the various photographs of Anna Karina taken by Michel Subor; in *One Plus One* (1968), the rehearsal with the Rolling Stones as in *Soigne ta droite* (1987) with Rita Mitsouko; and there are the different approaches to the same photographed image in *Letter to Jane* (1972), comparing her to herself and to other images related to her. This is a familiar play in Godard's films which are, broadly speaking, serial portraitures not unlike Warhol's portraits of Marilyn Monroe, Elizabeth Taylor and Campbell soup cans. Godard's *Nouvelle Vague* (1990) and *Hélas pour moi* (1993) are films about the return of the same. *Histoire(s)* similarly repeats the same image, word or sound and each time it is what it always was and completely different, once again, as with Pop.

Effectively, because *Histoire(s)* is composed entirely of citations in various guises, what is cited is a single fragment of a continuum of images that once were part of a larger unity (shot, scene, sequence, film). The citations are superabundant even if thought of horizontally in a line one after another, but most images and sounds in the film are composites, overlaps, multiples. There are few that stand alone and, even those that do, because they attract and project associations, they find, if not their

sense, their force by relation to other images that sustain them and transform them. All Godard's images are plural as a result of a process of a
disengagement from an original source and their freedom thereby to
connect with other images of different kinds in different directions. The
signs produced in *Histoire(s)* and the histories they suggest, because of
the nature of citations, always consort with an outside, not exactly beyond
the frame or off screen in a diegetic film world, but in the world, with
realities, hence with possibilities and uncertainties that can never be
finally resolved or settled.

The consequence of the superabundance of useless signs and the insufficiency of language and images in the face of these to be definitive – as if
language and expression, and with them reality, are submerged by signs,
weighed down by their copiousness and infinitude – is that *Histoire(s)*
throws doubt upon the adequacy not only of a history of the cinema but
of a history of cinema expressed in film and therefore creates doubt about
the adequacy and sufficiency of film. *Histoire(s)* is that demonstration
of such insufficiency in practice, of too much and not enough, which it
exemplifies and denies. It exemplifies it because it provokes permanent
dissatisfaction (nothing is complete). It denies it because it creates perpetual desire (infinite possibilities). The two together are the motor of the
film if not of the cinema.

Film and photography are reproductive, tied to imitation. The 'modern'
film and the 'avant-garde' film, including the New American Cinema
of the late 1950s and 1960s, sought to free itself from such illustrative,
mimetic practices. Modernism, understood generally as a move away
from representation and illusionism, towards a concern with art as its
own subject and as an autonomous reality rather than the reproduction
of a reality outside it, has been most difficult to realise in film in part
because of its reproductive vocation. The desire of 'modern' filmmakers
to reject such otherness (meaning, representation) and instead to emphasise the 'being-ness' of their films has been difficult to achieve. The films
were not popular and costs of production often considerable.

Pop art, later the work of Robert Rauschenberg and Jasper Johns,
shared the modernist concern with autonomy and self-reference, but did
so critically and to such a degree that, rather than rejecting imitation and
representation, they cultivated them and brought them into the heart of

their works where they were interrogated, cited, parodied, worked upon. In so far as they did so, they breached a boundary that modern art had vigorously defended, namely that relation between the art work and reality. The focusing by Rauschenberg and Johns on that boundary raised the question of what art is while refusing to provide an answer. Questions generated not answers but more questions. Whatever was proposed was provisional, open and inconclusive, namely, that art is a play with reality and the border and threshold between it and the world.

The crucial artistic movement that lay behind Pop and its immediate successors like Rauschenberg is Dada of the 1920s, specifically the work of Kurt Schwitters and Marcel Duchamp. Godard is the heir to these Dada/Pop/post-Pop/postmodern practices. His 2006 gallery exhibition at the Pompidou, *Voyage(s) en Utopie, Jean-Luc Godard, 1946–2006: À la recherche d'un théorème perdu (Journey(s) to Utopia, Jean-Luc Godard, 1946–2006: In Search of a Lost Theorem)*, resembles elements of Rauschenberg's Combines and his later installation pieces. The exhibition echoes Duchamp and Schwitters more than practices in the contemporary cinema, as if, in the exhibition and in *Histoire(s)* which it complements, the cinema entered a place beyond itself, not only where few filmmakers and few if any producers are willing or able to go, but to the museum, the gallery, the installation of real things.

One way of dealing with a mimetic and representational tradition is not to move toward abstraction or a purity of form but to move in the contrary direction toward impurity (the blurring of the distinction between art and document, art and reality) and excessive, even parodic imitation (the citation).

What is striking in *Histoire(s)* is its heterogeneity made up of different forms, objects, texts, sounds and images all with established meanings, traditions, contexts and expectations. Rather than emphasising a modernist concern with autonomy (chastity) and rather than asserting exclusive links with film (celibacy), *Histoire(s)* not only goes beyond the cinema, but does so by pressing on the line between illusion and the real, the interiority of a work and the exteriority that the film gathers within it to refashion, rework and re-project.

If this method is by now familiar and dated in the arts of painting and sculpture (installation works, happenings, found objects), it has not been a practice within avant-garde film whose radicalism is less concerned with stressing the impurities between art and reality evident in *Histoire(s)* than in formalism and abstraction: the works of Stan Brakhage, Hollis Frampton, Michael Snow.

Godard, as in Pop and the works of Rauschenberg, does not reject reproduction but emphasises it, accumulating its hodge-podge, detritus and especially the ruins from an illusionist past in film that he cites, as Rauschenberg incorporates chairs, light bulbs, car wrecks, old furniture, newsprint and toys. Similarly to Pop, Godard repositions and rearticulates existing imagery, making such re-membering the defining activity of his work, and not just recently as in *Histoire(s)* but from his very first films.

Many of the filmmakers of the French *Nouvelle Vague* openly recruited images from 'outside', thereby raising questions that had been central to theorisations of the 1950s (Bazin, Mitry) concerned with realism and reality in film. Though other filmmakers of the *Nouvelle Vague*, like Truffaut, took a path somewhat distant from such interrogation towards a more recognisable cinema, romantic, narrativised, theatrical and performative, Godard has continued in the direction in which he first set out.

Godard refuses to see language as the simple translation of a previously conceived idea. He has instead defined the directing of a movie as a creative form of thought. The foregrounding of form in Godard is characteristic of all modern art. It takes on a special resonance in Godard's work inasmuch as it allows for an investigation into the effectiveness and present-day chances of the means of expression. This investigation goes to the heart of Godard's creativity, it orients the general direction of his work and gives authenticity to its meaning.

The fact that *Histoire(s)* breaks established rules is not to suggest that other films must do the same. It is not like a manifesto characteristic of the avant-garde, but the creation of a sense of possibility for all films. After *Histoire(s)*, there are no rules and everything is open to question.

Investigations (1)

The credit sequence of Bertolucci's *Strategia del ragno* (1970) takes place against brightly coloured, schematic *naif* images of animals and objects painted by Ligabue. The opening entry into the film is to the make-believe fairyland of the primitive created by the painter. The narrative opens with the arrival of Athos Magnani, the younger, the son of Athos Magnani, the elder, with the same name, at the railway station in the town of Tara. The father is an anti-fascist hero, murdered, so the story goes, by fascists in 1936. Father and son, played in the film by the same actor, Guido Brogi, look exactly alike as their names are alike. The credit sequence sets the tone for a 'reality' that, as with the credit sequence, is an entry into the imaginary. Because characters and time are doubled, and literally so, they confound any reality whatsoever.

Tara, the name of the town in the film, is the town of Sabbioneta, a late sixteenth-century northern Italian town near Mantova built by Duke Vespasiano Gonzaga. Much of the action in the film occurs in the town centre, in the Piazza Ducale. Sabbioneta is near Parma where Bertolucci grew up. It is the setting for his *Prima della rivoluzione* (1964). The Piazza Ducale in Sabbioneta resembles the Palazzo del Comune in Parma. Both are real locations that are like each other, and also like theatre, at once real and fantastic. They resemble the Surrealist landscapes of Giorgio De Chirico and the strange, often erotic juxtapositions of figures, place and objects in the paintings of René Magritte that go to a beyond into an 'other' world as in the *naif* work of Henri Rousseau and Antonio Ligabue.

Sabbioneta is a Renaissance 'ideal' city. The Piazza Ducale was designed to be like a theatre, a setting of spectacle, ceremony, pageants, almost as if was wearing a mask, draped in masquerade. The film migrates in time across centuries, from the sixteenth during the Renaissance when Sabbioneta was built to the twentieth, and the consolidation of Italian fascism, going back and forth in time almost in a single camera movement, in the same gesture or by a cut, less a transition than an overlap, an answering shot which is not a reverse shot but a reply from another time, almost magical when Athos the son becomes Athos the father and the father the son, not unlike the overlap between Giacobbe 1 and Giacobbe 2 in *Partner*, where one becomes the other.

Becoming the other is everywhere in Bertolucci's films.

The name Tara for Sabbioneta is the name of a mythical place, the Kingship of Tara in Ireland, and the fictional plantation in the American South of the same name in *Gone with the Wind* (1939). The Irish connection with Borges's story is compelling. Historically, there was a Viscount Tara and a Baron Tara. Tara is an ancient Irish title of authority. The real becomes fictional without losing its reality, and reality becomes mythical, where limits between the real and the legendary, past and present, vacillate.

Athos Magnani, the son, comes to Tara at the invitation of Draifa, a former lover of Athos Magnani, the father. Draifa has two ages, when she was young, in love with the father, and now older, possibly in love with the son, the duplicate of his father. Draifa is also the duplicate of herself, the similar sense of a doubled identity as with Athos the elder and Athos the younger. Draifa, like the Magnani, is both. The transition from one state to another, one time to another, one identity to another, is fluid and indefinite, comparatives and analogies moving alongside each other in parallel lines that refuse to be still, as with Tara and Sabbioneta.

Differences are both parallels and vague intersections. The young Draifa is like the older Draifa reliving the past. She seems to offer herself sexually to Athos Magnani, the younger, as if the younger Athos was instead the older and still living.

When Athos, the son, comes to Tara to investigate the life of his father, he discovers that his father was not the hero that the town seems to have believed he was and that it had so honoured with plaques, engravings, speeches, place signs, celebrations, but instead a traitor, the negative of what appeared to be, where the negative is real and the positive an illusion. Like his father, the son chooses to defend the myth of the father as hero as concocted by the father, that is, not the fact, but the fiction, despite what the son discovers to be the truth. The son becomes, in loyalty to his father, a traitor to the truth and to reality. His loyalty to myth is a loyalty to story, more nearly true because poetic and close to Shakespeare. It is not the heroism of the father that the son is loyal to, but the staging of a theatrical death and heroism to deny the realities of suicide and treason. Athos the son, to be true to his father, shares and sustains his father's falsity, and becomes, as his father had been, false in order to be true, the sense of his father's staging of the entire masquerade of heroism and history. Athos Magnani the son, recreates himself in the image of his father.

It seems that not only are the companions of the father aware of the truth because they shared in the arranging of his death but so too is the entire town of Tara aware of it, and everyone therefore, like the father, is acting out a role that had already been 'written' by the father and that included a role for his son and his return to Tara in order to sustain the father's myth of himself, a myth he had concocted, and that the whole of Sabbioneta would (falsely) confirm as true. What is at stake and what is 'saved' is fiction.

Tara does not become theatre, but is theatre *from the beginning* as are the stories of father and son. All know the truth, yet all are loyal to the legend. The town is a theatrical set and a stage, and the people of the town are actors, defending not the truth but a script.

When the son, at the close of the film, goes to the railway station to finally leave Tara, the railway tracks are covered over with grass as if they had not functioned for some time. There is no train. Perhaps the son had never arrived in Tara, and Tara is truly mythical, and so too perhaps is Athos Magnani, the father, with no more an existence than Brigadoon in the Minnelli film or the 'Histories' staged by Shakespeare.

Bertolucci's camera is constantly in movement in shot sequence pans, tracking shots and zooms, as if his camera is in search of something, an inquest into a truth, a place to rest, an explanation and clarification. The movements, however, rather than elucidating what is sought, cause the already obscure, feigned, enigmatic, labyrinthine to become still more obscure and to the very end and beyond the end, the film by its movement, its seeking and restlessness, moving in opposite directions at once, towards something and away from it, or in a circle arriving at the end at the beginning, turning back on itself, trying to grasp what is already past and has been lost.

Nothing is more puzzling and opaque than the fixed, definitive, solid, the ostensibly clear. The decisive is often no more than what things appear to be, but seldom are, like Draifa's charming pretty young servant girl, who is a boy.

Investigations (2)

One of the loveliest yet seemingly inconsequential scenes in Antonioni's *La notte* (1961) is Lidia's walk from the centre of Milan to its periphery after she leaves the launch party for Giovanni's new book. During that party, as well as at the later party at the Gherardinis', and perhaps in most of the scenes with her, for example, at the night-club, in the hospital, even at home dressing and in the bath, there is the same sense as during her walk of Lidia observing what occurs and what catches her attention of what people do, how they react, however banal or seemingly unimportant the action: a car park attendant eating a sandwich, two workers giggling, snippets of conversation, a band play-ing, Giovanni's sadness, the illness of a friend. Lidia seems to have no apparent reaction to these events beyond momentarily attending to them. She seems both intent and removed, not exactly indifferent, but blank. In any case, it is difficult to find the significance of these events, in part because her reactions are unclear and because there is no mech-anism to underline her view (the lack of reverse shots), in part because the events seem to have no dramatic or narrative function. They lead nowhere and are without apparent importance for the narrative and its progression.

The insignificance, the lack of drama, the blankness is not only an attitude of Lidia's but an attitude of the film, as if it too is strolling with-out giving anything encountered particular importance, at least not in advance of the encounter. Yet, if you think about it, the lack of emphasis gives these small events solidity, concreteness and a presence that is exceedingly rare.

In traditional films, nothing occurs that is not part of the logic of events and a narrative dramatic progress. Each occurrence is a link to another and yet another still from the moment the film begins until the events conclude as if running their appointed course. There are two evident consequences of these procedures. The first is that however immediate and compelling traditional narratives may be, because of their directional, progressive nature they belong to the past. What you see is the telling of a story that has already occurred. It represents what has been and not what is. The film is not finding a story as it proceeds but telling a story that has already proceeded. *La notte* works differently – nothing is given in advance of its occurrence and certainly not a preordained significance. It is as if the film is finding itself in the course of its becoming. Because there is nothing that pre-exists the film there is nothing for the film to re-present. It is instead creating new realities as it moves along free from the demands of a narrative, of representation and above all of the obligation 'to signify'.

The second consequence in the traditional film is that each of its events, however grand, like a battle, a murder, an accident, or however infinitesimal, like a glance, a fiddling with an object, mixing a drink, lighting a cigarette, say in a film by Hawks, has significance narratively. Thus no event is there for itself but instead for something else to which it adheres. It is that adherence that lends it significance and meaning and is part of a narrative economy in which everything 'tells' and is clearly functional. Precisely because nothing tells in that way in *La notte*, it is the insignificance, the unrelatedness of things, the lack of evident function that gives things a presence and uniqueness and gives the film its freedom. They are simply 'there' – the rockets set off in the field in Breda, the pattern of light and water on the windscreen of the car taking Lidia and Roberto to nowhere in particular.

There is a lyrical, beautiful quality to *La notte* that can be felt and experienced but is difficult to specify. As Lidia, and with her the film, move from one thing to another during Lidia's walk after the book launch party, and in which none of the things encountered are in themselves important or of consequence and yet concretely present in part for their lack of consequence, the going between things and between events at once emphasises their separation and individuality and hence the gap (of significance, of temporality) between them as if they belong to a real space, but not to an imaginary progressive time and narrative, while other connectives of a different order are made possible. Rhythm is not quite the right word for it, but, if the objects are not connected, the images as a flow and fluidity and duration of intensities are connected, as if the concreteness of objects and gestures is left behind as they dissolve into the concreteness of the images of them.

It is a curious transformation of the solidity of things into the fragility of images, almost at the borders of abstraction like the paintings of Giorgio Morandi and the sculptures of Alberto Giacometti. Hence things in the film assume a quality that is both abstract and impermanent not despite, but because of their concreteness. The dissolution of connections, of relations, of place, of emotions that establish the possibility of each element to be itself and to be equally 'there' enables the film to engage in a perpetual transformation of the things it represents and of the film itself. If nothing is fixed, nothing made permanent, nothing irretrievably connected, joined, made to function and signify, then any number of new relations become possible and the film and the lives within its fiction are opened up and liberated. The price of that liberation for the characters is the dissolution of relations, the realisation of separateness, seeing the gap, perceiving the banalities and emptiness; the price of that liberation for the film is the breaking of representational and narrative ties whose yield is the possibility for images to freely relate, as occurs in Lidia's walk where a sandwich becomes laughter and laughter a pussy cat and a pussy cat a baby crying and then there are rockets in a field and ruins of a relation. What is so absorbing is the way each of these images of things seems to call to the others, rhythmically combining and then passing on, dissolving into something else, not for any direct function or clear purpose except for the beat and cadence of these new and surprising connections, of new realities.

Language

The Fascist party came to power in Italy in 1922. It remained in power until the middle of 1943 when Italy was invaded by a joint American and British force that landed in Sicily from North Africa and progressed from there, across the straits of Messina, to the Italian mainland. Effectively, fascist power came to an end in September 1943 as the Allies fought their way north first to Naples, then to Rome and then, in 1944, 'liberated' the whole of Italy from both Italian fascist rule and the Italians' allies the Germans who had become, with the surrender of the Italians in 1943, occupiers.

In the 1920s, the Italian film industry was essentially an industry of distributors and exhibitors of foreign films, mostly American. That situation began to change with the coming of sound in 1927 and markedly in 1938, when the Italian government banned the import of foreign films, mostly American, as an economic measure, but also as a political one while at the same time subsidising Italian film production by way of pre-production grants (thus stimulating production to make up for the shortfall in films for exhibition due to import restrictions), the building of a modern studio on the model of Hollywood and production subsidies based on box-office receipts. Until 1938, Italian production was relatively limited to around thirty films a year, but after that date production remarkably increased to nearly 120 films just before the collapse of the fascist government.

Until then, Italians were entertained to primarily American films dubbed into Italian, and after that date to films made on the model of American studio films: adventure films, war films, light romantic comedies, musicals, melodramas. The Italian cinema was a 'classical' cinema like the Hollywood cinema it imitated for reasons of economy as much as for fashion. For many, the American cinema was a model for a 'fascist' cinema because of its emphasis on action, movement, energy and its avoidance of reflectiveness and of ideas. The 'new' Italian cinema, like the American cinema, was primarily a cinema of narrative fictional fantasies. At the same time, a new cinema began to take shape different from the genre-based classical one. It tended to be more realistic in the sense of taking, if not its subject, its atmosphere and milieu from everyday Italian reality: its towns and cities, countryside and people. It first manifested itself in a documentary direction and in films not dissimilar to the dark and social dramas referred to as *film noir* in America and in France. These films, rather than emphasising romantic make-believe situations in artificial constructed locations, went out into the street, among ordinary people, and what they revealed was a new reality or rather a familiar one but not the one that had been the subjects of the cinema: poverty, social need, misery, distress, corruption, criminality, eroticism, the unhealthy, the underground, the dirty. There was little sunshine to these films.

This new cinema began to have linguistic features more reflective of the realities of Italy than the classical Italian cinema. The picture of Italy that emerged from the Italian cinema in the 1930s was of a unified and essentially contented, endearing people brightly lit. One sign of that unity (and it should not be underestimated) was a uniform Italian speech, the Italian being taught in schools and broadcast on the radio, but not spoken by most Italians. Until relatively recently, Italians spoke the language of their region or even their district as a 'first' language rather than 'Italian', or they spoke Italian in a pronounced accented regional, localised speech. The reality of Italian regionalism (cultural, linguistic, economic, social) contrasted with an image of unity and populist conformity that Italian fascism helped to promote (schools, radio, government) and certainly sought to project (in the cinema, in the press, in magazines).

A cinema that began to be concerned with Italian realities, as opposed to the artificiality of screen representations as they had been, necessarily concerned itself with Italy's linguistic and regional realities. What is notable about Italian films of this kind made after 1943 (for example, Visconti's *Ossessione* (1943), Rossellini's 'fascist' war trilogy, De Sica's *I bambini ci guardano* (1944), De Santis's *Riso amaro* (1949)) is their linguistic diversity in which characters either speak with noticeable regional accents (albeit in 'Italian') or speak in dialect (for example, the fishermen of Aci Trezza in *La terra trema* (1948) speaking a sub-dialect of Sicilian).

What the linguistic diversity of Italy revealed is contradictory: on the one hand the reality of a plurality of languages identified with regions and with class (dialect as the language of the Sicilian poor and the dispossessed in *La terra trema* and in the earlier films of Pasolini, in the Neapolitan sequence in Rossellini's *Paisà*) whereas 'Italian' is a language of the educated and the relatively comfortable, belonging to bourgeois culture and the bourgeois State (the language of the bureaucracy, of the police, of the Church, of intellectuals, of the media). The reality of Italy was a reality of disunity set against an ideal 'fascist' Italy of cultural and economic homogeneity for which language was an indicator ('Italian' a sign for unity, the nation; plural languages a sign of differences, backwardness, opposition to the nation for reasons of class). The contradictory aspect is that however realistic dialect may be it was a sign of separation and isolation, especially so in conditions where Italian was being promoted as dominant and national. Effectively, there were two nations (or many), broadly speaking, one Italian in culture and speech and the other dialectal. The division was particularly marked between the north (rich, industrial, urban, bourgeois) and the south (poor, agricultural, rural, peasant), and overlaid upon that division was another division that was social, historical and economic. To choose dialect to represent realities in literature (Pasolini, Gadda) was not simply a linguistic or artistic choice but also a political one.

There is not one but three 'languages' in play in Luchino Visconti's *La terra trema*. The first and most obvious is the Sicilian of Aci Trezza spoken by the men and women who act as themselves in the film; the second is Italian spoken within the fiction of the film by the members of the Church, the benefactors of the boats, the employees of the bank which is also the language spoken in the narrative summaries by an outside narrator and in three voices (those of Visconti, Pietrangeli and a Sardinian actor); the third is literary from the novel by Giovanni Verga, *Il Malvoglia*, on which *La terra trema* is based.

The three languages are always present in the film in various combinations and intensities essentially transposed one upon the other. For example, when the narrator in voice-over speaks, his Italian has been refashioned to approximate the rhythms and cadences of the Sicilian of

Aci Trezza as if, though on the outside, he is speaking like the characters on the inside, and though in Italian, like Sicilian, as if he is 'other', however indirectly: the language operates as a social shifter. And though the Sicilians speak in Sicilian, much of what they say is a direct translation from the literary language of Verga as if, though speaking Sicilian, they are speaking it as a novelistic and artistic speech and thus in that sense also a speech of the 'other' but inversely to that of the narrator. And finally, there is the language of Visconti (who takes the side of the fisherman).

What interests Visconti in the speech of Aci Trezza is not so much its authenticity as its musicality and archaic resonances ('like ancient Greek'). Just as the Sicilian speech is transformed into a literary language and Italian transformed in the narration into Sicilian cadences, Visconti transforms the Sicilian speech into an aesthetic equivalent of music, of pure sound (since its meaning is impenetrable). If you like, it speaks of something ancient, rich, beautiful and full of colour. The fishermen of Aci Trezza are also the fishermen of the film *La terra trema* (like themselves but other than themselves) and as such they are figures from a nineteenth-century novel and from nineteenth-century opera, aestheticised versions of fishermen as their village is aestheticised into a film set and they into mythic creatures of an isolated purified unreal past: absolute realism and absolute artifice together.

The scenes of the film were composed to follow the Verga novel. The fishermen and others of Aci Trezza were asked to improvise gestures and words for each of the scenes. Visconti then remodelled these improvisations for particular sound effects to correspond to indications in the novel. It was complicated and time-consuming work requiring more than six months of preparation. *La terra trema* then is not a film where the people play themselves improvising their lines and movements, but to the contrary a carefully wrought object, made up, however, of the realistic units and sounds of their speech.

La terra trema is as composed as *Il gattopardo* is and the person who plays 'Ntoni is as much acting as Burt Lancaster is as Fabrizio, the Prince of Salina, or Alain Delon as his nephew, Tancredi. This is true as well of the costuming. The torn shirts, mended trousers and coats of the fishermen are as carefully created as the gowns of Angelica in *Il gattopardo* while settings like the salting of the anchovies are constructed with as much detail and attention as the ball scene in *Il gattopardo*.

On the one hand, Visconti insists on the concrete reality of things in his films, on the other, he refashions these for emotional and spectacular effect. The house of the Valastros in Aci Trezza is a composite of three houses, one for the interior, one for the exterior and one for an effect of framing, not unlike the composite language that the Valastros speak and that the film speaks, made of realism and artifice, the exact formula and conflict at the heart of nineteenth-century melodrama.

Levels

Like Rivette, Renoir is a director of scenes, rather than of continuity. His films appear to be a mix of scenes rather than a combination of shots and each scene is relatively independent of the others in the sense not that there is no link (thematic or narrative) between scenes, but rather that there is no evident linear accord between them. It is for these reasons that Renoir's films (and Rivette's) are often described as 'theatrical', which is not to suggest that they are either primarily concerned with dialogue or that gestures and attitudes are exaggerated and false; on the contrary, what marks the theatricality of Renoir's films (and Rivette's) is the naturalness of their scenes and especially of the performances of the actors.

Renoir is particularly fond of long takes, often with wide shots and sometimes in depth of field. The reasons have to do with his essentially scenic concerns: that is, rather than 'building' up a scene by the joining of shots, he tends to allow the scenes to 'evolve' in accord with the life of the actor and performance. What is important then is the living moment, rather than moments constructed after the fact (edited).

This sense of the living moment is the source at once of the joy and bliss of Renoir's films (the emphasis on 'life') and their sadness and tenderness (the living moment is a passing one, caught in its movement yet left behind and lost thereby). These moments (his scenes) are precious and fragile.

One of the games or plays that dominate all of Renoir's films (*La Règle du jeu* (1939) is a variation of *Boudu sauvé des eaux* (1932)) is the disruption of a social order and social conventions, literally turning them upside-down by conduct that is often sexual, uninhibited, natural, asocial. On the one hand, as in melodrama, though Renoir is seldom melodramatic, the conventions of the social order incite by their very pressure impulses that threaten them, the consequent disorder and destructiveness are the very reasons that order is necessary. Each assumes and gives life to the other, which is why Renoir is never moralistic, never makes judgements, never takes sides and has extraordinary sympathy for every position.

Not only do Renoir's films play between these positions within the fictions and stories he creates, but he is also at the very heart of their creation, a matter equally of theme and style, in the sense that theatre (as convention) is juxtaposed to cinema (as naturalness) so that Renoir (and Rivette) set a stage that is set and a story that is a constraint and a limit, but in which action can take place, and action is so filmed (in sequences and scenes) as to allow for its own spirit of evolution, its own momentariness and naturalness to emerge, and that suggests another set of contradictory positions both of the story interior to the film and of the film exterior to the story: on the one hand that of constraint and on the other, that of the liberation from it, literally by the destruction of the social order and rules of the game (always a bourgeois game) and, more profoundly, the overturning of the theatrical and the narrowly fictional by what is immediate and, if not unplanned, at least free to develop, not exactly improvisation, but neither an obedience to the prescripted and preset.

It is as if, through theatre and fiction, Renoir allows one to see real life, possible only by means of the theatrical, not despite it but because of it. This results in a very strange and literally ingenious, genial occurrence, namely the accidents and passing of time that Renoir allows to occur by his staging and that make disappear the artifice, the staging that has made such chance and evanescence possible.

This happens at different levels in a Renoir film, the intrusion of disorderly elements in the fictions (André Jurieu, Marcel and thereby sexuality and desire in a ruled order where such unseemly things are kept hidden in La Règle du jeu; the presence of Boudu literally raised from drowning and brought into a bourgeois setting that he both animates and disrupts) and of action and movement in a scene that, no matter how carefully set and established, seems literally to begin anew, to burst at its seams or to have its composition and placements overturned (Schumacher chasing Marceau at the fête) or the pushing out of the boundaries of a frame by introducing lateral, exterior, even extraneous entrances, exits and movements. These different registers, between theatre, cinema, fiction and film and between different levels within them, play with one another, move between, at once contrary to each other and completely dependent, free and constrained like Boudu, or like Listingois. Each is within the other, a structural element and not simply a matter of character or story. The reality often remarked of in Renoir's films (and in Rivette's) is a consequence of the distortion and disruption not only of conventions but also of frames, shots, continuities without which reality would never appear.

Masquerade

Last Tango is a sort of tragic *An American in Paris*.

Bernardo Bertolucci[9]

In masquerade, an inside is hidden from view by an outside, by appearances, making the inside enigmatic because masked and the outside enigmatic because false. In classical films, the inside (the person, the actor) and the outside (the character) tend to merge as if there is no difference, instead, the illusion of sameness and transparency, character unified because there is no contrary.

Stars in film can be an exception because they are noticeable in their stardom, but what is exceptional in their performances, what makes them stars, is the success of their masquerade, of becoming other than they are, to become a character, if only momentarily, in order to return as a star.

Masquerade in Bertolucci's cinema is paradoxical, not only with regard to character but with regard to setting, plot, drama, citation. Masquerade becomes evident, displays its artifice. A citation is always on the outside, referring to what is beyond itself, external to it. In so doing, what is referred to seems to swell, to be itself and, simultaneously, to be more than it is, a double and an other. The expansion crosses a line that had kept it within boundaries. The inside that has been expanded and invaded by whatever is cited and added to incorporates what is outside of it, takes

9 Joan Mellen, 'A Conversation with Bernardo Bertolucci', in Fabien S. Gerard, T. Jefferson Kline and Bruce Sklarew (eds), *Bernardo Bertolucci: Interviews* (Jackson: University of Mississippi Press, 2000), p. 77 (originally in *Cinéaste* (Winter 1972–73)).

possession of the citation, and is also incorporated by it, as if in two
places at once, within and without the film. Bertolucci is a master of such
formations, reminiscent of Pasolini who delighted in creating analogies,
differences in likenesses on which Bertolucci's films depend.

Rosa's husband Paul, played by Marlon Brando in *Ultimo tango a Parigi*
(1972), had, before the film begins, just committed suicide by cutting
her throat. While the maid cleans Rosa's blood from the mirror in the
bathroom, she narrates the story of Paul, but to whom is not clear, most
probably to the police after Paul's murder:

> he was a fighter, but things went badly for him, then he became
> an actor, then a drug dealer on the waterfront in New York, then a
> revolutionary in South America, then a journalist in Japan, then he
> landed in Tahiti where he sorted things out, then caught malaria,
> then came to Paris where he met a woman with money and he
> married her.

The maid's monologue is like the maid's monologue in Louis-Ferdinand
Céline's *Journey to the End of the Night / Voyage au bout de la nuit* (1932) in
Jean-Luc Godard's *Une femme mariée* (1964): that is, it is a citation. In fact,
it is a citation doubled. The person the Brando maid describes is a voyager
in an exclusively fictional cinematic biography where Brando joins the
Bertoluccian cast of film travellers from *La via del petrolio* (1965) onwards.

The biography of Paul, in the Bertolucci film, is the biography of Marlon
Brando in other films by other directors, an already legendary Brando
that Bertolucci adds to by compacted overlapped citations. The biography of Brando is a biography of characters he played in Elia Kazan's *On
the Waterfront* (1954) and *Viva Zapata!* (1952), Joshua Logan's *Sayonara*
(1957), Lewis Milestone's *Mutiny on the Bounty* (1962) and *Ultimo tango
a Parigi*. His films are locations where citations, other references, jostle
for notice with the Brando ones: Samuel Taylor Coleridge's 'The Rime of
the Ancient Mariner', the whaler Captain Ahab in *Moby-Dick*, the arms
dealer Arthur Rimbaud. Inside and outside cease to matter in these intersections, serial associations, parallel universes that converge and cross,
extra- and intra-textual.

What the maid relates in *Ultimo tango* are myths and legends of Brando,
as the maid in *Une femme mariée* adds to a legendary Céline. Bertolucci

stacks references like library shelving. In *Strategia del ragno* and in *Ultimo tango* these are particularly marked by the ever-present citation of Verdi's *Un ballo in maschera* (1859). In *Strategia*, the play of masks, betrayals and murder in the Verdi opera is duplicated, like a second death. In the film, Athos Magnani dies twice, once in 1936, then again in a narrative that recalls Gina's observation in *Prima della rivoluzione* (1964), that the Parma bourgeoisie, after eating, recount their meal, thus eating twice over.

Brando in *Ultimo tango* plays the role of the actor Marlon Brando, who, in appearance, gesture, dress, is Brando to the letter, an actor playing a character who performs as an actor playing a character who is always himself, a double doubled, in masquerade, never himself as if the self-repeated, duplicated, added to, insisted upon, is equally denied, more becoming less, and unidentifiable by the fact of their superimposed fictional layers. The film is a masquerade that turns back toward a past that includes Brando and, like virtually all Bertolucci's films, is in parallel times, a past becoming a future and a future already of the past. In *Strategia*, the past is entwined in multiple other pasts, and multiple presents, one theatrical set within other sets, one series within other series. The film cuts in continuity between juxtaposed times as if distance, not difference, is the stake.

Masquerades in Bertolucci's films, especially *Ultimo tango*, *The Last Emperor* (1987), *Stealing Beauty* (1996), *Il conformista* (1970), *Novecento* (1976), *La tragedia di un uomo ridicolo* (1981) and *Strategia del ragno*, are masquerades not only by costume and decor but by time and history. The juxtaposition of the tango contest and Paul and Jeanne's parody of it in *Ultimo tango* takes place on the same set: two styles, two times, two kinds of couples side by side, both out of style, out of time, as with dance in Bertolucci's other films and, like them, where movement and the transition between times are a constant, always present, one becoming the other without a break. The dance is these opposites united, made possible in a Bertoluccian world of projected fantasies, spectacle and theatre caught and displayed in no longer fashionable, historically limited, styles of dancing: the 1930s–40s dance and costume of Julia and Anna in *Il conformista*, and Lucy's solo dance evoking the 1960s in *Stealing Beauty*, and the rock-and-roll dance of Primo in *Un uomo ridicolo*. All are, as with Bertolucci's other films, scenes of deceit, falsity and masque.

Melodrama

Visconti worked in theatre, lyric opera and film. In each of these pursuits, though especially in theatre and lyric opera, he put into play (put into scene) a pre-existing text. In theatre, these texts were ancient (Shakespeare), relatively recent (Chekhov, Strindberg), or contemporary (Cocteau, Anouilh, Miller, Williams). What was interesting in these theatrical productions were their visual, spectacular aspects (decor, lighting, costume, gesture), no matter what the period from which they came. Visconti sought to find visual and sound equivalents for the literary aspects of these theatre pieces so that what was seen was principally the instrument for understanding while patterns of speech and gesture in speaking were as important as the literal meaning of what was said. In lyric opera, Visconti was especially interested in nineteenth-century Italian opera, Verdi in particular, but also Puccini, Donizetti and Bellini. There are passages from Bellini in *La terra trema* (1948) (the salting of the anchovies sequence) and much of the music in *Il gattopardo* (1963) is from Verdi (a previously unrecorded Verdi waltz is the music of the nearly hour-long ball scene, and a Verdi march accompanies the Prince of Salina and his family as they enter Donnafugata).

In his theatre and opera productions, Visconti literally realised (made real) what pre-existed the performances, that is to say, he gave reality to a text and its ideas (a cultural object). At the same time he focused in these productions on the actors (their actions and gestures) and on decor and setting, seeking to present these both as realistically as possible and to the last detail as well as in their spectacular aspects. Visconti's intense realism touched on an extreme of spectacle and hence the unreal. Thus, there were two realities that interested Visconti: a cultural one (the text) and a performative one (setting and action). What made Visconti one of the greatest *metteurs en scène* of theatre and opera also made him one of the greatest *metteurs en scène* of the cinema: he imitated realities and brought them to life on stage or in front of a camera, putting them 'in scene', not exactly documenting them so much as spectacularising them, transfiguring them. This apparent opposition or *mélange* that mixed realism with theatricality, a punctilious concern with the real side by side with the artificial, is central to all his works and singles him out, not only in Italy but globally.

Film for him had specific qualities related to its ability to reproduce realities that theatre and opera did not have. Film was more apparently imitative and, interestingly, what Visconti seemed to concentrate upon in his films was to bring out and record what was before the camera as a world in itself. Thus, rather than 'writing' with film, he sought to find a way with the camera to reproduce the world that was presented to it and in the best and most effective way: its elements, gestures, passions, emotions, ideas, stories. What he manipulated was all that went before the camera. It is to that pro-filmic area of *mise en scène* that most of Visconti's efforts were devoted. In that sense the images of a Visconti film were essentially directly aligned with the reality they reproduced as if between the reality of his images and the images he made of reality there was a perfect accord, though the reality reproduced was markedly theatricalised. This imitative, mimetic impulse toward reproduction is evident in Visconti's use of the camera and his editing procedures. He favoured shooting in sequences with relatively little cutting within scenes, preferring instead compositions in depth, a moving camera or moving lenses.

Visconti's films were made at a time (the 1950s and 1960s) when the accord of reality and image and the mimetism of his work were at odds with what began to emerge as the modern cinema, where the relations and accords characteristic of Visconti's films were called into question, deconstructed, broken, reflected upon and made discontinuous: in Italy by Antonioni, Rossellini and Pasolini; in France, by Godard, Rivette, Rohmer; in America, by Welles, Ray, Cassavetes. For these directors the film itself had a presence and was not simply an instrument for imitation.

Visconti is a classicist in the sense of valuing the virtues of a tradition by maintaining it (not to innovate but to imitate and simulate, not to transform but to reconfirm) rather than a modernist concerned with questioning tradition and displacing it. His films are melodramas and he had recourse to music, painting, opera and the novel of the late nineteenth and early twentieth centuries, a *fin de siècle* romantic, nostalgic melancholy of emotional staging. Modernism tends to be interested in a renewal and transformation of what has been and primarily by work on stylistics and form. For Visconti, what is primary is content not form in the sense that his formal procedures are dictated by a content to be expressed in a performance and a spectacle given to him in a pre-existing text that he stages.

Whereas modernist films (Godard is exemplary and in a different way, so too Antonioni) create a purely filmic world, Visconti's cinema serves to reproduce in film a world that has been staged for it, as if the images you see are transparencies, like windows, that look out upon a world set before it. There is never in Visconti a discourse upon the world you see, no instance of self-reflection on material, technique or the act of filming, nothing to take you away from the world being reproduced to the activity and forms of its reproduction, in short, no strategy to make you see the film as distinct from the reality it proposes; nor does it question thereby the transformation of reality into images and by that questioning cause them to part company.

If modernism 'writes' with film, Visconti's classicism 'reproduces' with film.

Visconti adheres to procedures characteristic of the classical cinema: montage is invisible (not disruptive of action but rather subordinate to it in order to maintain its continuity and homogeneity, and the homogeneity of the space-time in which action occurs); there is an emphasis on the depth of an imaginary space (there is no surface in Visconti's films to indicate the screen or the frame – what are linked in his films are realities not shots, scenes of life not framed instances of film); cutting and breaks are kept to a minimum (Visconti prefers to move his camera or manipulate the lens rather than to disrupt a 'scene' in its unity and wholeness by a cut); a concentration on the spectacle and at some distance (Visconti is fond of long shots) that prevent details from overcoming a sense of the entirety and integrity of the whole.

Nevertheless, Visconti is a classicist in a modern world. His work stands out as a style as much a part of the past as the worlds that he reproduces and represents. It results in a tone and atmosphere to his films that are nostalgic for a past and melancholy at its passing, not simply the events of it but the culture of it, the way things are formed.

In every Visconti film what is seen and what the characters wish for, strive for, and are destroyed by are impossible dreams, things they cannot have except as wishes (images) that the world (reality) at once prevents and provokes. Visconti's heroes are always ones who hear distant voices (sirens) or dream distant dreams that set them off on voyages in search of these only to be shipwrecked, defeated, drowned.

The framework is a melodramatic one. Melodrama is always the story of passion and sentiments brought to an extreme, exacerbated by realities that incite them (the exploitation of the fishermen in Aci Trezza in *La terra trema*) and defeat them (the storm, the risk, the power of the wholesalers). The emotions unleashed by this conflict between the real of circumstance and the unreality of desire provoke the colour, energy, spectacle and centre of his films, as also occurs in grand opera. Visconti was as notable for his direction and staging of grand opera and of theatre as he was for film. Indeed, his films were operatic and melodramatic as his plays and opera productions were filmic. The clash between circumstance and desire is evident in Visconti's staging at the edge between the real (concrete, material) and its transfiguration and artifice, its theatre and cinema, their qualities of dream, emotion, passion, rhythm, exaggeration, gesture.

In most cases, though not in every case, Visconti's characters are between two worlds: one ancient and traditional put at risk by another that is coming into being (modern, bourgeois, rational, capitalist). It is the latter that causes so much destruction and is part of the modern that Visconti passionately rejects. What the new world lacks is exactly the passions of the melodrama that it evokes and thus what is passing in a Visconti film is not only a world that is represented with all its objects, be it of fishermen and their humble houses in *La terra trema* or aristocrats and their magnificent *palazzi* and possessions in *Il gattopardo*, but the culture that belongs to them (music, literature, theatre, the novel) and that are embedded and inscribed in every gesture of the characters, in what they wear and what they own and treasure. Visconti's spectacle is essentially a spectacle of things and it is in these that all passion is deposited. What melodrama does is to allow characters to live their desperation in the melodrama with its colour and hysteria, and what Visconti does, and simultaneously, is to present the reality of that desperation in the exaggerated forms of melodrama, both the physical reality that he animates and dramatises and the culture that frames it doomed by time and the modern. Every object and every movement is precious because historical and about to pass. The intensity embedded in things is an intensity all the greater for their impermanence.

Visconti's choice of melodrama is aesthetic and ideological, stylistic and political. 'Before' the modern cinema, before Rossellini, before Godard, classicism was a practice not a choice. But 'after' the modern cinema, after Rossellini, after Godard and after Welles, it is a style among others, an option. In Visconti's case (and it is the only tear in the fabric of the unity of his films) it is a consciousness that the forms he adopts and the passions he unleashes are already part of the past, as fragile as an image.

Minimalism

Mouchette (1967) and *Le Journal d'un curé de campagne* (1951) are returns to an ancient story, the Passion of Christ. In that story, as in Bresson's two films, there are similar elements: *chance* (a series of encounters none of which are particularly connected, but all of which lead to a pre-destined end); *predestination* (though the paths to a final end are matters of chance and coincidence, the end itself is predetermined); *freedom* (the characters embrace their fate freely, not mere acceptance but an active embrace as understanding and thereby liberation); *God's grace* (the final act and the entirety of the journey towards it are a gift, evidence of the grace of God).

The stories, as narrated by Bresson, appear to be predestined only after the fact, not before. Nothing that comes before determines the final out-come until the outcome is reached and then as a consequence can be read back into the events that preceded it. The outcome is neither logical nor exactly linear. It simply arrives. It arrives because it is in the nature of things, but that nature is an illumination, not a causal chain.

If, indeed, Bresson repeats the story of the Passion, returns to it, his loyalty to it, like his loyalty to the novels of Bernanos, is literal and redun-dant. He does not adapt the literary text or illustrate it. He repeats it. Particularly, in *Le Journal*, each act you see is the repetition of the act that has been spoken in the narration. Thus you have a series of different but related materials side by side that you can recognise because of their similarity, but most of all because of their redundancy: Bresson's film,

Bernanos's novels, the Passion or, in other terms, images and sounds, written words, a sacred text and, finally perhaps, the events that the text relate, that is, a memory.

Why do it this way? Why not adapt the Bernanos rather than present it literally, and why not present the story of the Passion rather than transform it and why, more generally, present things in so disconnected, undramatised, non-causal a manner as Bresson does?

Clearly, it is not possible to go back directly, and for a very simple reason. If the Bernanos were adapted, it would be falsified. The novel would be lost and be displaced, effaced, set aside by the film. You would neither hear the writing nor see it. It would disappear. Thus, the going back in this instance would not be a return, nor a repetition, but an imposture. Bresson is in any case very precise in not wanting any imposture in his films, thus his strictures against acting (interpreting) and against fictionalisations as illusions. He wears down and pares down interpretative performances and he defictionalises by presenting the elements of a fiction without their illusions and joins. It is as if stories are reduced to the gestures (the language and elements) that compose them, that is, the reality of their composition and enactment.

If any attempt at a realism would be illusory and false, what then are the alternatives? Certainly, Bresson is not a realist in the sense of seeking out the real-seeming; he is rather a realist in seeking out the truth of things, a truth often masked by realistic fiction and its conventions of realistic acting.

In a paradoxical way, Bresson pares down performance and story and text to their absolute minimum, a kind of nudity or bareness as if to reveal their essence (truth) and in so doing attains to an artifice that is more extreme than the most studied imitative performance; but whereas the latter reproduces (imitates) the former, Bresson's approach reveals, uncovers, unmasks: the reverse of imitation. In so doing, as with musicals (film or theatre), musical elments, gestures, words, sounds are purified and made abstract (they become music, dance, movement) no longer imitative and representational of something else, no longer narrative but themselves purities of gesture, rhythm stripped of representational rationale and, thus, in Bresson's case, of their realism.

Bresson gives the novels of Bernanos a second chance not by imitating but by composing by means of them, purifying their literariness into forms in film. He uses film in this case to abstract the literariness of the novels, to their writing; that writing then becomes a compositional element in his films just as he reduces performance, heretofore in the service of representation and imitation, to its gestures, its separated-out parts, its fragments of movement, body, voice, its components, and with these, he constructs a film. The film then is both the reality of the story and its abstraction, that is, the story, but the story as its forms. These forms, for him, point to a truth that can only be formally reached, the essence of things rather than their surface representation.

Film, for Bresson, registers at once the reality of things and their truth but only on condition that this register is revelatory rather than interpretative, that it strives toward a blankness, confident that the attainment of such blankness, of such stripping down, will reveal a truth otherwise imperceptible and certainly imperceptible by a covering over by fictional imitations and its corollary, fictional acting.

This is not only the second chance for Bernanos but the second chance for the Passion, the recovery of it by the recovery of means, of gestures, of acts, that returns to a past for a present in keeping these dimensions distinct in the redundancy of their actions, both a second chance, a repetition, and an eternal return.

Just as Bresson returns to us the Bernanos novels and the Passion of Christ, he gives us (returns us) to the cinema, perhaps to its original innocence and purity. The move away from representation and the move toward abstraction (the former is never completely effaced and the latter never completely dominant – they are in tension and in conflict and always in simultaneity) reveal, as few filmmakers ever have done, the forms of the cinema just as surely as the films reveal the writing of Bernanos. Bresson attains with the cinema a maximum of what might be described as a cinematic redundancy: the event and its duplication and nothing more – the very first films, the beginning of the history of the cinema and, another history that only the cinema, perhaps, the cinema alone, can recount.

If the novels of Bernanos had been adapted by Bresson, the images would function as a recording and thus be without a life even if they had the illusion of life, a kind of corpse activated. What gives Bresson's *Le Journal* life is the encounter between it and the novel, between film and literature. It is their juxtaposition, their coming together (but not in accord, not in effacement), that is the film and the energy and vitality of the film. Equally, it is the juxtaposition of shot and the subject, and of shot with shot, that is the magic of the Bresson film, where, without any foreknowledge, any clear notion of an outcome, such juxtapositions produce something entirely new and unforeseen, where writing in the radical sense of writing gives birth to ideas and to images and to sentiments not known in advance but produced at the moment of writing, not quite improvisation, but close to it, something approaching the sense of chance and accident, to be alive to chance occurrences, chance encounters and to seek out, be open to, what they might reveal and produce, what life gives us rather than what we try to enforce upon it. Bresson's method, by paring down, by extraction, is a method for making come alive (revelation) what is there, what, if you like, pre-exists the film but is also its mystery and secret, and that these juxtapositions of pared fragments ignite and open up, like the grace that suffuses the parish priest and little Mouchette descending the hillside. One thing, another thing ... and then something else ... revealed ... and that, that is grace.

Mise en scène

Sound comes to the cinema at the end of the 1920s. Its immediate impact on the cinema was to theatricalise it in the worst sense. Film became subject to the word, to the script, to dialogue which tended to immobilise it: both camera and actors. Much of cinema in the early years of sound (and not merely confined to the cinema of the United States) was a staging and recording of literary works (talkies).

At the same time as sound altered the cinema in a backward direction certainly in relation to the fluidity of films of the 1920s, theatre also changed, but in a forward direction where stagecraft, movement of actors, lighting, physical expression, costuming, in short, the visual aspects of theatre, became as important if not more so than the word and the play in the staging of theatrical works. While the cinema became 'theatricalised' and subject to the word in the early 1930s, theatre at the same time became 'cinematised' in the sense of moving closer than films of the period to the early history of the cinema before the introduction of sound.

The term 'classical' for the American cinema initially referred to the cinema of the 1930s, films of story pre-eminently whose sense was conveyed by dialogue (as in the theatre) and by binding the audience, imaginatively, into dialogic relations by a system of shot and counter-shot that captured an audience into exchanges between characters.

The radicalism of the theatre compared to the conservatism of the cinema in the early 1930s mirrored a situation that was true in the first few years of the cinema's history. The term *mise en scène* began to be used in France for new theatrical practices in the late nineteenth century and the early years of the twentieth to denote a more 'naturalist', sensual, physical and visual theatre than the theatre of the eighteenth and early nineteenth centuries. It is in this period that filmed theatre became particularly evident in the French cinema (*Film d'art*): the staging of famous literary and classical works. Filmed theatre was in essence a caricature of the theatre – exaggerated gestures, an immobile camera, long takes, dull sets.

It is not difficult to understand in this context the revolution in cinema marked by the films of Griffith and Eisenstein for their fluidity, movement and energy and realised with specifically cinematic means. It is important to notice in these two figures, their initial involvement with the theatre, in the case of Eisenstein with the avant-garde theatre of Meyerhold, and in the case of Griffith with the popular excesses of melodrama. The great period and splendour of Italian lyric opera is of this time in the nineteenth and early twentieth centures (Puccini, Verdi, Donizetti) where melodramatic theatre becomes spectacle, precisely the opera that Visconti revived in Italy (and whose forms he translated into his films), injecting into it a stronger realistic and melodramatic sense and a greater attention to performance, movement and gesture rather than simply attention to voice and to singers standing before an audience.

The notion of *mise en scène* applied to the cinema has perhaps never lost its original theatrical references to mean primarily the reciting of a text by actors on a stage to include their entrances and exits. When the term is revived by French critics after the war and most vigorously by the French *Nouvelle Vague* in the pages of *Cahiers du cinéma* and *Présence du cinéma*, it was done so polemically, as a catchphrase (much as the idea of the *auteur* was, and to which it is related). *Mise en scène* is nothing very specific. In general it denotes an attitude to the cinema and, for the French critics, a new and modern view. It is a cinema opposed to the literary and primarily montage or *découpage* (classical) cinema of the 1930s, a theatrical, dialogue-based cinema of the translation of scripts into images, a cinema of illustration essentially dependent on theatrical-literary conventions. *Mise en scène* referred to a specifically 'cinematic' and more natural, realistic rendering of emotion and expression where emotions and ideas were conveyed not primarily by dialogue and the script but by decor,

performance, expression linked on the one hand to the actor (movements, gestures) and settings and on the other to the use of the camera
and lighting. It is in this period that the silent cinema comes to be revived
critically and for obvious reasons. *Mise en scène* at one and the same time
was an insistence on what might be called (though difficult to define)
the 'specificity of the cinema' and a redefinition of the cinema as an art
of bodies in 'real', 'true' settings to reveal the beauty of the world, of the
real, of persons (the importance in the period, indeed the golden age, of
the body and the outdoors – the western, *film noir*, the musical – and the
critical privileging of modes of filmmaking that preserved the integrity of
this notion of the real: depth of field, cinemascope, the use of a moving
camera and cranes and the use of the zoom as opposed to montage which
was discontinuous and fragmentary).

Nicholas Ray, Orson Welles, Elia Kazan, and Joseph Losey (and not to
forget Luchino Visconti) are primarily men of the theatre and in the
1930s in the United States when theatre was (along with painting) one
of the most radical (politically and aesthetically) artistic pursuits at the
time (as opposed to the cinema – kitsch, conservative, populist). It might
also be reiterated that the theatre, to which these men belonged, not only
was innovative and experimental but that the nature of its experiments
was in a direction of greater realism and a visual sense, that is, it was like
what the cinema would become when these young men began to interest
themselves in film, precisely at the moment when the classical system
and the studios that underpinned them began to crumble and would
eventually disappear. Their cinema was a new and experimental cinema,
and especially that of Welles, Losey and Ray.

This is the beginning of a review in 1957 by Jean-Luc Godard in *Cahiers
du cinéma* of Nicholas Ray's *Hot Blood* (1956):

> Si le cinéma n'existait plus, Nicholas Ray, lui seul, donne l'im-
> pression de pouvoir le réinventer, et qui plus est, de le vouloir.
> Alors que l'on imagine volontiers John Ford amiral, Robert Aldrich
> à Wall Street, Anthony Mann sur les traces de Belliou la Fumée,
> Raoul Walsh nouvel Henry Morgan sous le ciel des Caraïbes, on
> voit très mal en rechance ce que le metteur en scène d'*A l'ombre
> des potences* donnerait dans quelque activité que ce soit, autre que

cinématographique. Un Logan, par example, ou un Tashlin, peuvent réussir dans le théâtre ou le music-hall, un Preminger dans le roman, un Brooks dans l'enseignement primaire, Cukor dans la publicité, mais pas un Nicholas Ray. La plupart des cinéastes, si le cinéma n'existait soudain plus, ne seraient point désemparés pour autant, Nicholas Ray, oui. Après la projection de *Johnny Guitar* ou de *La Fureur de vivre*, impossible de ne pas se dire: voilà qui n'existe que par le cinéma, voilà qui serait nul dans un roman, mais qui sur la scène, partout ailleurs, mais qui sur l'écran devient fantastiquement beau.

(If the cinema no longer existed, Nicholas Ray alone gives the impression of being capable of reinventing it, and what is more, of wanting to. While it is easy to imagine John Ford as an admiral, Robert Aldrich on Wall Street, Anthony Mann on the trail of Belliou la Fumée or Raoul Walsh as a latter-day Henry Morgan under Caribbean skies, it is difficult to see the director of *Run for Cover* doing anything but make films. A Logan or a Tashlin, for instance, might make good in the theatre or music-hall, Preminger as a novelist, Brooks as a schoolteacher, Cukor in advertising – but not Nicholas Ray. If the cinema suddenly ceased to exist, most directors would in no way be at a loss; Nicholas Ray would. After seeing *Johnny Guitar* or *Rebel Without a Cause*, one cannot but feel that here is something which exists only in the cinema, which would be nothing in a novel, the stage or anywhere else, but which becomes fantastically beautiful on the screen.)[10]

Godard again in 1958 writing about Ray's *Bitter Victory* (1957):

Il y avait le théâtre (Griffith), la poésie (Murnau), la peinture (Rossellini), la danse (Eisenstein), la musique (Renoir). Mais il y a désormais le cinéma. Et le cinéma, c'est Nicholas Ray.

(There was theatre (Griffith), poetry (Murnau), painting (Rossellini), dance (Eisenstein), music (Renoir). But henceforth there is cinema. And the cinema is Nicholas Ray.)[11]

10   In Alain Bergala (ed.), *Jean-Luc Godard par Jean-Luc Godard*, vol. 1, 1950–1984 (Paris: Cahiers du cinéma, 1998), pp. 96–8.
11   Jean-Luc Godard, 'Au delà des étoiles', *Cahiers du cinéma*, no. 79 (January 1958), p. 118.

These remarks by Godard, not untypical of the tautological and non-analytic writing on the American cinema by *Cahiers* critics of the late 1950s, nevertheless gives a sense of the concern of these critics with the specific means of the cinema to which the phrase *mise en scène* primarily relates in its vagueness and in its polemical edge and that needs to be understood first and foremost historically in the shift, characterised by *Cahiers du cinéma* and the *Nouvelle Vague*, from one kind of cinema (classical) to another (modern) and for which the 'new' American cinema of the 1950s was both evidence and an important stimulus.

Ray's themes (betrayal, loyalty, fragility, violence) are primarily realised physically and visually, that is within the framework of what the *Nouvelle Vague* called *mise en scène*. In *In a Lonely Place* (1950), Ray concentrates on the unbalanced, unstable relation between Bogart and Gloria Grahame with its temporary and precious momentary harmonies and joys (love). The path of that relation and the risk and explosiveness of it are conveyed by Ray primarily in three ways: by capturing shifts in expression and gesture (from tenderness to jealousy, from ease to violence, from violence to remorse); by the composition of shots (the graphic clash of lines and movement, an architecture in movement and contrast); by the rhythm of the editing (a sense of unfinished, inconclusive shots, fragmented and discontinuous, of action only at its highest point, literally 'caught'). It is these aspects of the film, closely related to improvisation not only in the acting but in the shooting (albeit improvisation that occurs in rehearsal and then finally decided upon and set into the structure of the film), that account for the power of Ray's films, not the script or the dialogue. It is a narrative that is primarily physical and visual in which the word is subordinate as in the final sequence of the film of the wordless destruction of the relation between the two lovers, or, as in *On Dangerous Ground* (1951), the equally visual and physical constitution of a relation between Ida Lupino and Robert Ryan, in a reverse direction from *In a Lonely Place*, not from tenderness to violence, but rather a growing tenderness from out of violence, in both cases evidence of a fragility that is not only a quality of the characters but a quality of the films, that everything is at stake and every moment precious because fragile. It is the new cinema of *mise en scène*.

Modernity

Griffith's editing spatialised time, and Griffith established a tension between the temporal linearity of the narrative and the spatial simultaneity of his parallel alternating editing. One of the interesting aspects of Welles's *F for Fake* (1973) is the circularity and overlapping of the editing as if the film was a spatial surface upon which various temporalities were edited together, the case with Griffith.

Welles has three roles in *The Lady from Shanghai* (1947) as he has in *F for Fake*, *Citizen Kane* (1941), *Mr Arkadin* (1955) and *The Immortal Story* (1968). He is its author (the filmmaker), its principal character (Michael O'Hara) and its narrator (Michael O'Hara). He is, simultaneously, in all three of these roles, in the film (character) and outside it (author), and neither fully inside nor outside (the narrator). Welles is a multitude of images and functions that overlap and issue from different directions. The other characters are similarly multiple (the situation in *F for Fake* and also the case in *Citizen Kane*).

Elsa Bannister is a character played by Rita Hayworth. Rita Hayworth is a Hollywood image of beauty, eroticism and fatality, a lure and doubly deceitful: she deceives as a character (betraying O'Hara and seducing him as Oja Kodar does to Picasso in *F for Fake*), though the seduction is imaginary and she deceives by the fact of being an actress and a star (acting, faking, simulating).

The duplicity and multiplicity of Hayworth–Bannister and Welles–O'Hara are part of the constituents of the other characters: Arthur Bannister deceives, plots and mystifies and is a grotesque, a distortion, a parody, a reflection-mirage of himself; the same is true of George

Grisby and Sidney Broom. In short, every image in the film is deceptive, deformed, divided and split while every figure proliferates into mirrored reflections so severe as to cast doubt on any reality whatsoever (as occurs in *F for Fake*, *Kane* and *Arkadin*). The proliferation of figures (and thereby the crisis and instability of identity and the similitudes in images) causes a split to appear between images and what they represent since no image is adequate or conclusive to the reality it supposedly depicts; indeed, the reverse is true: it is the inadequacy, the difference of image from reality that Welles establishes in this film (and in all his other films).

Its severity in *Lady from Shanghai* (and *F for Fake*) is directly related to Welles's narrative approach. If generally, in most films, images are by themselves ambiguous and seldom clear, words and stories usually function to stabilise and anchor the image to give it meaning and precise significance (dialogue, narration, description, story), true in silent and sound films. Welles uses words differently: to question an image, unsettle it with doubt. The words of characters and of the narrator are either confused or deliberately misleading, making uncertain and dubious what you see and hear. Rather than words being a support to the image, Welles's words tend to undermine the veracity of both: you cannot trust words, or images, or actions or persons in his films, especially since points of view (the way you look at what you are presented with) are distorted (the low angles, the wide lenses with short focal lengths) and overlapped or sepulchral, as if everything decomposes and shatters or is either coming from or dispersing towards an elsewhere. The narrator is neither centre nor guide but a character caught in a labyrinth of words and images mostly of his own making (his story is a story of being trapped, seduced, misled, a story of confusion and inadequacy, a victim of himself and of fate), a split where nothing holds together and no path is clear or direct.

The brilliance of the final scene in the Hall of Mirrors in the Crazy House is a culmination of the film and of the manner in which its vertiginous and labyrinthine story is told (the story is that labyrinth and the telling is the weaving of it, a story of split identities, mirrored reflections, impossible mirages narrated by Welles *and* by O'Hara) and by these very means (the inadequacy of image to reality, words to sense, sound to image, narration to story) results in an unreadability and opacity, the decomposition not only of figures but of time. The subject of the film is in its forms, and the sense of what is told resides in the structure of the telling.

Welles does not assume a definite relation of film to reality, either the classical one of imitation or the modernist one that retreats from reality towards the pure autonomy of the work. Instead, he opens up the question of that relation without providing an answer. It is a demonstration, like *F for Fake*, of possibilities and problems. The film is that opening up of the cinema to questions that can only be posed, but whose answers are the entire historie(s) of the cinema.

If Welles's films are named as 'modern' (as they tend to be) on the basis of the spectacle of their forms and their distance from and criticism of classical norms, it would impoverish and limit his films to do so since their forms have a mirrored not instrumental and certainly not inessential relation to his themes. The films are neither purely film nor securely representational, but in a constant shifting between the two like the identities of Rita Hayworth between character, star, schemer, seducer and the identities of the narrator(s), the knowing but not omniscient Welles and the innocent and trapped O'Hara, split identities, but inseparable, once again, as in Bertolucci's *Partner*, the doubles Giacobbe 1 and Giacobbe 2.

Montage (1)

At the very beginning of the cinema, strictly speaking, there were no shots nor, therefore, montage. The earliest films (documentaries as well as fictions) simply represented what went on in front of the camera. In that sense, fictions were documentaries (because they documented what occurred) and documentaries were fictions (because they suggested a story, or, at the very least, a logic and significance). In both cases, because these early films were fundamentally a record, the events that occurred in front of the camera had an accidental, unpredictable and unplanned aspect: for example, the charm of one of the earliest Lumière films of a train coming into a station is its openness and accidental 'found' quality (like 'reality'), and similarly for the early Méliès films, which involved a fixed camera at a fixed distance and which often 'found' in its lens the unexpected, and thereby were open, empty of logic or continuity, but filled with possibility.

These earliest experiences of the cinema suggest a situation that has always been addressed in film, but never satisfactorily nor definitively, namely the relation between the chaos of reality and the ordering of it by film. All films seek to provide an order by framing, perspective, editing, placement, juxtaposition, a combination of putting into scene and an editing of accords. And thus, for the most part, films when they create an order have tended to try to *simulate* reality, create likenesses of it, rather than truly represent it. As soon as a documentary, no matter how concerned with recording the truth of things, begins to give a shape and a significance, order and a logic to what it records, the reality of what it records is displaced. On the other hand, as often happens in fiction, a

slight gesture or movement by an actor is revealed by the camera and in
such a way as to separate the actor (in reality) from the character (in the
fiction). That gap between the real and the fictional, and their overlay, is
one of the qualities in Godard's *Une femme est une femme* (1964), particularly marked in the amateurishness of the performances by Anna Karina
(Angela), Jean-Claude Brialy (Émile) and Jean-Paul Belmondo (Alfred)
and the fact that they seem to be as much 'found' and 'discovered' as they
are 'planned'. Similarly, in the filming of such fictions, changes in light
and in colour values can occur, especially out of doors, beyond the control
of any programme. At the same time, during filming, a certain turn of
phrase or turn of gesture can suggest a path or an interest or an association that escapes a design or script set out in advance. It is precisely this
entry of the 'real' into the fictional that Renoir exclaimed was the essence
of cinema: 'C'est le cinéma!' The real, if it comes, is a disruption and the
very sign of what the cinema is. And thus the two, reality and film, are,
as in the best of films, both one (the same) and also distinct (different).

There is an essay by the novelist, filmmaker and art historian André
Malraux, written in 1939, 'Esquisse d'une psychologie du cinéma' ('Sketch
for a Psychology of the Cinema') where Malraux argues that the cinema
truly appears only with montage and, by implication, with the shot, and
thus the earliest films, before montage, were, according to Malraux, not
yet cinema, but only photographs of movement. That is, for Malraux,
cinema depends upon the breaking up and fragmentation of a single
unified theatrical space-time into a purely cinematic and heterogeneous
space-time which is constructed into some kind of discourse in which
each shot functions as a sign. The problem about such a view is that the
reality of things before filming is not only turned into images (and images
are not the real thing, but at best only similar to it, a representation), such
that the image relations of montage take precedence over what is originally there, in short, reality is shaped and manipulated, for example in the
parallel and alternate montage of last-minute rescues and chases as in the
films of Griffith and the associative montage in Eisenstein (the slaughter
of cattle and the slaughter of workers in *Strike* (1925)).

Bazin, in his essays 'Ontologie de l'image photographique' ('Ontology
of the Photographic Image') and 'L'Evolution du langage cinématographique' ('The Evolution of the Language of Cinema'), took a different
view, namely that procedures of editing either, of the associative kind

as with Eisenstein or of the dramatic-analytic kind as with Griffith and
later of the 'classic' Hollywood cinema of the 1930s with the coming of
sound, tended to ignore the essential reality of things because editing was
necessarily manipulative and thereby an artificial construction and, most
importantly for Bazin, it presumed a fragmentation and disruption of the
integrity of real space and time in order to reconstruct these as signs of a
discourse rather than as a revelation of the real. Bazin rewrote the history
of the cinema in terms of this view, singling out the films of Stroheim,
Murnau and Flaherty in the silent period as films that respected the
integrity of the real and typified the realist vocation of the cinema almost
at its very beginnings rather than what occurred in the films of Eisenstein
or Griffith or the classical films of the 1930s.

There is no question that, however interesting these positions are that
seek to define what is specific and essential to the cinema, they present
a problem, and simply because they are prescriptive, limited, offering a
singular view of what the cinema is in its essence and therefore what the
cinema should be in practice. Bazin was not simply recommending a
certain path for the cinema, however, or even a narrowly developmental
history, but crucially responding to what was, when he was writing, a new
development in the cinema that in part related to technical advances in
sound recording, in film emulsions, in lenses and a greater use of pan-
ning, tracking, the zoom, depth of field and, oddly enough, by directors
with a strong theatrical background like Renoir, Welles, Nicholas Ray,
Preminger, Ophuls and others like Bresson and Rossellini anxious to
substitute for the verisimilitude and simulated reality of films that characterised the classical cinema, a cinema that would be truly respectful of
the constituents of reality.

Among these various historical and theoretical perspectives (the theories were also histories and the histories were at the same time theories)
that involved relations between reality and fiction, the real and the artificial, the document and the fictional, the appearance of another and crucial distinction (and debate) appeared concerning a cinema of montage
and a cinema that primarily constructed a reality as opposed to a cinema
that merely registered one.

One of the virtues noticed by Bazin, and also by some of the writers
and later filmmakers of the *Nouvelle Vague* in the films of Preminger,
Ray, Welles, Rossellini and Renoir, was that a cinema based primarily on

the sequence (shot-sequences, a camera that followed action, a minimum of editing, the deployment of a moving camera or moving lenses and the addition of depth and the extended surface of cinemascope, and a narrativised stance that refused to interpret and instead desired only to record) rather than based principally on the shot as its essential unit resulted in a cinema where unities of space and time were more evident and the integrity of performances more respected and thereby were assumed to be more realistic.

This view, though it appeared to make sense, was problematic. The faithful rendering of a performance, rather than ensuring the reality of what was represented, often resulted in its disruption. For example, in *Une femme est une femme* (1961), what Godard's camera picks up in the sequences in the apartment of Emile and Angela, while respectful of the spatial and temporal integrity of the sequence, nevertheless disrupts it in various ways: the performances appear as performances and the actors thereby do not fully inhabit their characters, thus the accord between film and reality is not realised; the camera often takes arbitrary paths that seem inexplicable and, because inexplicable, noticeable, thus posing against 'reality' as a unity its division into different levels, that of the making of the film, the finding of things, and the fiction as represented; the desire to record a scene and the refusal to interpret it, to provide a perspective or point of view for fear of imposing a reality rather than revealing a reality, often gave the wholeness that was produced not simply an ambiguity but a blankness and opaqueness, in short it created obstacles to understanding, since reality unfiltered was not necessarily clear or transparent, on the contrary (the arbitrariness of action and of the movement of the camera in the scene in the apartment clarifies nothing and, rather than advancing a narrative and story, disrupts it); and the film easily loses control and coherence by the introduction of extraneous references and citations to other realities outside the fiction that the film picks up (for example, citations to the American musical, to comic books, to silent film slapstick) in the midst of differently organised and directed sequences.

It is as if Godard is intent not only to break things apart but to break them apart at the very line that was instituted by the first films (and is a constant in every film), namely that between the chaos of reality and the desire for orderliness in the film. If something is established in a Godard film, it is almost always interrupted, intruded upon, broken into, dismantled as if the messiness of reality (however conceived) is integral to the orderliness of the film and that this messiness inevitably makes its presence felt and in such a way – and it is a way out of a historical problem as posed by Bazin and Malraux – that Godard's films never settle on one side or the other of this historical divide, but instead gain strength and fascination by their between-ness, a between-ness that his films carefully cultivate and at the same time carelessly allow.

Interestingly, while Godard asserted that every documentary is also a fiction and the reverse, every fiction a documentary, he also, in his essay 'Montage, mon beau souci' ('Montage my fine care') observed that montage presumed a *mise en scène* and vice versa, not that they were the same, but rather that they were different and it was their juxtaposed differences that needed to be retained, understood and delighted in, indeed it is the pleasure of Godard's films.

The usual function of montage is to create accords between fragments in order to produce an appearance not only of continuity but of sense and significance. Godard's editing has different ends. It is to emphasise differences between shots, between sequences and within shots (between images and sounds, words and meanings, the artificial and the real, the staged and the spontaneous) and thus to preserve by means of such differences each term involved in the juxtapositions, and at all levels in which they occur, hence the need for disruption in order to indicate how things really are and never to fall into the trap of either a simulation of the real or empty chaos.

Sometimes Godard can produce an image of extraordinary lyrical beauty. Partly it is the result of his placing of things and his way of capturing, lighting, and recording them, but it is also by way of pointing to and underlining either by careful framing or/and by editing, by montage. What his montage does is to emphasise not simply what is represented but the fact that it is represented, that is, it points not simply to the object of the *mise en scène*, what is put into scene, but to the action of putting into scene, at once a reality and the film that has caused the reality to be seen and to occur, two realities, but at different poles apart. The lyricism is a matter of illuminating both elements without losing either, neither life nor film. It alters an entire historical view of the cinema. It recalls the earliest film comedies, Mack Sennett in particular, and much later the comedies of Jerry Lewis, much admired by Godard, the establishment of an order as a condition for its disruption.

Montage (2)

The juxtapositions of fragments in *Histoire(s) du cinéma* (1988–98) are of various kinds accomplished by various means. They involve angles, light, surface, depth, duration (acceleration, slow motion, flickering), graphic lines (verticality, horizontality), scale and dimension. Some are rhetorical, poetic or musical: condensations, inversions, correspondences, contraries, dissonances, contrasts, rhythms, pauses, repetitions, refrains, rhymes, succession, tempo, conflation. Some, while formal and rhetorical, specifically involve recurrent motifs and subjects: hands, eyes, monsters, aircraft, bestiality, savagery, executions, heroism, innocence, dance, war, slaughter, the Holocaust, Hitler, Mussolini, Hitchcock, Rossellini, John Ford, Jean Renoir, Nick Ray, D.W. Griffith, Sergei Eisenstein, Buster Keaton, Charlie Chaplin.

There had been a debate in the late 1950s and early 1960s originating from a reading of Bazin between those in favour of *mise en scène* (leaving scenes whole, the shot sequence, depth of field, the unity of surfaces, the integrity of space and time) and those who were partial to the use of montage (classical editing, the montage of Eisenstein). The two positions, however, can be regarded as equivalent, reversible and inseparable. As Godard pointed out, to divide or oppose them would be like opposing rhythm to melody. In any case, the extent and duration of a shot is already a montage decision, as is the choice of subject, setting, figures, background, foreground. And if the intent is to reveal what is going on in a scene, its 'reality', breaking the scene up into a number of shots might be more efficacious than an interrupted shot sequence, more the consequence of improvisation and inspiration at the editing table than improvisation before the camera. Montage, rather than being unnatural and unrealistic, can be a means to help to see and discover reality.

Montage is the principal means by which *Histoire(s)* is constructed and is also its subject. The film depends on montage and is an experiment in montage, an action and the consciousness of it. While the film brings fragments together and takes them apart and since there is seldom a natural connection between the citations and fragments so treated, the consequences of the montage in feeling, association, direction cannot be known in advance. Effectively, the montage lets loose, disperses, coalesces, arranges a field for associations, memories, incrustations, musings. It is ceaselessly active and present, but says little directly, since such saying is beyond its competence. It is the opposite of the classical use of montage. Its functions are elsewhere: to see, discover, investigate, question, open, undefine, put into play, destabilise, bring to life. Whereas, in the classical film, the film is obscured for the sake of a meaning, sense or drama, sense is the casualty of *Histoire(s)*. Its drama is its montage, as colour is in Van Gogh, framing and formal intersections in Cézanne, spatial and temporal perspectives in De Chirico and in Cubism, sound, space and movement in the films of Tati, music and dialogue in Demy.

Histoire(s) du cinéma never really ends, is never finished, even when the last image comes on the screen. The reason it never finishes and is unfinished at every moment is that, looked at in its entirety or in its least detail, nothing is ever completely consumed. Everything seems to retain an inexhaustible reserve. The montage is the means for discovering and pointing to that reserve, the virtual images, paths, associations in every image and any combination of them.

Every image and sound in the film is irreducible and singular, detached from where they originally were to become free, themselves, separate, 'other', as different not only from what they once had been (an element in another text) but different now in relation to what they encounter (other singular elements from other texts). They are at once intensely separate and independent and promiscuously plural. They touch, join other cited fragments. Their separateness is virtual, temporary. With each new encounter, they are altered, seen differently, even if or especially if they are repeated, newly contextualised and resituated.

Succession proceeds in the film as a reverse circularity. In most films, there is a progression, a perceptible continuous time of development and resolution achieved by a system of consequence at once formal, thematic, dramatic and narrational. The next image is anticipated in the prior one and so on to the conclusion of the film. This kind of continuity with its line of logic constrains every image to proceed along a determined path. In *Histoire(s)* something quite different occurs, succession moves backwards so the preceding image is the future of the successive one, since every new image that appears alters not only the one that preceded it but all that came before it. This alteration is not a matter of a forward, successive connection but is a reverse effect of the montage which discovers in the preceding image a virtuality that only becomes or could become apparent *after* a new image appears, not as a displacement of the previous one (succession causing every present to pass into the past) but as its revelation, making it present once again, rescuing it from any pastness whatsoever. And, because of an apparent infinite virtuality, every passing is a new beginning and every past a potential future, the reason why it is impossible to speak of *Histoire(s)* coming to an end. The film in not being self-contained is always more than itself.

Franz Schubert composed his Symphony number eight (the Unfinished) in 1822. It consists of two movements rather than the usual four. The first movement contains an open citation to Beethoven (the *Eroica*) and, as with other symphonies, returns in various ways to the beginning in recapitulations. The second movement is notable for its counterpoint between various instruments and the repetition of variations. The counterpoint functions as interruptions of the two dominant themes of the movement. Godard, in *Toutes les histoires*, 1A of *Histoire(s)* extensively cites passages from the first movement of Schubert's symphony. *Histoire(s)* has an aspect characteristic of Schubert's Unfinished, the recapitulations, the later modification of earlier passages by subsequent ones, repetitions that are varied on their returns and the role of counterpoint as digression.

By not insisting upon or providing links between shots or scenes, the independence of each shot or scene is enhanced and the montage in operation is linked more to that of Eisenstein (a montage of attractions) than to Pudovkin (a montage of consequence). The shot is no longer the sum of preceding shots, nor their conclusion.

There are scenes and shots of extreme beauty and lyricism in *Histoire(s)* as in all Godard's films. As these are interrupted, disrupted, dispersed, it is not that the lyricism, engagement and fascination with it are lost so much as transferred, as in music in the passage from one key, motif or melody to another that alters intensities, mood, depth, colour, line, duration, movement, silence, rhythm. A single note or figuration may be expanded into a new motif or a dominant or combined with others to effect a change in volume, depth, direction, or function as a counterpoint, or to create a series.

Alain Resnais remarked on the beauty of Jean Renoir's *La Règle du jeu* (1939), so intense and perfect as to bring him close to tears as if faced with the mysterious and the unknown. The perfection he felt was difficult to analyse and its attainment difficult to explain. It had to do for Resnais with Renoir's ability to know precisely how long a shot should be held, when to cut and the terms for creating the transition to a new image. For Resnais, Renoir was always right: a second less, a second more, the slightest change in framing, and the shot, sequence or scene, indeed the film, might falter or worse. This kind of rightness, essentially formal and abstract, more instinctive than planned, involving transfers and transfigurations of tone, line and shape, is true for *Histoire(s)*, despite or especially because of an apparent distance between images in time, space and subject, the radical heterogeneity of material and the immense effort and risk involved in connecting them.

The complement to the flow and grace of the transitions is the instant, a moment of pause, redirection, interruption, when whatever was, and in whatever course, stops, changes pace as if caught by a distant sound or sight. Such dissonances, changes of direction and counterpoint are as much part of the lyricism and precision of timing in *Histoire(s)* as the connectives in some lengthy passages.

Histoire(s) is an ideal postmodern work for its disjunctions, play with virtuality, openness to chance and by its avoidance of any manifesto, unlike the modern where the manifesto often seems its reason to be. *Histoire(s)* is also Romantic for its concentration on the purity of the moment, the beauty of the slightest gesture or note, what is waited for, yet arrives unheralded, unexpectedly, a question of duration, patience and the good sense to recognise when what is sought has indeed arrived and then to seize upon it, if only temporarily, and then to know when to let go and move on, and, how to move on.

As Godard said in a 1967 interview: 'I have only made a single discovery in the cinema, which is how to move easily from one shot to another beginning with two very different movements and, what is more difficult still, to move from a shot in movement to a still shot. In such a way you can join one shot to any other.'

Museum

Some paintings at the end of the nineteenth century, the work of Manet, for example, became what Foucault called 'museum paintings', paintings for other paintings, both contemporary and of the past. The historical dimension was not particularly chronological. The museum painting related to other paintings not by geography, time, or subject but as form and its transformation: light, brushstroke, colour, composition, surface.

The museum was not primarily educational, nor there to conserve and preserve works of art, but rather to exhibit art as sacred for admiration and worship. Two things were necessary: that the work be truly a work, that it was fabricated, and that it was exceptional (beautiful, skilful). These qualities defined what art was. A question arose about how works were to be exhibited. As with libraries, classification systems were instituted which had little to do with aesthetic value, but everything to do with place, subject, artist, genre and, later, movements.

Cinémathèques are film museums. Like the art museum they have similar modes of classification without which what would be left would be a heterogeneous collection of bric-a-brac, an essentially meaningless hodge-podge because not classified. Instead, categories would provide works, whether painted or on celluloid, a representational consistency, in effect, some kind of narrative significance, historical or not.

The Paris Cinémathèque directed by Henri Langlois was founded by him in 1935 with Georges Franju and Jean Mitry. Godard called it not only his home but his birthplace: 'On est né au musée, c'est la patrie.' Langlois's Cinémathèque collected films (the museum as archive) and screened them. What was unique about it was that it was primarily a place of exhibition different from most cinémathèques whose primary activity was archival, often at the expense of exhibition. Langlois's programming was impulsive, personal, associative, sometimes governed only by chance and opportunity in the belief that an odd, unclassifiable, disorderly screening of films without privileging any particular view shaped by systems of classification would be exciting, surprising and revealing, like a surprise encounter. Langlois was a Surrealist as his 'method' for the Cinémathèque attests. It was designed to suggest, indeed form, new relations between films rather than impose already familiar and institutionalised ones. Langlois was a poet of the cinema who brought films into contact with each other and with the past without reference to normal programming categories. Godard explicitly acknowledged his debt to Langlois and he does so extensively in *Histoire(s) du cinéma* (1988–98). The Godard film is a direct descendant of the Cinémathéque and thereby of Surrealism in spirit and in fact, and Godard is one of its children evident in his *Histoire(s)* and his 2006 Pompidou exhibition.

Langlois was dismissed in 1968 as director of the Paris Cinémathèque by the Gaullist Minister of Culture, André Malraux, because Langlois's direction was considered to be too personal, disorganised and unaccountable. Langlois kept few records and nothing was systematised or catalogued. After his dismissal, Langlois was invited to lecture at the Montréal Conservatoire d'art cinématographique on the history of the cinema. The lectures, which proved popular, were based on film extracts of films that Langlois brought with him from Paris.

Malraux had been forced to reinstate Langlois at the Cinémathèque under immense international pressure, including street demonstrations in Paris orchestrated by Godard and others of the French *Nouvelle Vague*, worthy of their own Surrealist inheritance. In December 1976, Godard and the producer Jean-Pierre Rassam suggested a project to Langlois to make a film on the history of the cinema to be released on film and video whose aim in part was to generate revenue for the Paris Cinémathèque. Rassam was to finance and produce the film and Langlois and Godard to write and direct it. Langlois died in 1977. Serge Losique, then the Director of the Conservatoire in Montréal, asked Godard if he would take up Langlois's lectures at the Conservatoire. He accepted the invitation as an opportunity to further the film project of a history of the cinema as a co-production between Godard's company, Sonimage, and the Montréal Conservatoire. The scenario was to be divided into ten chapters or voyages, each constituted by Godard's lectures. The scenario took the form of notes published in 1980 entitled *Introduction à une véritable histoire du cinéma et de la télévision* (*Introduction to a True History of the Cinema and of Television*) and intended as the first of seven volumes. No further volumes appeared and meanwhile, the Conservatoire, not able to find sufficient money, withdrew from the project which then became wholly the responsibility of Godard and Sonimage.

Godard's idea of a *véritable* (true) history of the cinema was one composed solely of images and sounds, film encountering film, acting upon film, film as a protagonist, a character even, not a receptacle, not words as commentary or narrative or explanation, but directly active, forms in themselves less to elucidate or be illustrated than to question and interact. Godard proposed a structure where fragments of film assumed a variety of positions and connections rather than being constrained in a single or homogeneous one as a representative example of something definite. Each 'voyage' of the *Histoire(s)* was to be a meeting between a film of Godard's and films by other directors to accompany it, both contemporary and from the past, few with an obvious, evident or necessary connection either to Godard's film or to the other films in each voyage. What governed Godard's choices is not clear, and what might arise from these was impossible to tell in advance. It was to be an adventure, literally a voyage to the unknown, with virtual consequences 'to be'. Even if the marks of the landscape were familiar, the effect of their conjunction and passing was not. Godard's conception for the film was akin to Langlois's programming, a juxtaposition-montage of unplanned differences:

> Voilà pourquoi la Cinémathèque est bien. Parce qu'on y voit pêle-mêle beaucoup de films, aussi bien un Cukor de 39 qu'un documentaire de 18.

> (This is the reason the Cinémathèque is so good. It is because you can see many films there, and pell-mell, a Cukor film of 1939 and a documentary of 1918.)

> **Godard**[12]

12 Jean-Louis Comolli, Michel Delahaye, Jean-André Fieschi, Gérard Guégan, 'Entretien avec Godard', *Cahiers du cinéma*, no.171 (October 1965), reprinted in Alain Bergala (ed.), *Jean-*

Myth

Ford is a filmmaker of dawn, dusk and night. Even in his brightly lit scenes, shadows intervene. His images are muted, on a shadow-line, depicting subjects from the past in the tones and atmosphere of the past, like old photographs, repetitions of earlier images, of what has been, memory not actuality, and, like memory, immobilised in time. If, in the stories told by Ford, events succeed each other and are consequent upon each other, the whole of the story issues from a frozen, eternal past. It is not only his characters who commune with the dead at a graveside but the audience watching his films.

Like the classical films of Hollywood, Ford's films transform realities of place, setting and persons into fictions, with the difference that his fictions are memorials, detached from the present and from history. Like the dead, Ford's images are eternal, caught in a time of perpetuity, his *Young Mr Lincoln* (1939) for example.

The present is a threat to the past for Ford: it involves change (history, passing) and loss (forgetting, effacement). His films are ideal memories of a lost paradise (the West, the family, the frontier, community, heroes, Indians, the cavalry, rural Ireland, the coalfields of Wales) kept intact from the disruptiveness of history (transformation) and reality (a different view) and subjectivity (plurality). The skill of Ford was to transform legend into 'fact', to make it seem more nearly true than any reality. He did so by rigorously objectifying the stories he told: the real settings of

---

Luc Godard par Jean-Luc Godard, vol.1, 1950–1984 (Paris: Cahiers du cinéma, 1998), p. 268.

Monument Valley, a landscape at once true and eternal. Ford followed and deepened the classical rules of continuity, linearity, simplicity, clarity, succession, nothing to disturb his smooth, homogeneous, essentially transparent surface (at once window and mirror). He managed to integrate the internal intimate scenes in his films of dialogue and story with the objectivity of setting, of shadowy, nostalgic, remembered landscapes and townscapes. The counter-shot to exchanges between characters was the landscape and the action within it (gunfights, Indians, ambushes). He easily moved between the two either in shots or in sequences of shots, scene to scene, of intimacy, plot development, character on the one hand and landscape and action on the other. This alternation and smooth transition are brought to perfection in *She Wore a Yellow Ribbon* (1949) and *Rio Grande* (1950).

The stories he told, especially in his westerns, were stories of heroes who helped settle the West (Kirby, Brittles, Doniphon, Abraham Lincoln), who brought law, peace, security, civility. It is at that point that the West Ford idealises ceases to exist. It becomes society, settlement, a different place, closer in time, no longer heroic and simple but complex, corrupt even, where his heroes and heroines who had made society possible have no longer a place within it, like Ethan Edwards in *The Searchers* (1956). They enter the legendary where they never die, or disappear, or are forgotten. They are at once objectified, sentimentalised and eternalised (*Fort Apache* (1948)), heroes who are condemned to wander.

Ford made his films in the modern industrial society of twentieth-century America, a disharmonic, diverse, complex place where sense was uncertain and individual identity in crisis. The realities of the modern world had displaced the epic world (as if it ever existed) and the myths of heroism and individuality that sustained it and that Ford depicted. It was the modern, the real, the historical, the subjective that Ford's films avoided. He was unlike Fritz Lang, Sam Fuller, Orson Welles, Nicholas Ray, who dealt with these areas as subjects in their films and in the forms of their films. For example, in the case of Welles's *Citizen Kane* (1941) and *The Magnificent Ambersons* (1942) or Lang's *Rancho Notorious* (1952), myths (of power, of the past, of the West) appear not as facts but as myths and are set off as such. Against these myths are posed time and the historical. These filmmakers were of a later generation to Ford, or, like Lang, had come from an urban, cultivated, sophisticated Europe. Lang, unlike Ford, rather than affirming the American dream, shattered it with the reality of things.

Ford gave his audiences the comfort of legends against the truths, realities and uncertainties of the modern. He was, as Welles commented, 'a maker of myths'.

Narrative

Most histories (*Histoires*), most histories of the cinema (*histoires du cinéma*) and most of the films that form part of that history and that tell stories (*histoires*) are narratives. They narrate events that have already occurred. The events so narrated are usually presented chronologically, a series of sequences, scenes, shots that progress in a more or less linear fashion, that begin and are concluded and resolved. One of the features of such narratives is that their elements belong to a hierarchy of importance and significance. Some passages are strong, others weak, some dominant, others merely transitional or intermediary like punctuations in a succession.

Narrative is the consequence of a historical situation largely codified in the nineteenth century in the novel and in History writing, though also in painting and in theatre, and, after the turn of that century, in film. Godard's films, from his first to his most recent, dismantle that tradition. His work is less a rejection of narrative as it had been practised (and largely still is) than it is a fragmentation and reordering of it, subjected to insistent interruptions, like a bell sounding or a telephone ringing in its midst.

In a Godard film, interruptions are not less important than what is interrupted, indeed the distinction between major and minor, representation and punctuation, *the* narrative and digressions from it, have little sense. All elements are equal (equally forms) and there is no classification system with all that implies of order and illustration. If his films, and especially his *Histoire(s) du cinéma* (1988–98), are dense with citations and examples from the past, these are more like a collection or artistic options than a museum or archive ordered by fictions of classification. The combination of the indifference of elements to hierarchy, their resistance to a fixed order and place and their apparent equality in Godard's work establishes each element as autonomous and particular and also as available for rearrangement, hence the instability, circularity and sense of possibility in his films, their lack of finish and their energetic ceaselessness, porosity and meandering, and thereby also the problem of speaking about them. How do you get hold of, begin to possess a Godard work which is so unfixed and opaque?

What had been crucial to narrative – its coherence, unity, homogeneity, linearity, continuity, sense and order – are, in Godard's work, broken apart, constantly intruded upon. The citations that compose his films – overwhelming in *Histoire(s) du cinéma* – arrive from elsewhere such that the films are always moving away towards and therefore back not only to where its elements originated but into new combinations and encounters with other elements, other citations; thus 'back' is also 'forward' and vice versa. The narrative (if it had ever existed) is consumed by such movements. Alternative arrangements created by the unorthodox and plural succession of materials are not connected as linear motivated consequences. They are simply and merely successive. Their true place is not limited, but depends on encounters difficult to state or foresee, and these are often simultaneous (the superimposition, fade, mix), disrupting time, or nearly so (rapid alternations, the flicker).

Most narratives, the grand narratives of History (*Histoire*) and the smaller histories (*histoires*), the stories and anecdotes they may contain, integrate the two. For example, to better understand Greek classical architecture, the political and social context of fifth-century Athens under Pericles might be discussed and, to the contrary, the political History of Athens might be illuminated by a detour through its architecture and sculpture. Similarly, the forms of the American cinema in the 1930s, might be incorporated into a history of the studio system, a discussion of the films of John Ford or an analysis of the Great Depression and the coming of sound to films. In these instances, the differences of Hollywood, the Depression, the studio system, John Ford, economy, ideology and art are grouped together within a homogeneous historical time with a foreground and background, the significant and less significant, marked lines of dependence and subordination. There is another way, that of associations (thematic, formal, remembrances) between discontinuous elements in sheets or layers of heterogeneous time and substance, as in, for example, André Malraux's *Le Musée imaginaire*, Walter Benjamin's *Arcades Project*, Aby Warburg's *Mnémosyne* and Godard's *Histoire(s) du cinéma*, collage-montages of non-contiguous and non-continuous fragments (citations), networks of echoes, resonances, rhythms, colours and space, like memories, or like pieces of music, in any case nothing very definite or fixed, as encounters which bear upon the present, suddenly appear and give witness, like Sergei Eisenstein's first, and best film, *Strike* (1925).

In *Histoire(s) du cinéma*, general history (wars, battles, economic arrangements, philosophical writings, the Holocaust, Hitler speaking, always a mixed bag), the history of the cinema (the films of the Soviet Union in the 1920s, Chaplin, the *Nouvelle Vague*, Italian neorealism, the studio system under Irving Thalberg) and the stories (*histoires*) of films evoked by cited fragments (from *The Searchers* (1956), *M* (1931), *Ordet* (1925), *Potemkin* (1925), *Broken Blossoms* (1919), *La Règle du jeu* (1939), *Cries and Whispers* (1972), *Gigi* (1958), *Paisà* (1946)), the history of art (Van Gogh, Picasso, Goya, Rembrandt, Utrillo, Matisse, pornography), all notable for their range, differences and distance from each other, are criss-crossed, intersected. They are not co-ordinated in the film, but overlap, are superimposed, flickered, appearing as simultaneous and distant, autonomous and in counterpoint like a musical composition, that is, they become forms. Taken together, they do not 'explain', but rather 'explode', act, come apart, dissonances that may coalesce or separate, forever being redrawn and not just occasionally, but constantly as new things are met and discovered. Godard brings things together not to explicate but to activate.

What is presented is a field of ceaseless movement where narrative and time are opened up, not exactly lost, but reconfigured as part of a composition, but not belonging to a narrative, nor a history, nor illustrations in the usual sense. The different cited histories, temporalities and instances that are brought into contact become multiple points of view, entries, appearances and disappearances, histories but not *a* history, still less *the* history, documents but not a documentary. The citations illustrate nothing, dense but not weighty, on the contrary. The fragments of histories, ruins of history and of narratives gathered in *Histoire(s)* work together to form not a new narrative and certainly not a new history. The history of the cinema as a narrative of narratives ceases to be sustainable.

Networks

> If the book is not conceived of as the arguing through of an idea or the exposition of a destiny, if it refuses to investigate itself, to anchor itself outside the signifier, it must be perpetual: not full stop to the text, no last word. And what is infinite in that book is not only its end; at every point the supplement is possible: something new can always grow later on in the interstices of the fabric, of the text. The book has holes, and therein lies its productivity ...; it is not going somewhere, it is going away, it never stops going away.[13]

Histoire(s) is a network of groupings and possible connections all of them in movement. The networks are of two kinds. One is spatial and topological, an effect of layering where points of contact as well as gaps, emptiness and breaks are visible. The vertical layers tend to be transparent, like fades and superimpositions. The layering is a matter of positions: even the slightest change or variation alters everything.

The other network is temporal, not progressive, as in a narrative dependent on the development of a drama, scene, character, or theme as consequence or causation, nor progressive simply by the linearity inherent in the projection of a film. The sense of succession is instead primarily one of possible connectives, sometimes horizontal, more often circular and

---

13 Jean-Louis Leutrat, 'The Declension', in Raymond Bellour and Mary Lee Bandy (eds), *Jean-Luc Godard: Son + Image 1974–1991* (New York: The Museum of Modern Art, 1992), p.25.

associative, frequently returning, retracing, interrupting, digressing, in any case constantly reconfigured.

It would be limiting to concentrate on the iconology of the elements in *Histoire(s)* in order to decipher a fixed sense to the film and to speculate on Godard's intentions or 'thought' in the usual sense. The created networks of possible, indeed infinite connections between different elements and varieties of signs are not suited to such definitions. The excitement of the film rests in its indefiniteness and the freedom it bestows opening entirely new realms of experience. What is offered is not a finished product but a process of formation, invention, searching, questioning, a work in progress.

Nowhere

In Rossellini's *Viaggio in Italia* (1954), the Joyces, Katherine and Alex, drive to Naples from England to settle an inheritance left them by their Uncle Homer. The film begins at a point in their journey just north of Naples. Three literary works from outside the fiction shadow their trip: a reference to James Joyce and by association to his *Ulysses* (a journey), and his novella, *The Dead* (a love lost, Katherine's story of her lover). And there is the reference to Homer's epic poem, the *Odyssey*.

Viaggio in Italia is a journey to a strange and marvellous world, to Italy, to the Italian South, a primitive Naples that disorients the pragmatic and sensible English couple who have arrived from the 'North', from 'civilization'.

The Joyces' voyage evokes multiple pasts (Homer, Joyce, the classical world and the world of the dead). In coming to Naples, they cross a line into an alien unknown. It is impossible to say, once the Joyces arrive at Uncle Homer's villa, where they have actually come to, still less where they are going, not only because of the multiple places that seem to proliferate out of the slightest, banal acts (driving, having dinner, eating breakfast, taking a siesta, sightseeing in Naples and Pompeii, a night spent in Capri) but because the deviations, interruptions, new stories that form along the way striate the central one (to sell the villa), cause it to veer off course in scenes of a marriage turning sour, compromised by other itineraries, geographical, emotional, a descent into an underworld, to the dead, a buried past, a primeval and a geological world that bubbles up from the depths of the earth (the sulphur fields).

Much of the fascination of Rossellini's film is its indirection and displacements that accumulate out of the everyday and from chance encounters: the smell of a cow, bugs on the car windscreen, a passing funeral, a casual remark, a dinner party, pregnant women. It is difficult to say not only where the Joyces may be going but where the film is going. Both are at times suspended in a nowhere.

In Jean Rouch's film *La Chasse au lion à l'arc* (1957–64), the film begins as a story told to wide-eyed children at a campfire about their ancestors who hunted lions with bow and arrow. The film is that story (mythological) and its actuality (a documentary). It is also a document of the telling of the story and of the document being filmed of it, at once a film and the idea of it, a film and its processes. The story told to the children is of a journey to the African bush in Mali (and before there ever was Mali), 'Further than far to the Land of Nowhere', the story of Nowhere and its lion hunters and the journey by Rouch to Nowhere in search of the hunters, in a magic land where anything is possible and everything true and imaginary.

The expedition to Nowhere 'crossing the great river, the Niger' by ferry comes to the other side where there are villages and where the Land Rovers, like thirsty animals, are given drink. The villages then disappear and there are no longer roads. The expedition finally arrives at Nowhere, surrounded by crystal magic mountains, an enchanted land of myth and ghosts and a real one of villagers, hunters, dust, scrub, giraffes, lions, crocodiles, ostriches, wild boar. There are giant boulders in Nowhere scratched with ancient drawings of animals and of circles with crosses inside them, indecipherable marks of a people Unknown, from before History, almost before Time. The marvellous is encountered once the line has been crossed, a real one (the river Niger) and a mythical one (the river Styx between Earth and Hades). For Rouch, it is a landscape as if from a De Chirico painting, the real seen through a borrowed image and transformed.

The river is a border between narration and action, past and present, the living and the dead, fiction and document, the fantastic and the real. It is the line crossed by the Joyces when they enter Naples to find themselves in a strange opaque magical world of Neapolitan miracles that disorient them.

To arrive Nowhere, to be in the Unknown, faced with the Unidentifiable, is a place richer than Somewhere. Because in not being mapped, or laid out and strange, it seems resistant to the reasonableness of the cartographic. Paths disappear, are erased or blurred, allowing new ones to spring to life, in fact and in fancy. You have to feel your way, as if in the dark, like a caress. It cleanses the eye to enable pure sight, freshens the ear to enable pure sound, is open to imaginings, lost voices, the whisperings and murmurings of the dead, and it is prompted by desire, liberated from reason.

Histoire(s) du cinéma (1988–98) is this kind of film on the Other side where nothing is certain or fixed and where there are no maps. It is so criss-crossed, as full of intersections and dead ends as the ancient uncharted African bush, the utopia of Nowhere. Pleasure is the state of being lost, to dream and imagine as the wide-eyed children imagine a land which is further than far.

Pop

Pop Art reached out not to real things but to images of things, and its aesthetic discipline has consisted in seeing objects as images or sculptures, so that the Bowery or the suburban kitchen becomes for the Pop artist an art exhibition ready for shipment to the international chain of art showcases. Basically, Pop Art is 'found' art, done over, but preserving its original appearance. Its most potent effect is the hallucination of mistaking the street for a museum or like the astonishment of Molière's character on learning that he has for a lifetime been speaking prose, but is unaware of it.

All the images in Godard's *Histoire(s) du cinéma* (1988–98) are almost entirely cited, found images, as are its sounds and speech. There are no real things in *Histoire(s)*, but rather pictures of things, duplicates of things. It is these images and duplications, the citations, that are concrete. The close relation in Godard's films between fiction and the real, the character and the actor, the object and its representation, History and history is like Pop.

> L'image est une création pure
> de l'esprit
> elle ne peut naître d'une comparaison
> c'est vrai
> mais du rapprochement
> de deux réalités
> plus ou moins

éloignées
plus les rapports
de deux réalités
rapprochées sont lointaines et justes
plus l'image sera forte.

(The image is a creation of the mind and is not born by a comparison but by the coming together of two realities more or less distant
from each other. The more the images are distant and just, the
stronger the image will be.)[14]

In effect the image is always constructed by the bringing together of
several elements in reality – an image is a relation which passes through
a process of thought. For Godard, an image does not exist alone. He
emphasises this, paraphrasing Pequignot, to the effect that the force of
an image is a function of the rightness and distance of the two realities
articulated in the image.

Two contrary realities cannot therefore come together. An image is
not strong because it is brutal or fantastic, but as a result of the association of distant and just ideas. For Godard we have only fragmentary
representations. The function of his cinema is to bring these fragments
into a relation with one another by means of its fundamental operation,
which is montage.

Photography alters history by introducing the monument into the document, the insignificant into the significant and by signifying the insignificant. Photography did not itself introduce the insignificant, did not
introduce the everyday and the banal into representation. That situation
was already, in part, a fact in painting (or would soon become so with
Impressionism), that is, its subjects were subjects that were no longer
'worthy' and significant, but rather were instead 'realistic'. This change
widened the subject of representation and at once democratised it, causing its aura to disappear. The very fact of insignificance, linked as it was
to a naturalism and realism, resulted (perhaps) in two things: one, by
reducing the importance of the subject, it gave greater emphasis to form;
and, second, because it was insignificant, it no longer could easily justify

14 Jean-Louis Comolli, Michel Delahaye, Jean-André Fieschi and Gérard Guégan,
'Entretien avec Godard', *Cahiers du cinéma*, no. 171 (October 1965), reprinted in Alain Bergala
(ed.), *Jean-Luc Godard par Jean-Luc Godard*, vol. I, 1950–1984 (Paris: Cahiers du cinéma,
1998), p. 268.

itself thus adding to the image, a commentary upon it, that would be built into it. The photographic work of Garry Winogrand of the 1960s and 1970s is exemplary in this regard.[15]

The usual course of most films is to interiorise an exterior, the real fictionalised. Godard (as critic) notices something quite different. Most generally the presence of an exterior not completely submerged by a fiction, therefore retaining its reality, its trace of an instant and, in doing so, in catching and capturing such moments, the film allows not simply reality, but history to enter into it. The moment is always real (life caught unawares): hence the concern with montage – these moments are always heterogeneous, disjoined – the real is always disruptive – the disconnections of De Chirico as if these objects were in different worlds, certainly different spaces, as with Cubism. And, once again, the trace of Vertov appears.

The image 'redeems' reality by doubling it, as does the citation, at once a cutting out and an emphasis, allowing it to be seen: as when you write, you see, it is a kind of attending to, an attentiveness, a underlining and pointing that allows you to see, like a mirror that doubles. The doubling by the image is also a memory, a rescuing of the image from time. And the image can be seen then as it never has been seen before, like the dance of Gene Kelly and Leslie Caron from *An American in Paris* (1951), because it appears within and side by side to a difference (the brutality and horror of an execution, made all the more horrible because accompanied by a dance of love that transforms and transfers the execution into a dance of death).

For the most part, images in *Histoire(s) du cinéma* are compound ones either because they are constructed by a variety of different kinds of superimpositions or because they are internally breached by a stuttering flicker or by disruptions caused by an extraneous or disjunctive sound, sometimes musical, sometimes natural, that creates a space for a new image to enter, not connected to the one breached. The compound image can also be an effect of a horizontal montage rather than the vertical one of superimpositions and fades, in a disconnection for example between

---

15   This was in 2014 on exhibition at the Metropolitan Museum of Art in New York.

intercut fragments from an American musical, an archival image of the death camps and a pornographic scene, that creates a sense of their co-presence. Even when one image is no longer on the screen, it never quite passes, a trace of it remains in the image that succeeds it as if compelling its return.

Most of the images in *Histoire(s)*, because they are cited (openly or not) and because they belong to a store of existing images, are, strictly speaking, documents, even if they are documents of fictions and other works of art. Though most of the material that composes *Histoire(s)* pre-exists it as images previously shot (and shot by others), the process of reshooting (a recycling), and the editing and arrangement of it in new combinations, no matter how manipulated, seems to suggest that nothing in fact pre-exists either operation. It appears instead (or is organised to appear) that the filming is a response to images and a questioning or marvelling at them, as is the editing. The film is a product of two operations that seem self-generated because the relation between images as projected is indirect and often opaque and because the principles that govern their presence and order are associative and remembered. It is as if the images were calling out to each other from a depth or underworld store of images *and* summoned by memories, personal and social, though between the two there is no strict boundary.

In so far as this may be true, a split is underlined between the reality of these images that pre-exist *Histoire(s)* and the operation of making them present. The split is vertiginous because the images represented by Godard are also representations of their reality that both pre-exist his film and are within it. In both instances, reality, as that which is prior to an image of it, is something that has already been transformed into an image, belonging thereby to the imaginary and to the double reality of itself as image and as reproduction. It marks out the fact, crucial for a history or histories of cinema, that history, rather than being a reflection of the real, is no more so than a film is. Both are representations, a discourse with a syntax (they are ordered) and an ideology (spontaneity or rationality). Yet, it is precisely as discourse that the films cited by *Histoire(s)* and *Histoire(s)* itself are historical since they register the world (document it) at a certain moment in time. Once that occurs they become part of the archive, become document. *Histoire(s)* simultaneously depends on the archive (it cites) and belongs to it. Its procedures are within history and constitute historical evidence by its material, intentions and immediateness. Later films by Godard cite passages and images from *Histoire(s)* as *Histoire(s)* does of earlier Godard films.

Jacques Rancière in an essay on *Histoire(s)* points to what he calls *the* central paradox of the film, namely the assertion by Godard that the cinema failed to live up to its vocation of documenting the real of the death camps and by such inaction betrayed itself, whereas *Histoire(s)* has, on the contrary, realised what it says the cinema has not been able to do. This apparent paradox belongs to a more comprehensive one, namely the position taken by *Histoire(s)* that the cinema, in not living up to its duties and the historical task of filming the world (of which the matter of the death camps is an aspect only), therefore cannot truly be called a modern cinema since modernity has to do with the entrance of the real with its disruptive and inexplicable force. In fact, for Godard, the cinema has renounced modernity in contrast to developments in the other arts. It has become inert, paralysed. In order to assert that denial of the cinema of itself and its promise and possibility, *Histoire(s)*, in the way it presents the history of the cinema effectively denies the denial. It is the contrary evidence of what it asserts.[16]

Every image in *Histoire(s)* represents something. Above all else it is mate-rial, a real concrete image bearing the imprint of the world and the culture from whence it came. No image in the film loses its materiality or exceeds it, in fact citation guarantees it. Even though the image is relocated in a series of images in *Histoire(s)*, that is, enters an artis-tic world, its place elsewhere and its materiality derived from that else-where are never compromised. The image might just as well be a sock, shoe or piece of newsprint implanted in an installation, for example, a Rauschenberg Combine. The reality of the image as image creates a new way of regarding *Histoire(s)* by locating it, as *Histoire(s)* locates every image it has borrowed, in a real space with definite volume, depth and a history beyond the artistic analogies for *Histoire(s)* that have been adopted from the other arts.

Histoire(s) is a real object, one of whose attributes is to register the world in a discourse that informs it primarily by the way the film reflects

16 Jacques Rancière, 'Le cinéma dans la "fin" de l'art', *Cahiers du cinéma*, no.552 (December 2000), pp. 50–1.

on the workings of the cinema and its possibilities to bring together incompatible and distant things in such a way as to affirm and secure their particularity and virtuality, a closeness of estrangement that functions in his film as a rule.

> Godard has no ideal aesthetic norm, nothing programmatic, no manifesto as is the case with modernism. His concern is to explore the nature of cinema as an instrument for encountering reality, and not a respect for some a priori conception of this instrument, however seductive or noble it might be.[17]

17 Jacques Aumont, 'The Medium', in Raymond Bellour and Mary Lee Bandy (eds), *Jean-Luc Godard: Son + Image 1974–1991* (New York: The Museum of Modern Art, 1992), p. 212.

Portraiture

The 'author–*auteur*' appears in the disjunctions and hiatuses not as the artist who creates the complete work but rather in the formula of Godard, 'the work and the idea of the work', 'the work and the theory of the work', the presence of the author as critic and as reflecting on the work and its processes, questioning what the work is and so completely as to efface the author – in the tradition of the *Nouvelle Vague*.

In the Poe story as related by the young man to Anna Karina, in Godard's *Vivre sa vie* (1962), the portrait takes life as it ebbs away symetrically from the young wife of the painter and, as he finishes the portrait, brings it and her to life, she, in life, dies. But this 'life' is purely fictional, itself only a mirror and this lure and feint is infinite. In the case of the film, that mirror is in the Nana from Renoir and the Nana from Zola and the Anna (Karina) who is the model for the artist (Godard). Her death in the film (a Hawksian death) brings her to life like Stracci's (and Christ's) in Pasolini's comedy, parody, blasphemy, *La ricotta* (1963). And of course it brings to life Oscar Wilde's 1891 enquiry into representation, *The Picture of Dorian Gray*.

Memories of films are always accompanied by their fictions, narratives and images. Memory is all of these things. If, on the one hand, in *Histoire(s) du cinéma* (1988–98) there are various strategies for creating simultaneity and verticality, one thing within, above or below another, between these occurrences at the same time is also a space, because what is emphasised, paradoxically, is that the images of things or images of other images, though occurring in the film at the same moment, are distant in time and in space. They are historically, and from certain points of view, remote, and, in ways not always explicable or clear, also close.

Every photographed and filmed image is a double of the reality of which it is the image. The modern arts have played with this duplicity, the conversion of reality into a sign. They have also resisted it, pointing to the process by serialisation, repetition, parody, excessive artifice, or by distortion. The double (the image) is always second to the original. This is true, and absurdly so, when a found object is simply displaced from the toilet or the bedroom to the museum floor. If, as in serialisation, staggering, stuttering, repetition, displacement, singularity is destroyed, so too along with it is the original in part for the deferral in time, in part for the seeming infinitude of duplication (mass production and serialisation), in part because the double introduces difference in the gap between it and the original, and because each repetition of the same is a divergence, especially if it coincides exactly with the original and so much so as to force a new point of view against any illusion, as with found objects or found images. The double is always a variant.

Most of Godard's actors play multiple roles within a single film, founded on the essential difference between the actor who plays a part and becomes a character and the character who makes it clear that the actor is ever present as when the character steps out of the fiction to become the actor once again commenting on the fiction and on his or her role within it. Or, Godard creates a situation where the character is a close double of the actor in reality, as if in imitation of self.

In *Histoire(s)*, there are many Godards, playing different roles being angry, reflective, comic, dressed, half-dressed, pensive, aggressive, shy, crude, lyrical, orchestrating, typing, editing, filming, and to each of these are attached different voices. The citations in the film can be thought of as so many impersonations by Godard issuing from his memories and associations as various as moods and the characters he plays. As with all self-portraits, the image is the consequence of an attempt to find the artist by the artist, but in *Histoire(s)* the doubling, tripling, multiplications by Godard of Godard are difficult to explain or locate. What appears are Godard traces, phantom Godards, and, in so far as the associations are not evident, motivated or close, their obscurity and distance lead to a distorted self-portraiture and to the question of what it was that created the associations and at what point in time. Since the pasts in the citations are historical, cultural and artistic, the film enters an immensity where nothing, least of all Godard, is definite.

Randomness

The cited images and sounds of Godard's *Histoire(s) du cinéma* (1988–98) are both random and ordered. They seem random because their relation to each other is obscure, distant and unpredictable. They seem ordered because there are themes, configurations and regularities, filled with semantic possibilities, that invite interpretation and codification yet frustrate the attempt at these because the regularities are tenuous and unstable, in constant transformation.

Any random series can become constrictive. Networks of associations form, necessarily, no matter how ungovernable they may appear. In *Histoire(s)*, because signs multiply and proliferate in abundance, they become dense and opaque. For example, Rossellini, Hitchcock, Jerry Lewis, neorealism, Lang, innocence, beauty, violence, childhood, monstrosities, hands, eyes, the camera, the gun, focusing, aiming, writing, spying, the Holocaust, Sarajevo, Mozart, Hollywood, Murnau, Dreyer, Welles, death, Rembrandt, Manet, greed, photography, technology, light, voyaging, discovery, experiment, time, control, the *Nouvelle Vague*, dancing, executions, massacres, and History and stories. These singular groupings in turn come into contact with each other, at some points coalesce, seep, spill over and associate, often by a hidden rhyme, rhythm or tone which alters everything. Such themes or subjects are reiterated and literally thicken. As they appear, new associations appear with them, new connections, and, as these occur, wanderings and disconnections begin to be made and the random series that seemed to have become regularised appears again as random.

One configuration is the relation between the visual and the verbal, not their mutual support but, on the contrary, their distance from each other and their irreducibility, particularly since the film suggests that one of the crimes of the past inflicted upon the cinema was the subordination of images to the literary, the word, the script, narrative, intrigue. In practice, the film does not renounce the verbal, but rather detaches it from its customary roles. *Histoire(s)* is not only a visual experience (freed from the word) nor an intellectual, discursive one (freed from interpretation, narration and commentary). Instead it is a play of the interaction of signs, verbal, visual, graphic, cited or staged, no matter what their construction, meandering and devastation and the participation of an audience in this operational process. It is precisely in the play that *Histoire(s)* dissociates itself from exclusively belonging to the cinema in order to take its place with the other arts and by doing so bringing the whole of the cinema with it.

There are singular ecstatic moments in the film, flashes of comprehension and discovery, when, as if from nowhere, or from far away, from an underworld of memory and the past, in the randomness of travelling and of perpetual multiple motion, a connection suddenly is found, at first dim, then, for an instant, bright, scintillating, and everything is illuminated, made clear, before obscurity descends again; the flash burns itself out, like Edmund's leap into nothingness in Rossellini's *Germania anno zero* (1947) that *Histoire(s)* replays and recalls.

Realism (1)

Classical art was considered art by the clarity of the order that it created (an artistic order). The terms which characterised it and the practices of it were harmony, symmetry, balance, lucidity, centring, hierarchy. It was an exceptionally rational and to that degree objective (impersonal) art. These qualities were evidence of the fabricated (artistic) nature of the work and the ideal order that was created. Nature was made over to conform to these ideals recognised and accepted as beautiful as defined by a tradition.

There was a potential dissonance and hence threat to classicism between the ideal of forms (abstract) and the nature that was being formed by it (concrete, disorderly). The dissonance was held back by a search for the ideal in nature such that the real and the artistic were not at odds but companions. The invention of perspective for example in the fifteenth century created a geometric space formed from a single fixed point of view that centred, measured all things along a line of sight. The ideal representation of space (balanced, harmonised) was taken to be a true representation of it, and that in turn at once necessary and beautiful (pleasing).

The arts of the nineteenth century (Romanticism, realism, naturalism) upset this system. They created a dissonance that had been present by pressing upon two essential aspects: the abstract (the work of art) and the concrete (nature, the real) and in such a way that the real issued forth as a direct criticism of the ideal and in so doing shifted the terms in which art was understood and appreciated. Impressionism, for example, tried to find what was in fact perceived, and alongside it the uncertainty of perception, and thus turned away from an objective rendering to a subjective one. While classicism celebrated the formality of its means to create an ideal picture, the new realism of Impressionism was primarily concerned with the act of perception and thereby the work of realising the action of painting and the time, light and colours that filled that time and came to be the subject of the work. On the one hand, it made the work of art its subject: not simply an instrument to represent something (nature, an idea), a set of procedures and relations (between art and reality) open to questioning and analysis. On the other hand, it was more responsive to reality, not as material to shape but as an activity to document, however disorderly, unfixed, multiple, heterogeneous and even ugly it might appear (the unnatural postures of figures in a Degas painting or of colours in a Van Gogh, or shapes and unbalanced lines in a Picasso). The characteristic of modern reality is its plurality and variability; classical reality was singular and fixed.

Thornton Wilder was an American poet, essayist, novelist and dramatist. In the late 1920s, he wrote *The Bridge of San Luis Rey*. The book is written in a pastiche of eighteenth-century French writing. It takes the form of writing from the past and points to it as if the novel is no more than a literary citation and at the same time a report of an actual event recorded at the time (a historical document). Thus, it has two features: classical perfection and elegance on the one hand and historical chronicle on the other. The story relates to the collapse of a bridge over a gorge in Peru in the eighteenth century resulting in the death of five people. A monk, who witnessed the tragedy, asks the question of why these five people were selected by God to suffer this fate. The answer, the monk supposes, lies in the particular histories of these five people. The novel is (ambiguously) the detailed account by the monk of the lives and characters of the five victims. It may also be the account of the writer. The telling of these stories, rather than clarifying the issue of why the five victims were chosen and what if anything they had in common, arrives at no clear explanation. The project of the writing – lucid, elegant, literary, beautiful – never attains its apparent end of clarification and explanation (its rationality and orderliness literally goes nowhere). To the contrary, what is left is a labyrinth of stories, interwoven fates, questions, possible pathways, hypothetical relations, at best separate disjoined narratives seeking explanations that prove elusive. The monk who initiates the inquest is burned at the stake by the Church for offering a view of the collapse of the bridge and the reasons for it that the Church regarded as unacceptable.

The project of the writing to reach a conclusion is thwarted as if the writing arrives empty-handed and in the end is only itself, only writing, since the facts surpass any attempt to give it a form and thereby all that remains is the writing as a trace of an attempt. What is represented in fact collapses, writing with no other object or pleasure than itself. The stories are at once what the writing produces and the background that exhibits the writing, albeit to little purpose, of little effective representation. All that is told tells very little.

Welles's America is not that of Hawks and Ford, not the film culture of Hollywood, but an intellectual, literary, theatrical, political and artistic America, the America of Thornton Wilder, for example, where a modern novel might echo with the diction of Mme de Sévigné or the America of Hemingway and Gertrude Stein and John Dos Passos where writing is a matter of rhythm and cadence rather than of significance, or the America of Jackson Pollock where the action and energy of painting rather than figuration are at the centre of his work.

Welles's films have four evident features. First, they bring together and overlap different techniques and styles either successively or in a single scene and sometimes within a single shot (depth of field and focal distortions in the attempted suicide of Susan in *Citizen Kane*). Second is the use of shot sequences and excessively detailed montage sequences, for example the opening of *Touch of Evil* and its close that create a gap between sounds and images (they have different references, different rhythms and seem to inhabit different spaces as in the scene of the recording by Vargas of Quinlan's dialogue with Menzies in *Touch of Evil*). Third, there are multiple points of focus in every scene. Welles's use of depth of field creates different pockets of interest that touch each other, collide or overlap, for example Thatcher's visit to the boarding house to take Charles away to be educated in *Citizen Kane*. Fourth is Welles's play with arrivals and exits (on-screen/off-screen), evident with the arrival of different groups at once scattered, dispersed and criss-crossed after the explosion in *Touch of Evil* (1958), and in the labyrinth of Cyprus in *Othello* (1952), where figures are distorted or overblown.

Realism (2)

Between 1943 and 1950, that is during the final years of the war, occupation, the Resistance, the Allied invasion of Italy, liberation (1944), the establishment of the Republic (1948), Antonioni made eleven, relatively short, documentary films. Before that, from 1938 onwards, he had been a film critic on the local paper of his home town of Ferrara, the *Corriere Padano*, and then, when he moved to Rome in 1939 on the journals *Cinema* and *Film d'oggi*.

Cinema was a fortnightly journal founded in the mid-1930s and directly subsidised by the Fascist government. The editor of the journal was Vittorio Mussolini, the son of the Fascist leader, Benito Mussolini. The editorial board of the journal, which included Luchino Visconti, also comprised critics who represented new and unconventional views on the cinema, some of whom were clandestine members of the Italian Communist Party (PCI) and the Italian Resistance. It was in *Cinema* from 1938 onwards that the first formulations of a new socially aware, socially committed Italian cinema, later referred to as *neorealismo*, began to appear. Though it is possible to see in these formulations and in neorealism a cultural and artistic opposition to fascism, it is equally possible to see that, because such formulations could take place during the fascist period, either fascism or neorealism or both have to be differently understood.

Antonioni's writings on film in this period of fascism, war, Resistance, social and economic distress were untypical of the writing about film at this time and on the journals and newspapers he wrote for. There is no indication in any of his writings of the events that were taking place in

Italy, or any trace of their consequences, nor is there any sense that he preferred or sought a cinema that was social, nationalist or political. He confined himself to discussions about the mechanisms and forms of film: colour, editing, performance, lighting, sound, music, structures of narration. And though, like his colleagues, particularly on *Cinema*, he called for a new and experimental cinema, it was form and structure, not subject and ideology, that interested him. If anything, there is in his writings on film a distaste for the kind of cinema that would be called neorealist, and not because he objected to its politics, on the contrary, but because he had a different view of the world than the one that informed neorealism and therefore a different view of the cinema.

Italian neorealism, best represented perhaps by the films of De Sica (not Rossellini), had two characteristics. One was the conventionality of its narratives and other was its rigorous objectivity. It told stories that directly reflected social situations and depicted men and women caught up in these situations. The stories were stories of how they coped with these social realities and in part of the characters as representative of these realities. Antonioni had a different interest and it is from that difference that the whole of his cinema derives. It is, in one sense, a very simple proposition, yet one characteristic of the modern cinema and perhaps of modernism more generally, namely that reality is a relation and that the relation involves our view of things (not simply as they are, but as they are imagined and felt to be) and that view is always necessarily personal and shifting. Fundamentally, for Antonioni, objective reality and thereby a stable reality were false, and part of their falsity was the sense of their singularity and homogeneity. The only true thing you could say about reality was that it was unstable, primarily subjective and thereby heterogeneous. Thus the subject that interested him was not the relation of characters to the world but the relation of characters to themselves and thereby to others and thereby to the world.

Rather than the emphasis characteristic of neorealism on social solidarity in a world to be transformed in a direction towards greater solidarity, progress and achievement, Antonioni depicted a world of individual separateness, psychological isolation, intense fragmentation and disconnection and an inability to find anything solid or permanent. Relations were both the sign of that difficulty, the consequence of it and, as well, the cause of it. Nothing in any case was clear, and certainly not beginnings or ends, causes or motives, and not only for stories and characters, but for films depicting these.

The dissatisfaction in De Sica's *Ladri di biciclette* (1948) ('Bicycle thieves' and not as in a characteristic American mistranslation 'Bicycle thief') is unemployment and all that followed from that (needing a bicycle, losing a bicycle, trying to recover a bicycle): that is, the dissatisfaction was primarily social, easily identified and resolvable. The narrative of it was straightforward and clear. However distressing the social reality depicted, it could be, unproblematically, depicted. Dissatisfaction in Antonioni's films is different: it is centred on an inability to grasp oneself and to relate to others and primarily because of the indefiniteness, the lack of clarity and the uncertainty of the boundary and outline to things and not only in what Antonioni depicted but in the manner of his depictions.

First, *Cronaca di un amore* (1950) concerns not the poor and the socially underprivileged but the very rich whose problems are not so clear-cut as a search for a bicycle so much as they are problems about a search for satisfactions of a different order, primarily psychological and emotional and which cannot be simply resolved but are a condition of existence. Second, it is not the reality of things that Antonioni stresses but rather their unreality, their lack of identity, their lack of clarity, their lack of order, their vagueness and ungraspability, not the fullness of the world but its emptiness, a void.

The film begins as a search for certainty based not on an objective reality but on an unease for which there is no concrete evidence except (and this is crucial) a group of photographs, the ambiguity of images. From this nothing or at least this nothing that is not anything very solid or precise, a story or perspective begins to emerge, a certain way of looking and understanding, that is, a certain security, but that security in turn dissolves, becomes decentred and unstable and not simply because of feelings and sentiments in the characters, a subjectivity that erodes the objective and concrete, but because Antonioni has a way of looking, of creating images that destabilise: an overlap between the objective and subjective, the use of multiple framings that divide and fragment (gates, windows, doorways, corridors, stairs), landscapes that have no centre, no activity, no action to give them sense and that appear as metaphysical, the obscuring of things by rain, fog, light reflections, unusual angles, rapid movement, locations that are disturbed by the constancy of movement, transport, accident and a certain way of holding shots beyond the point of their action and initiating shots before an action, stressing a shape and a narrative emptiness rather than mere background and the completeness of actions. Antonioni takes this process of dissolution further so that, for example, the reality that is dissolved is dissolved into something else that is abstract (lines, light, shape) and informal, while these, in turn, begin to coalesce into new shapes, new stories, new directions, new possibilities. The constant reshaping and dissolution are the story of *Cronaca di un amore* – the chronicle of a love affair – created out of nothing and into which it disappears. What remains, the only solidity, is the film as a record of that instability and that includes itself as if the film is its own document, not a mirror but a document, reportage.

Realities

Rossellini's *Paisà* was made in 1946, a few years after the events it depicts. It is composed of six episodes that trace the course of the war in Italy from the Allied invasion of Sicily in 1943 to the end of the Italian campaign in 1945. The film begins in Sicily, then moves north to Naples, then to Florence, then Emilia Romagna and concludes in the Po valley. Each episode is different in setting, in the events depicted and in their characters. The continuity between the episodes is purely geographical (south to north) and all involve a meeting of Italians with their particular culture and gestures and the Allied soldiers with theirs.

In the usual course of most films, 'realities' of location, persons, events outside the film are brought into its interior and fictionalised. These realities are transmuted: persons become characters, locations settings, events drama. From the late 1930s, and not only in film but also in painting and literature, the 'real' made an entry in its own right into works of art. The work was conceived no longer as a make-believe transformation of reality but as a space in which realities and fictions, different from each other and from different sources, were set side by side. (In literature the best examples are Hemingway and Dos Passos in America, Céline in France, Vittorini and Gadda in Italy.) If traditional works eliminated differences between realities and between the fictional and the real, these more contemporary ones emphasised them. The art work – this was especially true in painting and the novel – was like a collage of different and sometimes disconnected elements. In painting, and painting that increasingly resembled sculpture (the collages of Picasso, Robert Rauschenberg Combines,

Jasper Johns flags), the presence of such realities stood out. Paintings (and sculpture-paintings) contained 'real' objects: wheels, Coca-Cola bottles, Brillo boxes, bits of newspaper, stuffed chickens, stuffed goats, bicycle seats. Or banal things were reproduced in paint in which the paint, rather than hiding behind the object, was stressed and became an object in its own right (paint as the subject of painting, words and their sounds and rhythms as the subjects of writing). In this way the differences between the reality of things and the representation of them were simultaneously blurred and emphasised, for example, the series of American flag paintings and paintings of archery targets by Johns made in the 1950s.

Not only were 'real' objects made present but also the materials traditionally effaced by the scene painted were made to stand out, at times 'against' the scene even though responsible for having realised it (Johns's paintings again). The canvas or the board were no longer hidden by the scene painted upon it or the marble forgotten for the figures sculpted with it, but rather these materials were declared for what they were: canvas, metal, wood, cloth, paper or stone, as much a part of the painting as what it depicted. Often the subject of the word was ordinary and banal as to seem a parody, certainly of the exalted and the beautiful (Johns's flags, Warhol's Campbell Soup Cans). It is interesting in this regard that Rossellini so resisted the beautiful and the noble for the sake of the everyday.

The sharp division that had characterised the arts for centuries between the world and the art object, between an outside reality and an interior composition based upon it, between the real and the illusion of a verisimilitude, between the actual and its reflection, were called into question. Sometimes, this was an interrogation, sometimes a blurring. It involved not only the inclusion of real objects but the bringing into the art work of fragments of other works either artistic or belonging to the mass culture of reproductions: a postcard of a Leonardo, a passage from a novel, an imitation of a style, a photograph of Marilyn Monroe, a soup can, a citation from a film, the reproduction of an advertisement (the Esso signs, the Omo boxes, the razor clip in Godard's films).

Most importantly, these citations, the incorporation of an outside into the interior of a film or a painting, resulted in the marking out of a difference between the two as well as the difference between texts including the text that contained these citations, a text made up in its interior of all that was exterior to it and was emphasised to be exterior. The most crucial aspect of such citations was formal and, although some writers have attempted to engage in an iconological exercise of their meaning and associations (the references in Godard's films and especially his *Histoire(s) du cinéma* (1988–98) whose texture and substance is composed exclusively of references), their significance is elsewhere. It was not Marilyn Monroe that was important or Campbell soup cans in such citations but the differences in substance and appearance that her image constituted and the formal relational issues it raised of reality to painting, photograph to painting, duplication to original, thus they were not designed primarily to think about Marilyn as much as to think about painting, film, photography, images, methods, the ways of the text, how it was made and not what it signified.

Rossellini always had a general idea of the film he wanted before it was made, but never had a shooting script, never a *découpage*, never the film carefully laid out beforehand. His films developed as they were being made at the moment of their making rather than being a putting into image of a prior plan. He relied on the setting he had chosen to suggest how scenes were to be shot. The decision was, for the most part, last-minute: how an actor looked, walked, spoke, gestured in life determined for Rossellini what the actor would do and say in film. None of this could be planned in advance. He had to see the actor and then 'follow' what the actor inspired, rather than the actor following Rossellini. Dialogue and actions were given to an actor just before they were to be enacted and spoken to keep them fresh, not simply an illustration.

Rossellini's filming may seem rough. He did not rely on multiple takes in search of the right one or the beautiful one, but preferred an immediacy that would preserve the moment and glow of a performance and action. It was the momentary and thereby for him the real and true that were important not 'finish' in the usual sense. It was what he 'found' while filming (like Rauschenberg's objects found as he wandered through New York, and the bric-a-brac picked up by chance and placed in boxes by Joseph Cornell), rather than what he wished to demonstrate, that mattered: inspiration not planning, what arrived by chance rather than what was predetermined. And this included the situation he created for his actors, most of whom were not professionals (Carmela, Harriet, Massimo, the black soldier, the street urchin, the partisans in the Po valley, the monks in the monastery) and thus did not bring with them the conventions of making

believe, of 'acting' to convince, to express a soul. Filming (and performance) were adventures for Rossellini, a lightness of touch and being, a
sketch to seize the precious fragility and momentariness of reality.

The long takes and shot sequences noticeable in Rossellini's films have
two functions. One, to follow a scene as it develops rather than cutting it
up and reconstructing it, and, two, to find the rhythm of things.

In the first episode in Sicily, between Joe and Carmela in the lookout
tower, or in the Rome episode between Fred and Francesca in the hotel
room, or in the Florentine episode between Massimo and Harriet, in each
episode the search for someone or something that had been lost, Rossellini
builds up a sense of waiting and expectation, dilating and stretching time,
not by slowing it down but by drawing it out simply by having nothing
happen as if the sequence never quite 'arrives' or goes anywhere very
definite. But when it does, when at last it arrives, when the waiting is over,
when Joe is shot and Carmela sacrifices herself, when the partisan dies in
Harriet's arms and she discovers in his last words the fate of Lupo, when
Fred throws the note away before boarding a lorry back to the front and
Francesca waits for him in vain dressed as the young girl whom he had
forgotten, all the waiting and stretched-out time is illuminated in a sudden
flash and the whole of the film ignites. The illumination is not explanation
or interpretation but the illumination of a situation, of the facts of it and
its circumstance, in short, for Rossellini, its reality that asserts itself, that
'comes' and in all its multiplicity.

The usual sense of a cut in a film is to construct an accord of action and
sense, if only that of continuity between scenes and the shots that compose them. Rossellini tended to cut when actions seemed to be completed
and finished, exhausted. He cut seldom if ever to create an accord but
rather to establish an ellipsis between actions or moments, a difference
and a contrast, discords (Fred and Francesca) or blanks (in the conversation between Carmela and Joe, the black soldier and the Neapolitan boy).
Repugnance for Rossellini was explanation and interpretation. He cut
just before they might surface.

Rossellini's cinema is a cinema of subtraction, minimalisation almost
to the point of abstraction, a paring down to an unusual concreteness,
even banality: a cigarette lit by Joe in the dark, in the barrenness of the
tower to illuminate a photograph that causes his death, a piece of paper
thrown away by Fred with the address of Francesca, two English officers

discussing Giotto's Bell Tower like tourists as a bitter partisan struggle wages, a bar of chocolate in a monastery and the exaggerated gratefulness of a monk. Rossellini does not so much create scenes as drain them (the opposite of Visconti). Not only is there an ellipsis between one action and another but there are ellipses, disconnections, minimalisations within a given action and scene, reduced down to the idea of it and lacking the guidance of an explanation, of clear motivation or a precise logic of continuity, hence the sense that when something 'arrives', it seems to come from nowhere, or from 'reality' (or *is* reality): the black soldier in the bowels of the Neapolitan caves suddenly understands, the news of Lupo's death that comes to Harriet like a stray bullet that had come to the dying soldier she cradled in her arms.

The crucial act is not that Carmela will sacrifice herself or that Harriet discovers that Lupo is dead, or that Fred does not connect the Francesca he first met with his encounter six months later with Francesca the whore, or that the black soldier realises the truth of his situation and the situation of the Neapolitan boy and where each of them is placed, but how, and more importantly when, these moments of consciousness, revelation and sacrifice occur. It is not only Francesca, Harriet, the black soldier, the partisans, the American pastors and Carmela who wait, but the film that waits.

What are not joined in *Paisà* are the different levels of reality that are made evident, are not smoothed over, effaced or joined up, not completely thereby fictionalised and homogenised. In fact, it is these differences, the between of things, that is both the motor and the subject of the film. The final moments of the episodes, moments essentially of some kind of revelation, of a violent or profound change not so much in circumstance but in comprehension (the shabbiness, even faithlessness of the American chaplains in contrast to the innocence and nobility of the monk) are what emerges from out of the film's gaps and elisions, of what is not known, not seen when characters are faced with the realities of things and of themselves: war, distress, loneliness, isolation – where they are, who they are, what is going on, a confrontation with what is 'other' to them, beyond their usual understandings and culture.

There is not one reality in the film, but multiple ones of multiple differences, which resonate. *Paisà* mixes fictional occurrences with documentary material, the essential point of which (and it is here that there is a connection between Renoir and Rossellini, and Rossellini and Rivette) is a realisation (or not) by the characters (or the audience) of the 'reality' that surrounds them and that is the cause, in one form or another, of a crisis brought on by differences including that between the film and the reality it seeks to find, between fiction and document.

Carmela is not simply the character 'Carmela', but also Carmela Sazio, the daughter of a Sicilian fisherman, who simultaneously meets Joe from Jersey (in the film) and Robert Van Loon, the American soldier who plays him (in life). There is throughout the film this back-and-forth relation between the real and the make-believe in such a way that their difference is sensed, the one appearing in the other and the other making the one appear.

Such differences make strange. Out of that strangeness comes awareness. Rossellini's films, from first to last, are didactic, concerned with knowledge opposed to illusion and it is that relation, that confrontation, that his films press upon: hence, in *Paisà*, the search in almost every episode for something not there or at least not evident, only to be found, suddenly and tragically and miraculously – a reality that had always been there but unnoticed. To be found, to appear, required the time of waiting and watching to realise the falseness of what had been sought and the truth that had been lost, a realisation at once instantaneous and desperate.

Reproduction

There are scenes in Godard's film *Passion* (1982) that, at different points in the film, famous paintings from the seventeenth, eighteenth and nineteenth centuries by Velazquez, Manet, Rembrandt, Goya, Delacroix are set in scene by costumes, decor, lighting and the positioning of actors. In some of these scenes, the Requiem of Mozart or the Requiem of Gabriel Fauré can be heard. The scenes are staged replicas of the paintings, like living tableaux, without any attempt to dissemble the replication by absorbing what is staged into the fiction, for example the way Bertolucci does in *Novecento* (1967) where the strike of peasant workers is based on a painting of the same subject. Rather than the scenes of the Godard being naturalised as if issuing from a fictionalised reality, they seem, on the contrary, to be visible citations of works of art outside the film without being incorporated within it. In the Bertolucci, for example, the strike of the rural peasantry based on a painting is seamlessly connected with the fictional action as if the painting was at best only a scenic model. In the Godard, the paintings are stressed (to a degree they are parodied) rather than masked and hidden. In the Bertolucci, the painting is effaced as a painting; in the Godard, it is emphasised as a painting and as a citation. These are scenes filmed for a film being made within the film called *Passion* (a citation of the Passion of the Christ and of passions more generally, for art, for example, the passion of Godard). A series of mirrors and borders are constructed between painting and film, between one film and another, between different historical periods, and between what you see and what you hear: the music, the sounds of the set, the cues of the character who is the director within the film and the presence of Godard outside it. All of these elements are separated out, recognisable in their particularity and independence, rather than smoothed out such that any accords are seen exactly as accords (montage linkages) that have been shaped without any 'natural' necessity in their composition and connections. Montage, in this sense, is not simply an instrument illustrating a story but the subject of what is presented, hence not only are the paintings cited but the citation of them is cited, the montage that brings them into existence. Thus you have scenes that point to the painting that composes them (cited rather than represented) and point to the film and its mechanisms that picture them (the film citing itself) and also the music of Fauré and Mozart as equally citations.

What you see (and hear) in *Passion* is characteristic of much of Godard's work and of strategies of the modern cinema whereby what is given to the audience is given in fragments and everything seen and heard is made subject to some kind of dismantling in part by strategies of citation, by parody and by the juxtapositions of apparently unrelated objects, settings and historical periods. In one sequence, for example, you see a television camera crew filming the tableaux of a painting in turn being filmed by the film, you hear Fauré's Requiem and you see a scenic filmic reproduction by actors of Rembrandt's *The Night Watch*, all simultaneously, all on diffferent registers, all of different origins and all overlapped. The lines and differences between objects and materials are emphasised rather than hidden, nor is the film hidden. The relation between film and what is filmed is not transparent, that which is filmed effacing the filming of it, and, just as in the Godard film, differences are not effaced between the film and the making of it, between what is stated and the stating of it, so too nothing that is presented therefore is false or illusory or strictly speaking make-believe since make-believe and the putting into scene, and the act of filming, are indicated for what they are, in their separateness, independence and difference. It is precisely representational illusions and above all an illusion of relatedness, consequence and homogeneity that the film exposes. Everything is true and real, but what is lacking are the various strategies and rules of a verisimilitude and the façade of a realism. Even the fiction of the film, such as it is, has its fictional quality so underlined that the film seems to be citing itself and commenting upon itself as if it is its own subject rather than an instrument to illustrate some other subject, for example the fortunes of the Valastros in *La terra trema* or the house of Salina in *Il Gattopardo* (1963). In a Godard film, the reality

of the film and the reality of its images are set side by side as differences
rather than overlaid as sameness and made imperceptible.

In *Il gattopardo*, the scenes of the Garibaldini in their red shirts fighting
with Bourbon troops in the streets of Palermo are staged as a copy of a
nineteenth-century naturalist painting of the period; the same is true
of the scene of the picnic taken by the family of the house of Salina
as they proceed to Donnafugata; similarly the ball scene is a replica of
period paintings while the music of the scene is that of Verdi (a previously unperformed waltz) and the entire film mimics both theatrical
and operatic melodrama. In fact, much of *Il gattopardo* takes its visual
models from the Italian *macchiaioli* of the nineteenth century. But, as
with Bertolucci, these are neither references nor citations, but merely
material to be absorbed into the story and fiction. In Godard's film,
scenes are citations and are starred as such. In the Visconti film they
are woven into the fabric of the fiction (as if to say this is the way things
were in nineteenth-century Sicily), like a painting brought to life or more
exactly a memory recalled (cultural and actual simultaneously as in a
Proust novel) and re-enacted. At the picnic, the real (of the setting, the
decor, the implements, the food, accents) is doubly aestheticised: the
culture of an era of painting and the fact of the real both transformed on
the set into a narrative fiction. The image is at once a duplicate of the real
and a duplicate of the culture that produced that reality and of which the
culture is part, a culture that Visconti is attracted to while being aware at
the same time that it no longer exists. The film is not so much a revival
of the past as a melancholy remembrance of it, melancholy and nostalgia
touched by the funereal.

In the ball scene, which was shot in the Palazzo Gangi in Palermo, the
staging is meant to be taken as real, that is, really a nineteenth-century
Sicilian palazzo (which it is). Thus while the real is made to be like the
false or artificial (the palazzo as film set) and the false or staged like
the real (the film set as a palazzo), the two are so confounded as to be
indistinguishable, the opposite of the strategies of Godard. In Visconti,
the presence of the past can exist only in the illusions and fragility of
an image of reality. For Godard, the present of the past (Fauré, Mozart,
Rembrandt, Velazquez) exists only as style and form, not to evoke the
past but rather to be instruments for a new artistic future. The *macchiaioli*
painters, Verga, Lampedusa (the author of the novel *Il gattopardo*) are

brothers to Visconti who share similar values and culture. For Godard, the artists he cites are brothers of a different kind, artists who share a passion for capturing what is not yet rather than what has been. It is what has been that Visconti seeks to preserve and document, the film as its memory and its story of disappearance, and thereby the story of the need and provocation and origin of the film, hence the 'mimeticism' of Visconti and the 'writing' of Godard.

Returns

The citations in *Histoire(s) du cinéma* (1988–98) are not its models, nor exemplary, but simply material, elements in a surface assembly like a collage. The movement of the film forward is also a movement in reverse. Godard's montage transforms a previous image by a subsequent one such that the future does not come *after* but *before*. In general, and in its details, and at each moment, the film is a return to overlapping past(s) of the cinema, of the film, of Godard's own past. The returns are like memories, incursions into an unconscious depth that comes to the surface unannounced.

Literally, and constantly, the past is subjected to unforeseen transformations heading toward an unknown future. It is not that the past is the future but rather that the future is a rearrangement of returns. Such returns are neither stable nor controlled, but perpetual, shifting and open.

Every film of Godard's is so structured and, though, often, there is a principal underlying text, the films are not imitations or adaptations but a recycling of them as one element among others, recalled to be dismantled, dismembered, reconstructed and questioned, a return that moves forward.

Most films transform the world into images as if the world is the metaphor of cinema. Despite Godard's characterisation of the cinema as having a privileged relation to reality which he argues is its responsibility to maintain, not a single one of his films can be thought of as a documentary, at least not in the sense of simple reproduction. Nor are they narratives as is usually understood. Rather more than telling a story, they privilege the 'writing' of the film, discourse not representation, interrogation not chronicle or history. Though concerned with encountering reality and revealing it, it is an encounter mediated by images and their relation to each other that take precedence as if, to discover reality, you need first to change it into an image and then the image must change in its encounter with other images. What is primary is not the camera, recording, but the reconstruction, the montage.

The images in the film cited from other films are rendered as pure surface and form, like the repeated, staccato images of Ethan Edwards picking up Debbie in his arms in Ford's *The Searchers* (1956) or the montage of fragments from Italian postwar films to the beat of the music and words of Riccardo Cocciante. It is not that these images have been deprived of their former substance, but rather that their substance has been redefined. They are retained but reworked, recognisable but decontextualised, still figurative but functioning as forms. Because unencumbered by their former place, detached from previous contexts, they are free to encounter each other, to become part of new networks, having entered the depths of the past to return with a flower as evidence of having been.

The history of the cinema is not the subject of Godard's film but its instrument to conduct us to entirely unfamiliar places by means of the familiar made strange.

> La Nouvelle Vague s'est définie d'abord par le réalisme de ses thèmes et de son langage ... Mais rapidement, et grâce à Godard, cette revendication d'un cinéma davantage en prise directe avec la vie (donc plus réaliste), s'est transformée en une revendication d'une liberté d'écriture ... Tout se passe alors comme si la chose, la réalité, et la croyance qu'elles impliquent, étaient soudain évacuées au profit d'une interrogation sur l'image, sur les 'rapports de production' de l'image. L'image godardienne n'est plus (si elle fut jamais) transparente aux choses, elle s'opacifie et se simplifie dangereusement pour ne plus signifier qu'elle-même.
>
> (The *Nouvelle Vague* defined itself first of all by the realism of its themes and language ... But very soon, and thanks to Godard, this claim of a cinema that more directly seized upon life (and was

therefore more realistic) was transformed into a claim for the freedom of writing (*écriture*) ... It was as if the thing, the reality, and the
belief they involved, were suddenly emptied to the advantage of
a questioning of the image, of the 'relations of production' of the
image. The Godardian image is no longer (as if it ever was) transparent to things; it obscures and severely simplifies them in order to
signify nothing but itself.)[18]

18 Pascal Bonitzer, *Le Champ aveugle, essais sur le réalisme au cinéma* (Paris: Cahiers au
cinéma, 1999), pp. 92–3.

Theatre

There are three filmmakers who are present in every Rivette film: Renoir (for the sense of theatre and improvisation and the idea that the entry into the false, into play and theatre and roles, is a path to the truth of things), Rossellini (for the virtues of the imperfect, the heterogeneity and mismatch of different realities, chance and the arrival of the miraculous, the secret, the mystery ... suddenly, without apparent cause as the source of the energy and delight of cinema), and Bresson (for the purity of cin-ematic forms, *mise en scène* as an instrument to order space and time, to seek out and discover what the reality of things might yield – every film, then, an experiment).

These are less influences than presences. It is as if the cinema is a vast house, and in the house a family, and as you go about your business, you encounter the other members of the family and they remind you of things, and you chat with them, and you remember. *Va savoir* (2001), unmistakably, is a conversation with Renoir and in particular with *Le Carosse d'or* (1952) and *La Règle du jeu* (1939). There is the same to-ing and fro-ing between identities, the play of theatre and the play of life, and the inversion of the relation by Rivette in contrast to *Le Carosse d'or* and Renoir's homage to Italian theatre and the figure of Camille in the later film and Camilla (played by the Italian actress Anna Magnani) in the earlier one.

There are three aspects of the Rivettian method.

First, Rivette's films are lengthy, three – sometimes four – hours long, in one instance originally twelve hours. Watching them however is not difficult; they are long, but do not feel so. They seem to be aerated, lightened as if the length is necessary for the sense of momentariness and immediacy, of buoyancy. In part, this has to do with method. Rivette seldom cries out 'cut' to a performance. He permits it to run its course in order for it to arrive at something by itself, allowing the film its own life, not forcing it. Thus, Rivette adds (Bresson subtracts for similar reasons) in order to make more subtle, more nuanced, more playful and possible and thus, more aerial. Rivette's films fly, but to fly, they need to risk, at every moment, a possible disaster, a fall, *cadere*, a *cadenza*. It is the act of keeping them up that is the pleasure and magic of his films.

Second, Rivette always knows about tomorrow, the future. He knows today what he will seek tomorrow on the set, tomorrow's film. And he already knows yesterday, the past. But he never knows today, not in any detail. Today, the present is always an adventure, a stepping into the unknown. Rivette shoots in sequence. Yesterday will have an effect on today and today an effect on tomorrow. This is not the yesterday, today, tomorrow of the fiction but the yesterday, today, tomorrow of the film, of its shooting, its performances, its words, in short its play.

Knowing tomorrow is having not a script but an idea. Realising an idea is the *mise en scène* of the film, but becomes apparent only in its enactment, not before. Rivette's present is rigorously present and a matter of chance.

Third, Rivettian virtues are attentiveness and being *disponible* (open, expectant). To give an idea of a how a Rivette film is 'written' and the extreme danger that his films court, a danger unthinkable say in the Hollywood film: when Rivette comes on the set for a day of shooting, he is not at all clear about what will occur. There is no written script, no dialogue. The entry on to the set is not exactly work in the usual sense, but a non-work, a getting together, a setting to make things, as you might arrive at a party or in the playground. The set is an opportunity to play and the film the product of that play. In fact, the film is the play itself. There are two elements, the play that the film records and the play of the film in recording it, the world and the idea of it, the world and the discovery of it, both at once. His *mise en scène* is this interaction and tension.

The risk is obvious. The *metteur en scène* does not know exactly where he is going. The actors know little or nothing about their characters. They have their lines only day by day and sometimes only minute by minute, thus they, like the *metteur en scène*, must be able to react at the last minute, to discover themselves instantly and hope that things will work out.

The script writer is in the same situation. There is no script that has been written previously over months in advance of the film, but rather a script that is written on the set at the moment before a scene is shot and often as it is being shot. The film then emerges in this instantaneity and simultaneity, not as a record but as a performance based on the non-work of play.

Everyone takes a hand in the film. The actors, not only because they interact with each other and the decor and scene that surrounds them but because they also interact with the script writer and the director. The company plays together at making a film, and thus the outside of composition and structuring is at the inside of the film as if it is that *mise en scène* that is its subject.

The film is its very subject and the author of the work. The task of Rivette is not to force things, to direct things in a definite manner, but to watch and to listen to the way the film is going and the way dialogue and acting and story are proceeding, to be attentive to it and to accidents and associations and to then guide things, bring them to fruition and maturity and seize opportunities as they arise. This gives his films their concreteness, their play, their charm and their magic and generosity.

One of the most obvious qualities of Rivette's films is their ambiguity or rather ambivalence: there is no right or wrong, no good or bad, no black or white, but a floating between these, a delicacy that is at once aesthetic and ethical. And this ambiguity is connected to Rivette's manner of working, of both manipulating and not, exercising power and renouncing it. Power risks negating what might be, effacing what is and rejecting and excluding. Rivette's ambivalence allows shadows to emerge (*Va savoir* concerns doubles, shadows, mirrors that haunt the characters and the film), the forgotten to reappear (*Va savoir* concerns the return of actions, characters, events and their theatrical doubling), the excluded and hidden to be made present (*Va savoir* concerns the discovery of secrets and hidden objects in the Goldoni play made present by an accident in the kitchen and by the performance of the Pirandello play and by the failed

seduction of Ugo by Dominique, and the ring hidden in the sugar jar by
Arthur). The entry of spectres, ghosts, shadows, the excluded, the effaced
and the ambivalence of a *mise en scène* which permits these to appear is
what in part accounts for the combination of lengthiness and aeration in
a Rivette film.

> Un *réalisateur* est un cinéaste qui préfère le réel au vrai, la vrais-
> emblance à la vérité, la perfection de la réalisation à la maladresse
> pleine de vie de l'idée; il est insensible à la poésie de ces fautes
> d'orthographe (faux raccords, dédain pour le réalisme des éclai-
> rages) qui, pour le *metteur en scène*, sont la conséquence accessoire
> de son plaisir de filmer, d'inventer donc d'exagérer. Qu'importe au
> peintre que l'ombre sur la toile ne respecte pas les lois de l'optique
> (Rubens); qu'importent au metteur en scène la gaucherie d'une
> interprétation (il n'attend pas des acteurs, comme pourrait le faire
> le réalisateur, que leur jeu soit *impeccable*), ou la présence, dans son
> films, de surprises hasardeuses et fantaisistes …
>
> Si la Réalisation (adéquation entre un sujet et son traitement,
> ce qu'une convention nomme le style), vers lequel se porte tradi-
> tionnellement l'intérêt principal des critiques, compte moins que
> l'idée, et la réalité que la vérité, c'est parce que le metteur en scène
> véritable s'efforce, par cette invention jaillissante, par cette puissance
> de l'imprévu en laquelle réside la vie même, d'atteindre la figure
> secrète, but de toute oeuvre d'art.

> (A *film director* is a filmmaker who prefers the real to the true, the
> real-seeming to the truth, the perfection of direction to the awk-
> ward fullness of life in the idea; he is insensitive to the poetry of
> misspellings (mismatches, disdain for the realism of lighting)
> which, for the *metteur en scène*, are the unintended consequence
> of the pleasure of filming, to invent, and then to exaggerate. What
> does it matter to a painter that the shadows on a canvas do not
> follow the laws of optics (Rubens); what does the clumsiness of an
> intepretation matter to the *metteur en scène* (he does not demand
> of his actors as would a film director that their performance be
> *impeccable*), or the presence in his films of risky surprises and the
> unconventional …
>
> If 'direction' (the right match between a subject and its treatment,
> what is conventionally called style), that which traditionally is the

main concern of critics, counts less than the idea, and reality less than truth, it is because the *metteur en scène* truly strives, by this ebullient inventiveness, by this power of the unexpected, in which there is life itself, to attain to the secret end of all works of art.)[19]

19 Hélène Frappat, *Jacques Rivette, Secret compris* (Paris: Cahiers du cinéma, 2001), pp. 84–7.

Time

Tout le passé est nécessaire pour aimer le présent.

(The entire past is necessary in order to love the present.)

Annie Ernaux[20]

There is no single narrative to films by Bernardo Bertolucci, none that follows (or traces) a progressive, chronological line. For the most part, his films begin in a present already past or a past yet to be, but in dissolution, a future or a present becoming past, and becoming the past instantly, as each time is made apparent, and apparent at the same time. Each and every time contains other times, the multiplicities of time.

The line between different times is difficult to separate. Borders tend to blur. There are no simple flashbacks or flash forwards, not an exact before or a precise after that is not contaminated by a time alongside it or one that overtakes it until time itself is called into question. The interrogative is a function not a subject. All Bertolucci's films are questions.

No Bertolucci character – nor a Bertolucci film – is unified or seems to stand still. None in that sense is in the past. The films look forward irrespective of their stories. Every image, every occurrence, creates an uncertainty, not simply of this or that sequence but of an entire film, and, by extension, of all his films, the cinema itself marked by uncertainty.

Qu'est-ce que le cinéma? What is cinema?

20 Annie Ernaux, *Ecrire la vie* (Paris: Gallimard, 2011).

Though time and place alternate in the films, they and their alternations are not explications. A Bertolucci plot is never clear, not a plot at all perhaps, nor is plot or story an issue. The stories, at best, are a hinge. Sequences, sometimes as brief as a single shot, move back and forth as strata of times, an interrogative. What is given overlaps, intersects, modifies, dislocates, duplicates, doubles back, and, as they do so, time thickens. Bertolucci's narratives are never 'thin', never simply linear, or homogeneous, instead they are dense. Bertolucci: 'I work by addition'. Like his characters and his narratives, Bertolucci's films are perpetually in movement, are restless. Consequences in his films are neither caus- ative nor successive, but instead are rhymes, comparisons, repetitions, associations. They are tonal, linguistic functions, tenuous and flimsy, difficult to grasp, inhabiting a realm of the indefinite. There are sudden and fragile flashes of recognition of something that seems sure, but in fact very little of the continuous endures. Additions do not cumulate, or seem to add up. What has been made clear, a direction or a theme, just as suddenly becomes obscure, disappearing into permanent irresolution.

Some events, occurrences, shots, sequences, fragments of dialogue, light, patterns of colours, shapes, landscapes in the films are citations, some specific and tangible: the canvases of Francis Bacon, the settings and art of the Italian Renaissance, the films of Jean-Luc Godard, of Pier Paolo Pasolini, the paintings of Ligabue, the Fauves, the Primitives, Italian lyric opera, especially Verdi, Italian neo-impressionism, such as the canvas of peasants protesting that comes alive at the beginning of *Novecento* (1976). Though citations come from a past, it is always the present that cites, quotes, acts, that writes, but, once integrated into a fictional narrative, the past is displaced as it becomes the present of film.

Citations are always objective, belonging to time rescued, time brought back from time. Once invoked in film, a painting, a poem, a musical composition veers toward the insubstantial. However fanciful a cited painting may be by subject or intention, it remains, nevertheless, simply painting. By citing it, bringing it to the surface, cutting into it and refig- uring it within a new space and time, providing it with a new identity, it nevertheless remains itself (its origins leave a trace) and other than itself, a combine. What it once was and still is coexists with what it is coming to be, but is not yet, neither one nor the other.

Truth

In the late 1930s, Orson Welles already had a distinguished and exceptionally brilliant career in theatre and in radio theatre while still in his late
teens and early twenties. He became famous, indeed infamous, by a radio
play based on the science fiction novel *The War of the Worlds* by the British
novelist H.G. Wells. Welles dramatised the H.G. Wells novel as a radio
documentary of an invasion by Martians of the United States that parodied the form: the report of the fictional invasion was presented as a news
event taking place at the moment of broadcast. It was made to interrupt a
light entertainment swing band programme. The false broadcast of a fictional invasion seemed to many to be a true report of a real invasion and so
convincing that there was panic in the United States, mostly in the north-
east where the invasion from Mars was being reported as having occurred.

The War of the Worlds was organised to seem true because it was like
current radio broadcasts of spectacular breaking news. In fact, it was a
travesty of such broadcasts and of their documentary form, a form that
in any case verged on the spectacular. Precisely because of the thin line
between truth and spectacle, the real and the fictional, in such broadcasts,
Welles was able to succeed in making spectacle seem true just as radio
broadcasts, inversely, made the real into spectacle. Fundamentally, his
broadcast was a commentary, a criticism of what already existed as a
form. In effect, he transformed an apparent substance (an invasion by
aliens) into a form (documentary) and a commentary (on documentary
and on spectacle and on the mechanisms of radio).

Welles's *Citizen Kane* (1941) is similar to *War of the Worlds* in this
regard: it is a spoof of the great man biography and of the rags-to-riches

story, a commentary on an existing form. At the same time it hovers on the line, as *War of the Worlds* does, between reportage and fiction, exemplified by the reportorial structure of investigation in *Kane* and by the 'News on the March' sequence and also because, however it was vigorously denied, it comes close to the real-life story of the newspaper magnate William Randolph Hearst, so close in fact as to result in a boycott by the Hearst papers of the Welles film and an unsuccessful attempt by Hearst to have the film withdrawn and destroyed. (The Hearst suggestion in *Kane* is reduplicated in Welles's *F for Fake* (1973) involving mystery, fakery and myth.)

As with *War of the Worlds*, the spoof parody of reality that *Citizen Kane* practised had real effects in the actual world: panic in the streets in the one case and outrage in the boardroom and press in the other, in any case notoriety. Welles became news just as Kane–Hearst and the hoax invasion of New Jersey by Martians had been news. Welles had the magical ability to make nothing into something and something into nothing: precisely the theme of his *Immortal Story* (1968) (making a story true) and also of *Touch of Evil* (1958), *Lady from Shanghai* (1947), *Mr Arkadin* (1955), *Othello* (1952), and Carol Reed's *The Third Man* (1949). *F for Fake* directly cites *War of the Worlds* and as well it cites *Kane* in its own parodic 'News on the March' but edited to substitute for Kane–Hearst, Howard Hughes, a millionaire recluse, like Kane and Hearst, about whom stories were told and invented, as Welles had invented a story about Hearst, and because it seemed true it suffered the accusations of inaccuracies, libel and fradulence that are the subject of *F for Fake*: the forged biography by Clifford Irving of Howard Hughes and his possibly equally fradulent biography of the painter Elmyr de Hory, himself a notorious and successful forger of great paintings and a monumental liar. Welles, like these forgers and like the heroes in his films, has provoked stories about himself and has created himself as a personality larger than life like a Macbeth, an Othello, a Quinlan, a Kane, forgers, illusionists, liars and mischief makers all.

Welles died in 1985. He was seventy years old. *Kane*, his first film, was made in 1941. His last film, *F for Fake*, was made in 1973. Between these two dates, Welles made only nine other films and all under difficult circumstances of studio interference for those films he made in Hollywood and problems of money and distribution for those he made outside the United States. Whatever he did in Hollywood, with the exception of *Kane*,

was butchered by the studio, fundamentally because Welles did not conform to the rules, formal or otherwise, of the American industry and
the studio butchery reasserted those rules. Because Welles was different and thought and made films differently from the norms within the
industry, he was forced to work outside of it, independently of it, largely
in Europe where his films were better appreciated. From 1973 until his
death in 1985, Welles was unable to make a single film. And between *The
Immortal Story* and *F for Fake*, there is a gap of five years.

There are five principal characters in *F for Fake*: Welles, the Yugoslavian
actress Oja Kodar, the art forger Elmyr de Hory, the writer Clifford Irving,
and the former art dealer turned filmmaker François Reichenbach. All the
'characters' play themselves as they are in real life, but in real life their role
is not to be who they are: de Hory is a forger, Irving a liar and hoaxster,
Welles a magician and maker of films, a peddler of stories and illusions,
and Reichenbach a maker of images and a peddler of paintings, Kodar an
actress and seductress. None of the characters either in life or in the film
which is documenting their lives can be believed. Thereby, the film as a
record is in doubt; on the other hand, and strictly speaking, though *F for
Fake* is not a fiction film in any usual sense, nor is it a documentary.

Indeed, it could be argued, as when Welles, in the last sequence of the
film, removes the sheet from Oja Kodar's levitated grandfather, that there
is nothing there, that the film is literally empty, an illusion of presence.
Rather than a film, there is instead a discourse about it that replaces it.
Everything 'in' the film seems to be curiously 'outside' it as if the film
lacks interiority, is no more than a location, simply a space through
which various objects, gestures, stories, persons pass and connect or
disconnect, resonate or are flattened out, meet or fail to meet. The film
in effect is a void. Whatever is – de Hory, Kodar, Irving, Reichenbach,
Welles, Chartres, Ibiza, Toussaint, Paris – is made to disappear as surely
as the little boy's key and the coin that displaces it at the opening of the
film, or Oja's sister standing in for Oja, or Oja vanishing into a valise and
her grandfather vanishing into thin air (as if he ever was) while whatever
is not is made to appear as if it is by a series of displacements and era-
sures (coin for key, image for object, shadow for person, paintings that
are copies or that never were signed by artists who didn't paint them; de
Hory literally invents Giacometti paintings that were never painted and
the fictional grandfather invents an entire Picasso 'period').

Most of the material in the film was shot not by Welles but by Reichenbach for a film he was making on Elmyr de Hory. Some of the sequences were indeed shot by Welles but most of the film, in so far as it is a Welles film, is a film made in the editing room. If the characters are difficult to identify because they are never true, so too is the film, since it is composed of other films and found footage and because its words (interviews, asides, commentaries – as with *Citizen Kane, The Immortal Story, The Lady from Shanghai, Touch of Evil, The Magnificent Ambersons* and, interestingly, *Othello*) not only are the words of unreliable witnesses but issue from places well outside the film and its temporality.

The film involves essentially three stories: the story of Elmyr de Hory, the art forger, about whose life Irving has written a book. (de Hory paints post-Impressionist, 'modern' painters like Matisse, Derain, Soutine, Picasso and Giacometti and so convincingly that he is able to sell them to galleries and dealers); and there is the story of Clifford Irving who wrote a book that purported to be the official biography of Howard Hughes complete with interviews (the interviews were fake and the autobiographical elements of the book invention); and there is the story of Oja Kodar's seduction of Picasso enabling her, in return for posing in the nude for the artist, to be presented with twenty-two Picasso paintings, which her grandfather, an art forger, is said to have copied, then exhibiting the copies as genuine Picasso paintings and then burning the Picasso originals so that only the fakes existed (Kodar's seduction and story about Picasso is as untrue as Irving's book on Hughes and de Hory's paintings, while the grandfather probably never existed and is only an actor).

The material of which the film is made is various and none of it coheres. It is even difficult to say where the film actually begins. Does it begin at the station? At the moviola? With Elmyr? In Ibiza? In Paris? In Toussaint? With Reichenbach's film? The film is difficult to locate or hold on to in part because it is a parody and commentary on all its forms: on film, on art, on originality, on beginnings, on ends, on theory, on commentary itself. As with D.W. Griffith's film *Intolerance* (1916), all the elements of the film are co-present at every point of it, but unlike Griffith's film this co-presence never enters a progressive time, instead there is a constant separation and division of all that might be united and a union of all that is effectively separate. The documentary is not only falsified but is a pursuit of false trails as false and elusive as the identity of Kane or Arkadin or the character of Desdemona. Arkadin is who he is not and who he is not is who he is, thus to uncover or discover him, to certify him, is to lose him, because his character is one of elusiveness, illusion and negation, like the character of Kane, hence the emptiness in *Citizen Kane* of the childhood sledge that literally represents both nothing and everything.

F for Fake proclaims it is true but its truth is its falsity. This negative posing as a positive is what it is, an identity that is unspeakable and unlocatable. It negates itself as Arkadin does once he is 'revealed'.

Vertigo

At the opening of Hitchcock's *Vertigo* (1958) there is a chase at night by a uniformed policeman and Scottie of the fleeing criminal across the rooftops of buildings in San Francisco followed by the fall of Scottie suspended above the building hanging on to its guttering and then the policeman, returning to rescue Scottie, falling to his death. The 'reality' of the one scene (the chase) is derailed by the 'reality' occurring within it of another (the slip, the fall) which in turn becomes (for Scottie) a fear of heights (vertigo), a feeling of guilt (Scottie blames himself) and a transference (Scottie identifies with the policeman who died, and with his death, vertigo, guilt and even a certain voyeurism of identification come together). This scene in turn is 'like' (as if in a mirror, a pure reflection though in reverse) Scottie's relation to Judy/Madeleine/Carlotta and by extension to Kim Novak who moves in and outside the film as multiple characters and as one who acts; this is Judy's performance as Madeleine opens up the question of Novak's performance as the false Madeleine and then as the 'true' Judy.

What occurs at the opening reoccurs in other instances throughout the film, the metamorphosis of one thing into another then back again: realities into images, events into emotions, duplications and shifts of identities, imitations of appearances, the past in the present, the pursuit of chimeras (of things that do not in fact exist), the constant play of objectivity and subjectivity until the subjective becomes the objective and the fictional the only reality. Thus, as different spaces and different events (in reality) become likenesses of each other, they simultaneously give depth to the film (scenes thicken, events congeal, characters merge), give it a

musicality (events rhyme, resonate, become variations of each other, a
dominant becomes a minor, a minor a dominant, the transfer, for example, of Madeleine for Midge and then Madeleine for Judy and then Judy
back to Madeleine and in the midst of these the grotesque painted image
of Midge as Carlotta/Madeleine) and, in so far as these relations are 'true',
that is, in so far as such metamorphoses occur in the fiction of the film,
the content of things in the film (events, characters, emotions, objects, in
effect appearances) become less important than their forms (the tonality,
the transfers, the reflections), as 'reality' (a great concern of Hitchcock's)
dissolves into fiction and images (a greater concern of Hitchcock's), until,
for the spectators and/or the characters (Scottie and Judy/ Madeleine/
Carlotta) with whom one identifies, reality not only loses substance, and
is displaced by the fictional and the unreal, and the fictional reveals itself
as forms whose content is almost irrelevant and whose reality is essentially formal and abstract, thus negating a classical difference of form and
content. It is astonishing almost to view Hitchcock's works as a play of
abstract forms, not something the film begins as, but that it becomes in
the course of dissolving any and every reality except the reality of itself,
exactly what happened with modern painting in its rejection and compromising of representation until one begins with the dissolutions achieved
by Cubism and ends with the apparent chaos of installation artists like
Robert Rauschenberg and Jean-Luc Godard.

The irrelevance that Hitchcock *perpetrates* (like a crime) or *imposes*
(sadistically, grotesquely as reality is feigned, only imitated) turns around
a void, hence the vertigo, the dizziness, the loss of focus – is crucial to
Vertigo and all his films where story, emotions, characters, occurrences
are at once realistic and improbable, as if a Hitchcock film is looking
at itself, pursuing itself as intently as Scottie pursues Judy/Madeleine/
Carlotta. The regard and the pursuit are interrogative (the film marvels
at itself, seeks itself in amazement) and mocking (this is absurd, all the
more so when Scottie 'believes' it), turning improbability (in a word, the
fiction) into the only truth.

The world of Hitchcock's films is littered with a profusion of signs
(which indicate something, but are usually false, deceptive, misleading, confusing – what do they indicate? – that is, they are illusions,
McGuffins, pretexts and a lure because everything is at once realistic and
feigned, which is at the heart of the cinema, the very nature of film) and
these signs confront the character who looks at them and the audience

who sees the character looking. Both character and audience are like deceivers, *interpreters* of signs. Particularly exemplary in this regard is the English detective story, the whodunit, an imperiously intellectual form which reached its peak in the work of Agatha Christie and of which Conan Doyle's Sherlock Holmes adventures are one of the traditions behind Hitchcock's works. (What does this mean? Where will it lead? What is true?) The real questions though are less objective and are overwhelmed by *desire*, by the characters and by the spectator (what do I want?). It is precisely what is desired that constructs what is seen and responds to a presented objectivity of what is seen by the subjectivity of what is wanted that thus plunges the character and film into fiction, turns objects into signs and persons into images.

Such impositions by Hitchcock are what motivated Jean-Luc Godard to title section 4A of his *Histoire(s) du cinéma* (1988–98), which he devoted principally to Hitchcock, *Le Contrôle de l'univers*, thereby implicitly declaring him to be more powerful than any Napoléon or Alexander the Great or even perhaps God, the almighty, a mastery, literally of fictive creations made to seem not only real but as *the* world, the fantastic as reality, not by chance, an inheritance of a peculiarly English version of Surrealism. If some still worship God the Father, the French *Nouvelle Vague* worshipped Hitchcock, and its heirs still worship him. It is only at the close of the Hitchcock film when the fiction, improbability, subjectivity, the appearances of things, are literally shut down and the reality of the film (not the realities within the films, not their representations, certainly not anything so ordinary as a message or a significance) is revealed to be the only objectivity that endures. The film reasserts itself (against its representations) to become what it had always been from its first image, a fiction, and, despite its zig-zags between places, identities and times, is always and emphatically of the present.

Judy/Madeleine/Carlotta/Kim Novak are unstable identities in the film primarily because they are only images, only appearances and therefore, if not interchangeable, 'like' each other. Besides, their linkages are not causal but associative; that is, they are essentially, even as they converge, independent of each other, autonomous. Each identity, each image easily becomes the other (slides, skids) and even the one 'true' image, Judy as Judy in all her splendid vulgarity and banality, becomes her true 'other' self, the false Madeleine and twice over, once as Elster's invention and then what Scottie desires her to be (to be not herself), a desire she accepts, that is the desire, in effect, to be nothing but an image which is the desire of the 'other', of Scottie. 'Je désir le désir de l'autre.' ('I desire the desire of the other.') This self-effacement by Judy is to truly venture back to the past, to become Madeleine once again and reproduce herself, bring herself back from the dead into the present, co-operate with the desire of her lover to be, improbably, and terrifyingly, what he wants her to be, to return to the past in the present, to live with a dead lover, a kinky and desperate necrophilia. But then, would we not all want to commune with the dead? Ask Chris Marker, Jean-Luc Godard. Similarly, and because of these met-amorphoses of identities, possible only because identity is defined in the film by appearances (mere signs: clothes, make-up, hair, walk, gesture, objects), time in the film is in a constant (and, as Marker said, vertiginous) play of overlappings, interminglings and returns so that every present is also a past and every past another past again, and each of these invades the present as the future and past incessantly switch positions in accord with desires as if the characters are willing their fictions and then performing and acting them out as if they are their own fictional creations in a fantasy. Is this not a film, after all, where the dead come back to life (are dou-bled, duplicated, imitated) and then return to death, to non-existence?: the doubled gravestones (Madeleine, Carlotta), the doubled, indeed trebled, deaths and falls, some real, some fake (policeman, Madeleine, Judy), the doubled manipulations of imitation and appearance (the re-creation of Madeleine by Elster and by Scottie, the re-semblance of deaths, the re-sem-blance of similar pasts, the re-semblance of similar futures, a future past, that temporal mix Marker is so fond of, as he is of this film by Hitchcock).

Madeleine Elster dies and Judy as Madeleine 'repeats' her death and 'truly' becomes Madeleine for Scottie when he recognises Carlotta's (!) necklace and therefore Madeleine/Judy must die another death (this time real) to release Scottie from the past to which he was subject as Judy was subject (like him, both in reality and fictively) until both characters, Scottie and Judy, by this manner, come to resemble each other, like echoes, and by so resonating with each other that no original, no funda-mental, referential 'reality' any longer exists.

And there is as well the constant shift between objectivity and subjec-tivity in the film regarding Scottie's position(s), the audience's position(s) following him and Judy's position(s) being followed and then herself following Scottie's lead. Since everything in the film is doubled and more than once and mirrored in reflections that are constant, including those in time and in space and the regards across space and times, a labyrinth is created, and hence vertigo. Not only is it impossible to believe in the impression of reality that is put forward (a manufactured verisimilitude so familiar in most films but in this film made radically improbable) but it is also impossible to believe in the realities of the images in the film since every image, every sign (images here are less representations then they are signs to be deciphered) is enveloped, indeed consumed, by hallucinations of desire and is therefore deceptive.

These hallucinations recall the experiments by Lev Kuleshov in the 1920s in the Soviet Union where what is looked at by the blank stare of an actor determines what the audience imagines and therefore sees, so if the look is juxtaposed with a plate of food, he seems hungry, with a pretty girl, he seems lustful, with a revolver, he seems murderous and thereby every image is made potentially different not only by what might precede or follow it but by and alongside with the projections and imaginations of the spectator, who is vital in constructing an image and who is manipulated by Kuleshov and his insight into the mechanisms of montage and hence of cinema. In such a way, and by the profusion of signs and forms and their imbrication by Hitchcock, are his films purely film, hence their validation by the French *Nouvelle Vague* including by Godard, whose films can be taken to be, like the films of Hitchcock, and quite literally, reflections on the cinema.

Chris Marker noted the excitement of Soviet filmmakers, in the 1920s, including Aleksandr Medvedkin to whom Marker's *Le Tombeau d'Alexandre* (1992) is addressed, namely, that, if you put two images together, a third is created by the juxtaposition, and beyond that third, inside the two images, others begin to take shape by association. It is the principle, demonstration and genius of Godard's *Histoire(s) du cinéma* and of his remark written on a frame of the film and the title of an early essay in the 1960s, *Montage, mon beau souci* (*Montage, my fine care*). Hitchcock proceeds slightly differently. He binds the spectator for the entire length of the film within its fiction (to be taken as a reality) and by a very simple and exceedingly conventional procedure of shot/reverse-shot whereby every look is 'answered' by its object (either a thing or a person or simply a view): in essence, the Kuleshov effect. There is no outside then to his film, only this interior constructed by looks and by their objects which sustain and reinforce the fictionality of the film, in short its imaginary. His editing pattern is logical and essentially linear and consequential and so much so that it is therefore 'realistic' and 'motivated' in a classical manner such that the incredible realities he presents are more believable and acceptable. Sometimes his strategies are mixed and, rather than his relying simply on subjectivity to intrude upon an objectivity, the object becomes a projected fantasy, he creates a transition, as in Midge's apartment and Gavin Elster's office, whereby objective shots of the spaces and their order and harmony come to seem slightly, almost unnoticeably askew (the less noticed, the more effective as a disturbance of and within 'reality') and out of balance as if there is something else, some flaw, disharmony within the shot. Hitchcock uses the most conventional of cinematic procedures carefully regulated in the most conventional of film industries, Hollywood, to become a procedure not exactly to make the fabulous seem real but to make the real fabulous and to undermine the rules of the industry while employing all its devices – it is mockery and improbability made into reality as its key gesture.

Hitchcock's films are in part a return to the past, before sound, principally to Kuleshov and the Soviet cinema, while looking forward to the French cinema. It was in France and by French intellectuals and filmmakers, it needs to be remembered, that he was most truly appreciated and understood. His films privilege the forms of the cinema (his main interest) and bring these forward as his true subject. In doing so, like the best of films, his films, like Godard's films, are sustained reflections on the cinema, because they are experiments, and all experiments are at once critical and interrogative and thereby *historical*. Few filmmakers besides these two plus Rossellini so fundamentally incorporate the past in their present.

There is always a gap between an image and what it represents (in 'reality', 'outside' it). The gap is a gap in time (the image comes after) and in space (the space comes before). It is indicative of much of what can be called 'modern' cinema (Godard, Marker, Resnais, Welles are exemplary) as opposed to 'classical' cinema (Hawks, Ford, Preminger and, to an extent, Hitchcock) that, whereas the classical cinema sought to efface the gap between reality and image, past and present, content and form, by various strategies of continuity (logic, motivation, linearity), the modern cinema has tended not only to stress the gap but to exhibit it, flaunt it. Such exhibition is its very subject, whereas the effacement of it was at the heart of classicism. Godard and Marker, for example, not only made films whose images had a variety of origins, that is, their films were composed neither of similar objects nor of objects and events that inhabited the same space or times, their films always being a *mélange* of differences. In short, the images were decontextualised and sometimes deconstructed (flickering, superimpositions) and these, by being autonomous, by being taken out of context, were, in some cases, without a referent (context was disrupted, continuity avoided, logic confounded and all these interrupted – Godard's work is a work of interruptions) – and in part this was the case because of a mix of the fictional, artificial, false with the real, true and documentary, by which each otherness and difference posed a question to what it was different from and what is was other to. The central problem raised by Godard's *Histoire(s) du cinéma* was the question 'What is the cinema?' and 'How do you define it?' The answer to these questions not only was impossible to find but was necessarily tentative, provisional, subject to be questioned. Hence, without a definite response, the history or histories of the cinema were also subject to questioning and so too, necessarily, it was Godard's film that had raised the question.

In the Kuleshov effect (which Hitchcock duplicates), the link between shots is provided by the imagination of the spectator, that is, the ellipses of time, space, even reality *between* images are 'filled', essentially effaced, by the desire to create in the succession of images a similitude (*verisimilitude*) with reality, though the only realities are the gaps between the images and the imagination of the viewer. The fact that, in the Kuleshov effect, one image seems to naturally belong with another is a constructed not natural necessity and thereby essentially artificial, veering on the false, whatever the gap may be (that between the dead and the living, for example, or the past and the present, a gap stressed, indeed central to Rossellini's *Viaggio in Italia* (1954) and which thereby sets into play new continuities, new possibilities, a notion at the very heart of the wanderings and chance encounters built into the Rossellini film, into Marker's films and all of Godard's films).

What is fascinating about Hitchcock's *Vertigo* is not only the play between the improbable, the false, the desired and the real-seeming but the separations and gaps of time, reference, space and identities. The double and the repetition are always marks of a gap and a difference. For example,

the images of Judy/Madeleine/Carlotta/Kim Novak are not only multiple, compound images (past and present, here and now, reality and
image) but fundamentally false. Besides, every image juxtaposes within it
other alternatives and does so as simultaneities. The result is not only to
underline the distance between every image and the various realities each
supposedly refers to, but that reality itself and all its referents are called
into question and made unstable. The genius of Hitchcock is to maintain
these oppositions as relations so that either term in the oppositions is
only temporary, and because they become something else and take on a
life of their own as images do, especially images that are at once liberated
from reality and flirt with reality as if every event in the films is full (they
seem real) and empty (they are false).

Hitchcock uses every resource and rule of continuity editing between
shots and sequences to bind the spectator (and the characters) within
worlds and within a narrative that seem to be true (continuous, transparent, logical, motivated, detailed) – he is a Hollywood director – and then
to exhibit, press upon, reveal that an 'other' continuity was simultaneously at work either below the surface, hidden away or by means of time,
cached in reserve, and that what had been taken to be true was patently
false, what had been present was in the past and what was past was in the
present, and the only truth then was the falsity and the fictional in which
persons, spectators, characters, actors (but not Hitchcock) were trapped
because, rather than images reflecting reality, they only reflected and
mirrored other images that masqueraded, like them, to be realities (the
doublings, the coincidences, the encounters, the repetitions) and what
seemed straightforward was instead a maze in a hall of mirrors.

In *Vertigo*, at Ernie's, there is a shot in close-up of Madeleine (Kim Novak)
pausing for a moment before she leaves the restaurant with Elster. Scottie
(James Stewart) is at the bar looking at her. His look is also in close-up.
The paired shots of Madeleine looked at and of Scottie looking are remarkable. They are in close-up and thus break a pattern of medium and long
shots that have composed the scene. They disrupt a pattern (the close-ups
are marked as separate) and recompose it (they have a dramatic and psychological motive) so that the disruption, as an unease and as something
more than merely a look, conveys a double meaning, but one recovered,
rebalanced by the film. The close-up 'troubles' the scene, but it is only
a slight disturbance. The rhythms of the scene shift – a shift reinforced

by the close-up and dependent on it. The exchanges of the close-ups, of looking and looked upon, are dilated, slowed down, intensified. This change of tempo is also a break and disruption of pattern as if something is occurring that goes beyond appearance and description and yet is kept within believable bounds. Furthermore the image of Madeleine is not an objective description but a subjective one: not only is Madeleine overly posed and overly still but there seems to be a veil of peculiar light before her as if the image is unreal.

The images presented are not what they appear to be since something else is going on. The reality that is represented in the image and the reality of the image are both placed in doubt, because the image is incomplete and because it wavers between being objective (descriptive) and being subjective (a projection). What you see is not entirely what is there because what is there goes beyond the image into a past and towards a future. The past and future press on the shots and cause an uncertainty about what it is they describe, as if they exist at the 'outside' of the shots, but the externality to which they point is an exterior that nevertheless is contained within the boundaries of the fiction of the film and will become part of its continuity. What is missing, what is not told, what troubles the shot by the duplicity it evokes and the discontinuity by which it evokes it, is at the heart of the film, is its essential subject, the fundamental component of the condition of suspense (suspension, duplicity, unease, dissembling) characteristic of Hitchcock's films.

The scene is deepened in the succeeding two sequences when Scottie follows Madeleine by introducing a doubling of looks: Madeleine looks at an object (a bouquet, a painting, a gravestone) and Scottie looks at Madeleine looking. Between the look and the object, whether it is a gravestone or Madeleine herself, the gap is between what is and what can be, at once continuous and not, within which questions arise and answers can be speculated upon. It is that gap that involves the audience and brings it *into* the fiction to *cover* the gap. The audience is a *third* that completes the pairing of shot and counter-shot, look and object, subject and object. Scottie is a third as well. He is between Madeleine and her look and thereby enters into the appearance she presents with his desires. It completes their fiction and is bound within it.

Hitchcock began to make films in the early 1920s. He made fifty-two films over more than half a century. He worked, and successfully, within the commercial film industry, first in Britain (initially for an American company, Famous Players Lasky), then in the United States from 1940. His films were popular and profitable and, however distinct ('Hitchcock films' became a genre of their own), conformed to the patterns of the Hollywood film. Welles, to the contrary, who did not conform to those patterns, but challenged them, was able to make only eleven films, and these often with considerable difficulty.

Hitchcock's and Welles's films have a number of definite similarities. *Vertigo*, for example, plays upon identity, subjectivity, guilt, crime, gullibility and duplicity, as do *F for Fake*, *Othello* and *The Lady from Shanghai*, whose principal characters are caught in a labyrinth of deceit and false appearances in pursuit of what turns out to be murderous and treacherous.

In a Hitchcock film, the film is not simply a representation or illustration of a story in the usual sense. In the example of the close-up exchange of shots at the beginning of *Vertigo*, the form and structure of that exchange is a mirror of the themes and concerns of the film as if the subject is its form and the form its content, both conflated; hence the description of Hitchcock's films as 'pure' cinema. That purity and conflation has a name, 'suspense', at once a subject and a form.

In *Vertigo*, in the fiction of it, Scottie is the victim of his own desires. What he sees is what he projects, not their reality but their appearance, their image, the illusions they evoke and nourish. The concern of a Hitchcock film is with its images and the fictions that belong to them and are inherent in them. Necessarily, Hitchcock's films turn back upon their own style and forms without being so reflexive as to upset them. Strictly speaking, the crisis in appearances in his films is provoked from within the fiction by the force of imaginings and fantasies of his characters and by the audience: that is, while it breaks with the most obvious naturalism, it naturalises and motivates nevertheless.

Hitchcock raises differences central to the forms of film but he does so in such a way as to reconcile them while Welles breaks these accords by taking his films beyond the boundaries of their fictions, boundaries that Hitchcock not only rigorously respects but exploits (his films concern appearances). Hitchcock is an intermediary between a classical cinema whose forms he adheres to (and exacerbates) and what comes after Hitchcock and reflects on those forms, as notably with Welles. It marks a crucial historical shift.

Voyages (1)

Alla storia preferisco la mitologia, perché la storia parte dalla verità
e finisce nelle menzogna, mentre la mitologia parte dalla menzogna
e va verso la vérità.

(I prefer mythology to history, because history begins with truth and
ends in lies, while mythology begins with lies and arrives at the truth.)

Jean Cocteau[21]

Bernardo Bertolucci's *La via del petrolio* (1965) is a documentary made
for RAI television in 1965. The film was commissioned by the Italian
oil company Eni (Ente Nazionale Idrocarburi) in 1964. It is in three
parts: 'Origins' / 'Le origini', 'The Voyage' / 'Il viaggio', 'Across Europe' /
'Attraverso l'Europa'.

'Le origini' takes place in Iran. It begins with Fire, the burning off of
natural gas as a by-product of oil drilling. The burning off is at the top
of towers in a mountainous terrain. The gas is set alight by gun-flares at
night, like a pistol shot followed by a mini explosion at ignition. The film
opens with the gas burned off, a *coup de théâtre*. The burning is part of
the extraction process, but the visual effect seems a fantasy like the story
of Aladdin and his magic lamp in *One Thousand and One Nights*. The film
is in two worlds at once, a modern industrial one and an ancient legendary one. The burning off of gas is never completely accounted for by the
event. It goes beyond itself towards the mythical.

---

21 Quoted in Bernardo Bertolucci, *La mia magnifica ossessione: scritti, ricordi, interventi
(1962–2010)* (Milan: Garzanti, 2010), p. 109.

What follow are sequences from the streets and marketplaces of Iran: young children gawking at the camera and laughing, men with long beards hurrying away, leaving behind them shadowy tails of sidelong glances, carpet sellers on bicycles or pulling a cart or carrying carpets on their back. Such small, everyday events are more than descriptive. They belong to an antiquity that tends toward the fairy tale and make-believe, fragments of a present reality and of the past. However, practical and actual, scenes are never simply that. The street sequence is part of a formal pair that fluctuates between the factual and the fictional. The images of the film emerge into another time and in another world, and though temporary have the permanence of legend.

Iran is one of the oldest civilisations in the world, dating back nearly five thousand years. The mountains in the oil fields recall Monument Valley in John Ford's westerns, films of the passage of time.

The second part, 'Il viaggio', takes place at sea following a loaded oil tanker proceeding through the Suez Canal to the Mediterranean, and then the straits of Messina between Sicily and Calabria to Genoa, where the oil is pumped into tanks for distribution through pipelines: a criss-crossed webbing overland up mountains, down to valleys in Italy, to Switzerland, to Lake Como, and finally to German refineries at Ingolstadt.

The elemental aspects of the zig-zags of the Oil Road call up memories and associations beyond the range and confines of an industrial journey. Its elements derive from the sacred, from ancient myth, the epic, the time of the Gods before History: Earth Water, Air, and Fire.

When the tanker passes through the Suez Canal, everything is silent. It calls up the ghost ship in Rimbaud's poem 'The Drunken Boat'/'Le bateau ivre'. When the tanker enters Italy through the Straits of Messina, another classical journey is evoked: Ulysses, Scylla and Charybdis.

As soon as the oil travels by pipeline from Genoa through Switzerland to Germany, it is accompanied by Mario Trejo, an Argentine journalist, poet and voyager. Trejo comes to Genoa to travel the Oil Road. He brings with him memories, historical associations: the Milanese Romantic nineteenth-century Italian novelist and poet Alessandro Manzoni, whose novel *The Betrothed*/*I promessi sposi* (1827) is set on the banks of Lake Como, near the oil; the magical journeys to faraway lands and beneath the sea in the novels of Jules Verne; Herman Melville's epic pursuit of Moby-Dick; Marco Polo's voyage from Venice to Asia on the Silk

Road; Joseph Conrad's *Heart of Darkness*; the adventure tales of Salgarian pirates; the poetry of Paul Valéry; Goethe's journey to Italy; and the later journey to Italy by Henry James, the nineteenth-century Grand Tour of Europe; Roberto Rossellini's *Viaggio in Italia* (1954); Martin Luther and the German Reformation. Every step forward along the Oil Road by Mario Trejo is a step back into time, well beyond the road of the oil.

In 1926, the then Italian Fascist government established the energy and gas company Agip (Azienda Generale Italiana Petroli). In 1945, Enrico Mattei, who had worked for the Fascists during the war, but was an anti-fascist before the war ended, was appointed to run Agip by the provisional Italian government, the Comitato di Liberazione Nazionale (CLN). Mattei was instructed by the CLN to dissolve Agip because of its fascist past. Instead, he further developed and expanded it. In 1953, a new Italian oil and gas public company, Eni, was founded by Mattei, with Mattei as director. Agip was incorporated within Eni as its subsidiary, responsible for marketing and refining, while Eni had overall responsibility.

Part one of the Bertolucci film is dedicated to Mattei, who died in 1962 in a plane crash in Italy. The plane was blown up by a bomb, probably attached to the landing gear and detonated when the plane came in for landing. The bomb may have been planted by the OAS of the French right, or by the French secret service (Mattei opposed the war in Algeria, and more generally opposed French colonialism), or it may have been the work of the Italian Mafia on contract either to the French or to the large American oil companies (Mattei's 'the seven sisters'). Many of those involved in the murder investigation – members of the Italian police, the Carabinieri and, in one instance, a journalist – were murdered. All evidence at the crash site was destroyed.

Mattei had powerful enemies, both economic and political. With respect to the Algerian situation and to American dominance of the oil market – to say nothing of the Cold War and Soviet negotiations with Eni in the 1960s – the line between the economic and the political was murky.

In 1972, Francesco Rosi made *The Mattei Affair / Il caso Mattei*, centred on Mattei's work and the events related to his murder. Mauro De Mauro, a journalist who was working on the investigation of Mattei's death for the film, had discovered a recording made by Mattei just before he was assassinated. In mid-September 1970, Mauro De Mauro disappeared. Neither he nor the tape recording have ever been found.

The Bertolucci film, not simply its first part, is a memorial to Mattei, and to Eni. Bertolucci knew Mattei because of his close friendship with Bertolucci's father, the poet Attilio Bertolucci. In 1955, Attilio was appointed by Mattei to direct the Eni house journal, a cultural review with articles equally devoted to reporting on the Italian company and the oil industry.

The name of the journal, suggested by Attilio Bertolucci to Mattei, was *Il gatto selvatico* (*Wildcat*). 'Wildcatters' was the name in America of those who were among the first to drill for oil. The journal title, *Il gatto selvatico*, referred to the early experience of oil drilling, to the drill itself and to the oil-rigs. *Il gatto selvatico* suggested oil exploration, pioneering, the discovery of the new, adventure, travel and a history.

Attilio, who administered *Il gatto selvatico*, commissioned writers and discussed their articles; in addition, he wrote for it, mostly on the fine arts: the medieval period, the Renaissance, the Baroque, Impressionism, modernism.

Those whom Attilio commissioned to write for *Il gatto selvatico* were distinguished Italian literary figures. Besides Attilio, there was Anna Banti, Giorgio Bassani, Italo Calvino, Carlo Emilio Gadda, Natalia Ginzburg, Leonardo Sciascia, Enzo Siciliano and Mario Soldati. *Il gatto selvatico* was literary, artistic, informative, culturally influential, respected and popular. It was intended as an accord between the traditional humanities and modern industry, between culture and capitalism.

When Attilio Bertolucci was appointed to direct *Il gatto selvatico* for Eni in 1955, Mattei's precondition was that the notion of *avventuriero* with its connotations of adventurer, speculator, soldier of fortune, the potential lyricism of the story of oil, in short, its poetry and imaginary, had to be linked unequivocally to Eni's main concerns of business and industry. Attilio's brief was to integrate the one aspect with the other.

There were to be two facets to *Il gatto selvatico*, one related to the animal, the *gatto selvatico* (self-reliant, canny, romantic, savage, mythical), the other to the oil industry (rigs, drilling, pipelines, tankers), to the corporate business of oil. *Il gatto selvatico* was to be both, such that every barrel of oil would promote histories, stories, legends, literature, art and not just crude. The project, and its realisation by Attilio was years later paid homage to by son to father in *La via del petrolio*.

The film is a documentary on the exploration, drilling, extraction, transport and commerce of oil, and, by its lyricism, its cultural humanism and the fantastic, it is also memory and history made of mythical heroes and writers as heroes: Herman Melville, Jules Verne, Homer, Odysseus, Marco Polo. The voyage of oil, as the ancient journey on the Silk Road or the voyage home of Odysseus, is a romance, real and fictional, an actual voyage, and a voyage of the mind and spirit: Méliès, Rimbaud, the *Odyssey*. *La via del petrolio*'s three parts are like three acts in theatre.

The Iran in *La via del petrolio* recalls Rossellini's *Viaggio in Italia*, particularly the excavation scenes at Pompeii with its references to Vesuvius, and is the setting of the Rossellini film in Naples where the ancient and the classical overlap with the contemporary as in Iran. The scene in *Viaggio in Italia* of the ignition of the bubbling up of vapours from the earth is like the opening sequence in *La via del petrolio* of natural gas being burned off. In both sequences, the everyday becomes fantasy and dreamlike, Surrealist.

Viaggio in Italia leaves a trace in other Bertolucci films where past and present intersect and where what emerges is just below the surface like an archaeological dig uncovering fragments from the past, buried strata of rocks and ruins and of emotions as in the discovery of the lovers from Pompeii, from centuries ago, locked in each other's arms at death in *Viaggio in Italia*, which resonates for Katherine Joyce in the present, specifically, her relation to her husband Alex and to a former lover lost. The bringing to the surface of the buried lovers brings to the surface Katherine's present predicament as if the ancient past and the present are mirrors.

Mattei's major accomplishment was the negotiation of oil deals for Italy with Iran and with the countries of the Middle East, also with China and the Soviet Union. Mattei offered generous terms to suppliers in contrast to what American companies had offered. It threatened the American global oil monopoly, a reason perhaps for Mattei's assassination. In the 1950s and early 1960s, the Cold War was at its height, NATO had recently been established, an inheritance from the Marshall Plan, and, in America, there was the anti-Communist witch-hunt of Senator Joseph McCarthy and the House Un-American Activities Committee, and the trial and execution of the Rosenbergs for espionage.

Both Attilio and Bernardo Bertolucci had an affectionate relation with Pier Paolo Pasolini. All three were poets. Bernardo and Pasolini were, in addition to being writers, also filmmakers. Bernardo had won the Premio Viareggio in 1962 for his first published book of collected poetry, *In Search of Mystery/In cerca del mistero*. He was twenty-two years old. Attilio helped Pasolini publish his first novel, *Ragazzi di vita*, in 1955. Bernardo worked as Pasolini's assistant for Pasolini's first film, *Accattone* (1961). Pasolini wrote the story on which Bertolucci's first film is based, *La Commare secca* (1962).

In 1972, three years before Pasolini died – beaten to death, then run over, by a seventeen-year-old thug and prostitute, Giuseppe Pelosi – Pasolini began writing what he regarded as his most important work. He wrote to Alberto Moravia in January 1975: 'I have begun writing a book that will probably absorb me for years to come, if not for the rest of my life. I don't want to talk about it, however, it is enough to say that is a kind of *"summa"* of my entire life and of all my memories.' Some months later Pasolini was dead and the book, a manuscript of 522 pages, unfinished, in fragments. The title was *Petrolio*. Einaudi published the book as it was in 1992.

The central character of the Pasolini novel is a Catholic Communist, Carlo di Polis, described by Pasolini as like an angel and very social. Carlo works for Eni. He has a double, Carlo di Tetis, who, Pasolini wrote, is diabolical and sensual. Though the two Carlos are different, they exchange roles with each other, go back and forth to being one then the other, as if, though divided, they are a single character, a living contradiction. The novel is reminiscent of Dostoevsky's *The Double* (1846), on which Bertolucci's *Partner* is based, made in 1968, three years after *La via del petrolio*. Carlo di Tetis has sex with his mother, sisters, grandmother and the servants of the house as in the 'scandalous' seductions of the family members, including the father, by the mysterious visitor in Pasolini's *Teorema* (1968). One day, looking at himself in a mirror, Carlo finds that he has become a woman.

Petrolio is a reference to Mattei, and to his murder. In 1962, a few years after Mattei's death, Bertolucci started shooting *La via del petrolio* for

Eni. In 1964, Pasolini began making notes for *Petrolio*. He regarded the
murder of Mattei as characteristic of modern Italy. For him, Mattei's
assassination was related to Italian capitalism, a position he reiterated
in his other films, most explicitly in the brutal Sadean tortures, perver-
sions and murders in his *Salò*, released in October 1975, a month before
Pasolini's body was discovered in Ostia outside of Rome.

There is a perpetual play in Pasolini's work between the 'other' and the
'same', the 'other', either literally in fact, a double, or imaginatively a
double, a theme in *Petrolio*. What is not the same, what is other, is made
to be like the other. The form is analogical and metaphorical, based on a
comparative. What is different in fact can be similar in imagination, the
other as likeness and likeness as other. A similar paradox and contradiction involving doubling informs Bertolucci's *Partner* and his *Strategia del
ragno* (1970).

The journey from Genoa is the third part of the film, 'Across Europe'. *Fire*
in Iran, *Water* in the voyage to Italy, *Earth* to Germany, three of the four
elements. The film shifts the structure of *La via del petrolio*. A subjective
and openly poetic, citational view by Mario Trejo displaces the appearance of documentary objectivity in parts one and two of the film, which
opens up a different kind of road made of memory fragments. What
Trejo gathers from those he encounters in towns and landmarks along
way is not conveyed simply as information or fact, but as dream, poetry,
memories. The journey ends in an imaginary return to its beginnings, a
journey to the impossible.

Voyages (2)

The geography of Godard's *Histoire(s) du cinéma* (1988–98) is difficult to discover for lack of a stable structure. Time, space and dimension are telescoped; far away is brought close and the near made distant, the future can arrive before the present, and the past may come after either, and all may appear simultaneously. Prior images more often than not are the consequence of successive ones and the gap between the two considerable or blurred horizontally in time or vertically in space. Journeys may begin in the future or the present or an ill-defined, overlapping time or place seemingly moving towards the past to a land for which there are no maps. The journey consists of pauses, detours, straying, returns, criss-crossing, where terms such as direct and indirect have little sense.

There are two rules for travellers: you may not ask questions about where you are going, and, if you do, there will be no answer; you may not look back to see what is behind you and where you have been, and, if you do, it will not be clear. The pleasure of the journey is to lose yourself not to arrive. It is uncertain, boundless, the map non-existent, the topology impermanent. If you cannot accept the terms, the journey comes to an end and the imaginary world on the other side of where you have been will vanish, leaving you in doubt.

The last few minutes of 4B *Les Signes parmi nous* (*The Signs Among Us*), almost at the end of the film and of the journey of Godard, is a fragment from Orson Welles's *Othello* (1952) in which Desdemona is made to seem to have discovered a yellow rose. The rose is in close-up,

from Godard's *Allemagne année 90 neuf zero* (1991). It is followed by a
fragment from Francis Bacon's *Study for a Portrait of Van Gogh* (1957), a
silhouette of a man in a Fauve landscape flickered with the yellow rose
and the face of Godard. Then Bacon's painting appears alone, passing
to a fade-in of Godard's face once more. The music is a slow, lyrical
piano passage from *The Sea* (1995) by Kevin Bjornstad heard throughout *4B*. Godard speaks in a voice-over citing Borges's *Book of Dreams*
(1976): 'Si un homme traversait le paradis en songe, qu'il reçût une
fleur comme preuve de son passage et qu'à son reveil il trouvât cette
fleur dans ses mains que dire alors. J'étais cet homme' ('If a man having
passed through Paradise dreams that he received a flower as proof of his
journey and that upon waking finds the flower in his hands what is there
to say? I am that man').

In Cocteau's *Le Testament d'Orphée* (1960), the Poet (Cocteau) is given
a photograph by gypsies of the poet Cégeste, whom he had left behind
in his *Orphée* (1950) in a world between the living and the dead, the
price paid for the immortality of Orphée, the 'other' poet to Cégeste in
that film. Cocteau tears up the photograph of Cégeste he receives in *Le
Testament* and throws the scraps into the sea. The sea begins to boil; out
of it emerges Cégeste with a hibiscus flower which he gives to Cocteau
to give to Minerva, the goddess of reason, then turns his back and walks
away. Minerva throws her spear at Cocteau and he dies. The death is a
poet's death . The Poet is not a Cartesian and Minerva has no time for his
fancies and fiddle-faddle.

Like Cégeste, and like Cocteau, Godard in *Histoire(s)* enters another
world, one imagined as in a dream composed of sheets of time and place
from the antique to the present and beyond where anything can occur.
The sheets of time overlap: Desdemona is in Germany in 1990 and
Borges, Cocteau and Godard sail the same sea, visit the same kingdom
and bring back a flower as proof of having been there.

Dreams seem to come not from us but to us, as if from an outside.
Histoire(s) has that quality. Coming from us, images are manipulated,
under control, and, in so far as they are, they appear as logical, conjoined,
a narrative. Coming to us, pursuing the analogy of a dream, they seem
to lose their logic and the conjunctions which fabricate these. Instead
they are disjointed and dislocated. The advantage of images coming from
us is that they can be definite, secure and reassuring. The advantage
of images coming to us is that lack of control enables associations and

configurations that are not logical, definite or held in check. It is the lack of logic that permits any number of itineraries, voyages and geographies without limits of time or space; nevertheless, like a dream, the relations are patterned.

Writing

It is difficult if not impossible to know how Godard's *Histoire(s) du cinéma* (1988–98) was made. Certainly it is not a film in the ordinary way which follows a plan, still less a script, not at all a story or a narrative and it is hardly an essay, and it destroys most systems of reference in the usual sense. What then determines not simply the images and sounds that appear but their relations to each other? Much of these seem illogical, undirected, and, though it is possible sometimes to perceive an association, for the most part these are extremely distant and obscure even if these remote elements 'suddenly' fuse and coalesce. The film is not a representation but a manifestation, a demonstration (but of what?), a collection of documents whose order can be stated but whose significance is hard to discern. Above all, the film seems to be a record of the direct experience of making the film itself, an immediacy which results in an abundance of metaphors and signs but outside of the logical or the significant, even beyond control as if the film, in the instantaneities of its associations and linkages, has *written* itself.

Every film reconstitutes reality into signs, that is, the real is made into writing, thus leading to two kinds of critical discourse in part dependent on the way in which the film works: the relation of signs to the real (often as a simulacrum, a verisimilitude) and the relation of signs to each other, film as a way of thinking, like a language, but not this or that thought in particular. In *Histoire(s)* these signs in images and sounds are almost never direct, are already signs, already writing (films, literature, painting, music), that is, citations, carrying with them resonances and meanings from a prior origin. The signs then are ready-mades, like

Warhol's recasting, serialising images of Marilyn Monroe, or the objects long since discarded, now useless, functionless, that Rauschenberg brings together in his Combines made of strikingly oddly placed left-overs, brought back to life, absorbed into language, functioning as form, the real as writing but establishing nothing except that which is already a great deal.

Histoire(s) then is a vast undertaking of remaking, repositioning, restating the already written. In doing so, it dismantles a functional writing. It de-writes, breaks logical connectives, gives writing back to film and makes film an instrument. Whatever is in the film is concretely itself (because disconnected, extracted, literally excavated) and at the same time potentially, like a word or sound or, better yet, a phoneme, an independent unit on its own to serve within elsewheres, to be transferred and reused, resurrected, sent off on a myriad of pathways. Not any longer a scene in a narrative but a tool for creating a discourse. In that sense, these signs are indeed empty (potential) and this emptiness is their possibility, like a phoneme, a not-yet sign but the material for an infinite number of signs.

Most films are written first in stages (the treatment, the script, the shooting script), then filmed, with the filming, the images, being essentially an illustration of the writing (the writing come to life as visible scenes) and its effacement (the images cover over the writing which has been written in order to disappear, which is what a script is, a writing never to be fully realised as writing but only as a provisional plan or outline for filming). It is precisely the traditional role of the script with its apparent subordination of filming for the primacy of the word (and of literature) that Godard explicitly challenges in Histoire(s), not only by direct statements and cited examples but in practice, converting images and sounds into an autonomous *writing*, film as writing, the experience of it and thereby a different kind of primacy. If traditional writing *for* film was self-effacing, Godard's writing *with* film is declamatory. The first kind of writing constructed a make-believe and thus it was forced to hide. Godard's writing is a dialogue with the real and thus must be evident. It is the very purpose and project of his film. The writing has two related practices. There are actual words projected, written and spoken (words become images) and then dismantled, to function as provocations, anagrams, elisions, opacity, the source of new words, phrases, images, signs all jumbled, their elements dispersed, then, reworded, reassigned, coming together differently. The other practice involves the conversion (a transfer, relocation) of images and sounds into constituents of signs so that they are writing, and a writing not to represent or signify, but to be manifest, demonstrative.

Bibliography

Amengual, Barthélemy, 'Portrait de l'artiste en jeune homme d'avant la trentaine', in *Du Réalisme au cinéma* (Paris: Nathan, 1997)

——'Jean-Luc Godard et la remise en cause de notre civilisation de l'image', in *Du Réalisme au cinéma* (Paris: Nathan, 1997), pp. 555–603

Antonioni, Michelangelo (colloquio con), 'La malattia dei sentimenti', *Bianco e nero*, vol. XXII, nos 2–3 (February–March 1961), pp, 75–6

Aprà, Adriano (ed.), *Bernardo Bertolucci: il cinema e i film* (Venice: Marsilio, 2010)

Aumont, Jacques, *Les Théories des cinéastes* (Paris: Nathan, 2002)

——'Mortal Beauty', in Michael Temple and James S. Williams (eds), *The Cinema Alone: Essays on the Work of Jean-Luc Godard 1985–2000* (Amsterdam: Amsterdam University Press, 2000)

——*Amnésies: Fictions du cinéma d'après Jean-Luc Godard* (Paris: P.O.L., 1999), pp. 97–112

Baldelli, Pio, *Luchino Visconti* (Milan: Gabriella Mazzotta Editore, 1973)

Bellour, Raymond, and Mary Lee Bandy, *Jean-Luc Godard: Son + Image 1974–1991* (New York: The Museum of Modern Art, 1992)

Bergala, Alain, *Nul mieux que Godard* (Paris: Editions Cahiers du cinéma, 1999)

——(ed.) *Jean-Luc Godard par Jean-Luc Godard*, vol. 1, 1950–1984, vol. 2, 1984–1998 (Paris: Cahiers du cinéma, 1998)

Bertolucci, Bernardo, *La mia magnifica ossessione: scritti, ricordi, interventi (1962–2010)* (Milan: Garzanti, 2010)

Bordwell, David, *Narration in the Fiction Film* (London: Methuen, 1985)

Brenez, Nicole, 'The Forms of the Question', in Michael Temple, James S. Williams and Michael Witt (eds), *For Ever Godard* (London: Black Dog Publishing, 2004), pp. 160–77

Brenez, Nicole, 'For It Is the Critical Faculty That Invents Fresh forms', in Michael Temple and Michael Witt (eds),*The French Cinema Book* (London: BFI Publishing, 2004), pp. 230–46

Brenez, Nicole, and Godard, Jean-Luc, *Documents* (Paris, Centre Pompidou, 2006)

Casetti, Francesco, *Bernardo Bertolucci* (Florence: La Nuova Italia, 1978)

Cerisuelo, Marc, *Jean-Luc Godard* (Paris: Lherminier, Editions des Quatre-Vents, 1989)

Chateau, Dominique, A. Gardies and F. Jost (eds), *Cinéma de la modernité: films, théories* (Colloque à Cerisy) (Paris: Klincksieck, 1981)

Comolli, Jean-Louis, and Jacques Rancière, *Arrêt sur histoire* (Paris: Editions du Centre Pompidou, 1997)

Cuccu, Lorenzo, *La visione come problema* (Rome: Bulzoni, 1973)

Danto, Arthur C., *After the End of Art* (Princeton: Princeton University Press, 1997)

de Baecque, Antoine, *Godard: biographie* (Paris: Bernard Grasset, 2010)

Deleuze, Gilles, *Cinema2: The Time-Image* (Minneapolis: University of Minnesota Press, 1989)

Delavaud, Gilles, Jean-Pierre Esquenazi and Marie-Françoise Grange (eds), *Godard et le métier d'artiste* (Paris: L'Harmattan, 2001)

di Carlo, Carlo, *Michelangelo Antonioni* (Rome: Edizioni Bianco e Nero, 1964)

Didi-Huberman, Georges, *Images malgré tout* (Paris: Les Editions de Minuit, 2003)

Eisenschitz, Bernard, *Chris Marker* (Pesaro: Dino Audino, 1996)

Ernaux, Annie, *Ecrire la vie* (Paris: Gallimard, 2011)

Frappat, Hélène, *Jacques Rivette, Secret compris* (Paris: Cahiers du cinéma, 2001)

Gerard, Fabien S., T. Jefferson Kline and Bruce Sklarew, *Bernardo Bertolucci: Interviews* (Jackson: University of Mississippi Press, 2000)

Gili, Jean A., *Howard Hawks*, Cinéma d'Aujourd'hui (Paris: Editions Seghers, 1971)

——and Christian Viviani, 'Interview with Bernardo Bertolucci', *Positif*, no. 424 (June 1996)

Godard, Jean-Luc, *Introduction à une véritable histoire du cinéma*, vol. I (Paris: Editions Albatros, 1980)

——and Youssef Ishaghpour. *Archéologie du cinéma et mémoire du siècle* (Tours: Farrago, 2000)

Jousse, Thierry. *Pendant les travaux le cinéma reste ouvert* (Paris: Cahiers du cinéma, 2003)

Leutrat, Jean-Louis, *Hiroshima mon amour* (Paris: Nathan, 1994)

Liandrat-Guigues, Suzanne, and Jean-Louis Leutrat, *Alain Resnais: Liaisons secrètes, accords vagabonds* (Paris: Cahiers du Cinéma, 2006)

MacCabe, Colin, *Godard: Images, Sounds, Politics* (Basingstoke: Macmillan, 1980)

Mancini, Michele et al., 'Conversazione con Michelangelo Antonioni', *Filmcritica*, no. 231 (January–February 1973)

Païni, Dominique et al., 'Guide pour *Histoire(s) du cinéma*', *Cahiers du cinéma* (November 1998), Art Press (hors série)

Rancière, Jacques, 'Le cinéma dans la "fin" de l'art', *Cahiers du cinéma*, no. 552 (December 2000), pp. 50–1

——'Une fable sans morale: Godard, le cinéma, les histoires' in *La Fable cinématographique* (Paris: Editions du Seuil, 2001)

Schérer, Maurice (Eric Rohmer), 'Les maîtres de l'aventure' *Cahiers du Cinéma*, no. 5.29 (December 1953)

Silverman, Kaja, and Harun Farocki, *Speaking about Godard* (New York: New York University Press, 1998)

Socci, Stefano, *Bernardo Bertolucci* (Milan: Il Castoro Cinema, 2008)

Sterrit, David, *Jean-Luc Godard: Interviews* (Jackson: University of Mississippi Press: 1998)

Tesson, Charles, 'Entretien avec Jean-Luc Godard: Avenir(s) du cinéma', *Cahiers du Cinéma* (April 2000) (hors-série)

Tinazzi, Giorgio, *Antonioni* (Rome and Milan: Il Castoro Cinema, 1974)

Toffetti, Sergio, 'La scoperta dell'altrove: La via del petrolio', in Sergio Toffetti (ed.), *La scoperta dell'altrove* (Milan: Feltrinelli, 2010)

Williams, James S., *Jean Cocteau* (Manchester: Manchester University Press, 2006)

Wilson, Emma, *Alain Resnais* (Manchester University Press: Manchester, 2006)

Filmography

The filmography refers only to films cited in the text. In the title of some of the films, the Italian or French titles are the same as the English titles.

Michelangelo Antonioni
Cronaca di un amore (Story of a Love Affair) 1950
Le amiche (The Girl Friends) 1955
La notte (The Night) 1961

Ingmar Bergman
Persona 1966
Cries and Whispers 1972

Bernardo Bertolucci
La commare secca (The Grim Reaper) 1962
Prima della rivoluzione (Before the Revolution) 1964
La via del petrolio (The Oil Road) 1965
Partner 1968
Agonia (Agony) 1969
Strategia del ragno (Spider's Stratagem) 1970
Il conformista (The Conformist) 1970
Ultimo tango a Parigi (Last Tango in Paris) 1972
Novecento (1900) 1976
La luna 1979
La tragedia di un uomo ridicolo (Tragedy of a Ridiculous Man) 1981
The Sheltering Sky 1990

Little Buddha 1993
The Last Emperor 1987
Stealing Beauty 1996
Besieged 1999
The Dreamers 2003
Io e te (Me and You) 2012

Robert Bresson
Les Dames de Bois de Boulogne 1945
Le Journal d'un curé de campagne (Diary of a Country Priest) 1951
Mouchette 1967

John Cassavetes
The Killing of a Chinese Bookie 1976

Jean Cocteau
Orphée (Orpheus) 1950
Le Testament d'Orphée (The Testament of Orpheus) 1960

Joseph Cornell
Rose Hobart 1936

Jacques Demy
Les Demoiselles de Rochefort (The Young Girls of Rochefort) 1967

Claire Denis
Chocolat (Chocolate) 1988
J'ai pas sommeil (I Can't Sleep) 1994
Beau travail (Good Work) 1999

Carl Theodor Dreyer
Ordet 1925

Sergei Eisenstein
The Battleship Potemkin 1925
Strike 1925

John Ford
Young Mr Lincoln 1939
Fort Apache 1948
She Wore a Yellow Ribbon 1949
Rio Grande 1950
The Searchers 1956

Jean-Luc Godard
A bout de souffle (Breathless) 1960
Le Petit Soldat (The Little Soldier) 1960
Vivre sa vie (Her Life to Live) 1962
Le Mépris (Contempt) 1963
Une femme est une femme (A Woman Is a Woman) 1961
Une femme mariée (A Married Woman) 1964
Made in USA 1966
2 ou 3 choses que je sais d'elle (Two or Three Things I Know About Her) 1966
Loin du Vietnam (Far from Vietnam) 1967
La Chinoise 1967
One Plus One 1968
Tout va bien 1972
Letter to Jane 1972
Ici et ailleurs (Here and Elsewhere) 1974
Passion 1982
Soigne ta droit (Keep Your Right Up) 1987
Nouvelle Vague (New Wave) 1990
Allemagne année 90 neuf zéro (Germany Year 90 Nine Zero) 1991
Hélas pour moi (Woe is Me) 1993
For Ever Mozart 1996
Histoire(s) du cinéma (Historie(s) of the Cinema) 1988–98

D.W. Griffith
Broken Blossoms 1919

Howard Hawks
Only Angels Have Wings 1939
Red River 1948
To Have and Have Not 1944

The Big Sleep 1946
Rio Bravo 1959

Alfred Hitchcock
Rear Window 1954
Vertigo 1958
North by Northwest 1959
The Birds 1963

Elia Kazan
Viva Zapata! 1952
On the Waterfront 1954

Gene Kelly
Singin' in the Rain 1952

Fritz Lang
M 1931
Rancho Notorious 1952

Claude Lanzmann
Shoah 1985

Joshua Logan
Sayonara 1957

Auguste and Louis Lumière
L'Arrivée d'un train en gare de La Ciotat (The Arrival of a Train at La Ciotat
    Station) 1895

Louis Malle
Zazie dans le Métro (Zazie in the Métro) 1960

Chris Marker
Le Tombeau d'Alexandre (The Last Bolshevik) 1992

George Melford
East of Borneo 1931

Lewis Milestone
Mutiny on the Bounty 1962

Vincente Minnelli
An American in Paris 1951
Gigi 1958

João César Monteiro
Vai e Vem (Going and Coming) 2002

Pier Paolo Pasolini
Accattone 1961
Mamma Roma 1962
La ricotta (Curd Cheese) 1963
Teorema (Theorem) 1968
Salò o le 120 giornate di Sodoma (Salò, or The 120 Days of Sodom) 1975

Nicholas Ray
In a Lonely Place 1950
On Dangerous Ground 1951
Johnny Guitar 1954
Rebel Without a Cause 1955
Hot Blood 1956
Bitter Victory 1957

Carol Reed
The Third Man 1949

Jean Renoir
Boudu sauvé des eaux (Boudu Saved from Drowning) 1932
La Règle du jeu (Rules of the Game) 1939
Le Carosse d'or (The Golden Coach) 1952
French Cancan 1954

Alain Resnais
Nuit et brouillard (Night and Fog) 1955
Toute la mémoire du monde (All the Memory in the World) 1956

Jacques Rivette
Va savoir (Who Knows?) 2001

Roberto Rossellini
Roma città aperta (Rome Open City) 1945
Paisà 1946
Germania anno zero (Germany Year Zero) 1947
Stromboli 1949
Francesco, giullare di Dio (The Flowers of Saint Francis) 1950
Europa '51 (Europe '51) 1952
Viaggio in Italia (Journey to Italy) 1954

Jean Rouch
Jaguar (1954–67)
La Chasse au lion à l'arc (The Lion Hunters) 1957–64
Moi, un noir (I, a Negro) 1958
Chronique d'un été (Chronicle of a Summer) 1960

Giuseppe De Santis
Riso amaro (Bitter Rice) 1949

Vittorio De Sica
I bambini ci guardano (The Children Are Watching Us) 1944
Ladri di biciclette (Bicycle Thieves) 1948

François Truffaut
Tirez sur le pianiste (Shoot the Pianist) 1960

Luchino Visconti
Ossessione (Obsession) 1943
La terra trema (The Earth Trembles) 1948
Bellissima (Bellissima) 1951
Senso (Senso) 1954
Rocco e i suoi fratelli (Rocco and His Brothers) 1960
Il gattopardo (The Leopard) 1963
Vaghe stelle dell'Orsa (Sandra) 1965
Lo straniero (The Stranger) 1967
La caduta degli dei (The Damned) 1969

Ludwig 1972
Morte a Venezia (Death in Venice) 1971
Gruppo di famiglia in un interno (Conversation Piece) 1974
L'innocente (The Innocent) 1976

Orson Welles
Citizen Kane 1941
The Magnificent Ambersons 1942
The Stranger 1946
The Lady from Shanghai 1947
Macbeth 1948
Othello 1952
Mr Arkadin 1955
Touch of Evil 1958
The Immortal Story 1968
F for Fake 1973